HANSARD SOCIETY SERIES IN POLITICS AND GOVERNMENT

Edited by
F. F. Ridley

The Hansard Society Series in Politics and Government brings to the wider public the debates and analyses of important issues first discussed in the pages of its journal, *Parliamentary Affairs*

Britain Votes 1997

Edited by
Pippa Norris and Neil T. Gavin

Series Editor
F. F. Ridley

OXFORD UNIVERSITY PRESS
in association with
THE HANSARD SOCIETY FOR
PARLIAMENTARY GOVERNMENT

Oxford University Press, Walton Street, Oxford OX2 6DP
Oxford New York
Athens Auckland Bangkok Bombay
Calcutta Cape Town Dar es Salaam Delhi
Florence Hong Kong Istanbul Karachi
Kuala Lumpur Madras Madrid Melbourne
Mexico City Nairobi Paris Singapore
Taipei Tokyo Toronto
and associated companies in
Berlin Ibadan

Oxford is a trade mark of Oxford University Press

Published in the United States
by Oxford University Press Inc., New York

© Oxford University Press, 1997

First published in Parliamentary Affairs, 1997
New as paperback, 1997

A catalogue for this book is available from the British Library

Library of Congress Cataloging in Publication Data
(Data available)

ISBN 0–19–922322–X

Printed in Great Britain
by Headley Brothers Limited, The Invicta Press,
Ashford, Kent and London

CONTENTS

CONTRIBUTORS TO THIS VOLUME

Hugh Berrington is Professor of Politics (Emeritus) at Newcastle University. He is currently editing and contributing to *Britain in the Nineties: Paradox in British Politics*.

Alice Brown is Professor of Politics at Edinburgh University and co-author of *Politics and Society in Scotland* (1996).

Ivor Crewe is Vice Chancellor of the University of Essex and Professor of Government. He co-authored *SDP: The Birth, Life and Death of the Social Democratic Party* (1995) and *Decade of Dealignment* (1983).

David Denver is Reader in Politics at Lancaster University. His books include *Elections and Voting Behaviour in Britain* (1994).

Patrick Dunleavy is Professor of Government at the London School of Economics and Political Science. His books include *Developments in British Politics 5* (1997), *Democracy, Bureaucracy and Public Choice* (1991) and *Prime Minister, Cabinet and Core Executive* (1995).

Geoffrey Evans is a Fellow of Nuffield College, Oxford. His books include co-authoring *Understanding Political Change* (1991), and editing *The End of Class Politics?* (forthcoming).

Neil T. Gavin is a Lecturer in Politics at Liverpool University and his books include *Economy, Media and Public Knowledge* (forthcoming).

Peter Goddard is a Research Assistant in Communication Studies at Liverpool University.

Rod Hague is a Senior Lecturer in Politics at Newcastle University. He is co-author of *Comparative Government and Politics* (1992).

Gordon Hands is Senior Lecturer in Politics at Lancaster University. Together with David Denver he has recently published *Modern Constituency Electioneering: Local Campaigning in the 1992 General Election* (1994).

Dennis Kavanagh is Professor of Politics at Liverpool University. His books include *Election Campaigning* (1995) and he is co-author of *The British General Election of 1997* (1997).

Peter Kellner is political correspondent for BBC Television and *The Independent*.

Joni Lovenduski is Professor of Politics at Southampton University. Her books include *Contemporary Feminist Politics* (1993) and she is co-author of *Political Recruitment* (1995).

Helen Margetts is Lecturer in Politics at Birkbeck College. She is co-author of *Turning Japanese?* (1994) and *Replaying the 1992 General Election* (1992).

Ian McAllister is Director of the Research School of Social Sciences at the Australian National University and his books include (with Richard Rose) *The Loyalties of Voters* (Sage, 1990).

Pippa Norris teaches at Harvard University. She co-directs the *British Election Study, 1997* and recent books include *Electoral Change Since 1945* (1996) and *Passages to Power* (1997).

Brendan O'Leary is Professor of Political Science at the London School of Economics and Political Science. He is co-author of *Explaining Northern Ireland: Broken Images* (1995) and *The Politics of Ethnic Conflict Regulation: Case Studies of Protracted Ethnic Conflict* (1993).

Colin Rallings is Professor of Politics at the University of Plymouth. He is co-author with Michael Thrasher of *Local Elections in Britain* (1997).

Richard Rose, Director of the Centre for the Study of Public Policy, University of Strathclyde, published his first books on the 1959 British general election. Most recently he is co-author, with Stephen White and Ian McAllister, of *How Russia Votes* (1997)

Shamit Saggar is a Senior Lecturer in Government at Queen Mary and Westfield College, University of London. He is the editor of *Race and British Electoral Politics* (1997).

David Sanders is Pro-Vice Chancellor and Professor of Government at Essex University. His books include *Losing an Empire, Finding a Role: British Foreign Policy since 1945* (1990).

Margaret Scammell is a Senior Lecturer in Communication Studies at Liverpool University. She is the author of *Designer Politics* (1996).

Holli Semetko is Professor of Communications at the University of Amsterdam. Her books include *The Formation of Campaign Agendas* (1991) and *Germany's Unity Election* (1994).

Colin Seymour-Ure is Professor of Government and former Dean of Social Sciences at the University of Kent at Canterbury. His most recent book is *The British Press and Broadcasting since 1945* (1996).

Michael Thrasher is Professor of Politics at the University of Plymouth. Together with Colin Rallings he directs the University's Local Government Chronicle Elections Center.

Paul Whiteley is Professor of Politics at Sheffield University. He is co-author of *True Blues* (1994) and *Labour's Grass Roots* (1992).

Preface

This book is doubly important—as an account of British politics at its most dramatic and as a substantial contribution to the political science of British politics. It is the sixth book in the *Hansard Society Series in Politics and Government* drawn from special issues of *Parliamentary Affairs*. Ten special issues since 1991 have covered matters of current debate such as Constitutional Reform, the Extreme Right in Europe, Building Democracies, Abortion and Politics, Quangos, Women in Politics and the Scott Report—plus two on the general elections of 1992 and 1997.

Pippa Norris, then as now a British political scientist at Harvard, co-edited the 1992 issue; we are fortunate to have her again as editor of this volume, ably assisted by Neil Gavin of Liverpool University. She has used her contacts effectively, giving us a star-studded cast (quite a few return performances from 1992), all well qualified for the chapters under their names. Picking names out is always invidious, though perhaps good advertising, but here one would be tempted to list the entire cast, so the reader is referred to the contents page.

The 1992 issue of *Parliamentary Affairs* had a dozen articles; here we have 18 chapters, a comprehensive cover in a very substantial book. The contributions are authoritative yet produced at a speed rare for academics, the product of advance planning, editorial persuasion and good-will of authors. The Oxford University Press has also pulled out all stops to get us quickly into libraries and bookshops.

Other books will appear, some academic with good pedigree, other quality journalism but ephemeral. I believe *Britain Votes 1997* will remain the most comprehensive collection of authoritative chapters by the largest group of reputed specialists however. It should be a standard text for students of British politics, here and abroad, a source of information for writers now and researchers over the years to come—and it has much to offer the sometimes forgotten citizen who reads books for interest rather than as a profession.

The last is worth saying 1997 was a more gripping election than most. Remember watching television till dawn, well after Labour's overwhelming victory was clear, to hear the fate of prominent (or notorious) Conservatives. A landslide election certainly. A sea-change in public opinion. Parliament transformed. new faces in power, old faces almost forgotten. A Cabinet that hit the ground running, that may change the system of government (the British constitution in other words) as well as government policies. But that is looking ahead and the study of politics teaches one some scepticism. This book is about the 1997 general election, self-contained, and will remain an authoritative analysis of that whatever the future brings.

F.F. Ridley

Anatomy of a Labour Landslide

BY PIPPA NORRIS*

THE LONG campaign was flat, the opinion polls unwavering, the public overwhelmed by political ennui. Yet on 1 May 1997, and well into the following morning, as Tory after Tory was defeated, and defeated badly, at the polls, commentators floundered to pinpoint the appropriate adjective to describe the scale of the Labour victory, whether a 'landslide', a 'political earthquake' or a 'sea change in British politics'. The government lost a quarter of its 1992 vote, a third of its Cabinet and over half its seats (178). The Conservative share of the UK vote fell from 41.9% to 30.7%, their worst result since modern party politics began in 1832. The party was reduced to an English rump, obliterated in Scotland and Wales, and in most major cities. With only 165 MPs, Conservative representation was the lowest since 1906.

After eighteen years in the opposition wilderness, Labour surged to power with 419 MPs (including the Speaker), their highest number ever, overflowing the government benches in the Commons. Tony Blair won an overall majority of 179, the largest for any administration since the National government of 1935, and the biggest in Labour history. Labour recovered most in areas where the party had been weakest throughout the Thatcher years, storming back in Greater London, the South East and the Midlands. Blair's landslide was in seats, not votes: Labour's share of the UK vote (43.3%) was about the same as they achieved when they lost in 1970 (32.1%), and less than their peak in 1966 (48.0%). The centre parties also triumphed, with the election of 46 Liberal Democrats, their best result since 1929, despite a drop of one per cent in their vote. Scotland elected six SNP MPs, their strongest showing since October 1974, with 22% of the Scottish vote, while four Plaid Cymru MPs were returned in Wales. There were more candidates than ever before (3,717). Most fringe parties had their moment of glory but lost their deposits. The eurosceptic Referendum Party got three per cent of the vote, but only after spending £20 million, or £24.68 per vote. Ironically the net effect was probably to let in a few more europhile Labour members. All-in-all, the record books of modern British politics were less broken than smashed and overturned. So, after four successive victories, what produced the Conservative rout on 1 May 1997? After being written off in the early eighties, how did Labour recover middle England? And what are the implications of the results

---

* Lecturer at Harvard University.

for the future of British party politics? Let us summarise the long-term run up to the election, the impact of the campaign, and then who shifted, where, when, and why.

1. The share of the vote, 1992–97 (%)

	1992 UK	1997 UK	Percentage UK Change UK	1997 GB	St Dev of GB mean
Con	41.9	30.7	−11.2	31.0	12.2
Lab	34.4	43.3	8.9	44.4	17.9
Lib Dem	17.8	16.8	−1.0	17.2	10.9
SNP	1.8	2.0	0.2	2.0	7.6
PC	0.5	0.5	0.0	0.5	4.2
Other	3.5	6.8	3.3	4.4	3.7
Turnout	77.7	71.5	−6.2	71.6	5.56
Butler swing				−10.5	

2. The change in seats, 1992–97 (UK)

	Seats Actual 1992	Notional 1992	Seats Gains	Losses	1 May 1997	% 1997
Lab (*)	271	273	146	0	419	63.6
Con	336	343	0	178	165	25.0
Lib Dem	20	18	30	2	46	7.0
SNP	3	3	3	0	6	0.9
PC	4	4	0	0	4	0.6
N. Ireland	17	18	4	4	18	2.7
Independent	0	0	1	0	1	0.2
Total	651	659	184	184	659	100.0
Overall majority	Con 21	Con 27			Lab 179	

Note: (*) including the Speaker. Notional results based on the new constituency boundaries are derived from Colin Rallings and Michael Thrasher Media Guide to the New Parliamentary Constituencies (BBC/ITN/PA News/Sky 1995).

The long-term Conservative collapse

The headline story of the election was the disastrous long-term collapse of Conservative support, which started on 'Black Wednesday' (16 September 1992) with the withdrawal of Britain from the European Monetary Union. On a single day base interest rates at the bank bounced from 10 to 12%, then 15% a few hours later, then back to 12% by the end of the day. As Paul Whiteley argues later, the ERM debacle destroyed notions of Conservative economic competence and simultaneously sowed the seeds for bitter internal divisions within the government over Britain's future within the European Union.[1] After this, poll after poll reported the government in the doldrums. Labour support hovered comfortably between 40 to 50%. The election of Tony Blair as Labour leader after the sudden death of John Smith, in May 1994, and the transformation of 'new Labour', consolidated and boosted their lead in the opinion polls. Throughout 1995 the Conservatives languished at the lowest point for any government since regular polling began in 1945 (see Figure 1).

Conservative fortunes were also reflected in real votes at the ballot box. By-elections are usually an opportunity for people to protest

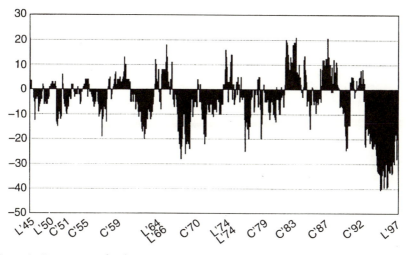

Figure 1. Government lead 1945–97
Source: Con-Lab lead in Gallup polls

against the government but from 1992–97 the Conservative share of the by-election vote plummeted by 20%, almost twice the drop experienced by successive governments under Mrs Thatcher. Minor parties commonly benefit and during 1992–97 the Liberal Democrats won Newbury, Christchurch, Eastleigh and Littleborough and Saddlesworth, while the SNP took Perth and Kinross. Nevertheless it was Labour which increased their share of the by-election vote most significantly (+ 7.4%), while gaining Dudley West, South East Staffs, and Wirral South. The last by-election won by the Conservatives was in 1988.

Successive local elections, maintaining the grassroots party machine, wiped out Tories in town halls up and down the land. In 1979, when Mrs Thatcher first won power, Conservatives had 12,143 councillors, and control of such major cities as Greater London, Birmingham, and Edinburgh, as well as metropolitan counties like Greater Manchester, Merseyside and the West Midlands. After the May 1996 local elections the party was left with only 4,400 councillors, well behind Labour (11,000) and the Liberal Democrats (5,100). While Labour controlled 212 local authorities in England, Scotland and Wales, and the Liberal Democrats held 55, the Conservatives were left with just 13 (see Rallings and Thrasher in this volume). The June 1994 European elections underlined Conservative decline: they held only 18 out of 89 seats (none in Scotland and Wales), with 26.9% of the UK vote. In 1992–97, Conservative party membership plummeted from 780,000 to under 400,000, falling below Labour for the first time this century (*The Times*, 6.6.97). The writing on the wall was plain for all to see (see Figure 2). The question obsessing journalists and commentators in the long, long run up to polling day was whether the Major government was suffering from another bad case of 'mid-term blues', from which they could

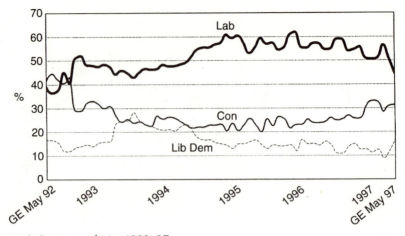

Figure 2. Party popularity 1992–97
Source: Gallup opinion polls

recover along with the economic 'feel-good' factor, or whether this signified a more fundamental challenge to almost two decades of Conservative predominance.

Stability and change in the election campaign

As the six-week campaign opened, despite the accumulated evidence, few contemporary observers seemed to expect that Labour could achieve such an overwhelming victory, not even Tony Blair, according to insider accounts (Robert Harris, *Sunday Times*, 3.5.97). Memories of the opinion poll fiasco in 1992, discussed in this volume by Ivor Crewe, meant commentators cautiously hedged their bets. The panel of twenty psephologists appointed by Reuters predicted an average Labour majority of 92. Earlier models by David Sanders had estimated that given the 'feel-good' factor in the economy the Conservatives should get around 37% of the vote.[2] Even on election day Michael Heseltine was boasting of a Conservative majority of around 60 seats, some commentators clung to predictions of a hung parliament, while pollsters like Bob Worcester expected a Labour majority of 101. Few expected a melt-down by the once-formidable Conservative election machine. Given the insistent drumbeat from opinion polls, local, European and by-elections, the defeat of the Major government should not have surprised anyone. Yet the size and scale of the Conservative rout did.

The launch of the official election on 17 March resulted in the longest campaign in recent history. John Major wanted to allow the Conservatives to build momentum by a triple strategy: by emphasising the positive economic performance of the government, by reassuring voters to trust John Major rather than the inexperienced and untested Tony Blair, and by attacking Labour on the old issues of taxes and trade unions. As discussed by Paul Whiteley and Dennis Kavanagh in this volume, the Conservative campaign was dogged throughout by stories of sleaze and derailed by European divisions, while the Mandelson Millbank machine stayed resolutely and tightly 'on message' throughout most of the campaign, and Paddy Ashdown fought an energetic, positive albeit largely one-man campaign for the Liberal Democrats. An analysis of the major issues covered by television and the press during the campaign found that the conduct of the election (including opinion polls, discussions of party strategy and the role of the media) occupied a third of all coverage, and substantive discussion of policy issues focussed on Europe, sleaze, education, taxation, constitutional reform, privatisation, health, social security, and Northern Ireland, in that order (*Guardian*, 2.5.97). The dominance of sleaze stories during the first two weeks, and the subsequent rise of Europe to the top of the media agenda in the third week, was particularly notable. Both stories provided negative coverage of the government, and prevented them from trumpeting their own message about the health of the British economy. Indeed it is striking how another content analysis study of the press found that when the economy was reported, bad news slightly outweighed good, despite the 'objective' economic indicators looking remarkably healthy[3] (see also Gavin and Sanders in this volume).

The Conservatives usually enter the campaign assured of a sympathetic press, so they can be confident of getting their message across. Yet in this election, as Colin Seymour-Ure points out, six out of ten national dailies gave Labour largely unqualified support. The papers' party backing first began to shift in the 1992 election, but they became heavily hostile to John Major following Black Wednesday, and the government never really recaptured their loyalties. The shift was most dramatically symbolised by the defection of the *Sun* ('THE SUN BACKS BLAIR') on the first day of the official campaign, although it is not clear how long Blair's honeymoon with the press will last. One intriguing issue which needs to be explored further is why this shift occurred, and in particular whether papers led or followed their readers' surge to Labour.

Despite increased pressures from the proliferation of satellite and cable stations, the main terrestrial channels on television maintained high standards of public service broadcasting in Britain. Given the flatness of the horse-race, as well as the lessons of the 1992 fiasco, broadcast news devoted less time to opinion polls, down from 14% of stories in 1992 to only seven per cent in 1997 (*Guardian*, 5.5.97). Television could not resist covering some of the trivia and fluff (the headless chicken fight, sex in the park for one MP, the debate about television debates). Nevertheless much news was devoted to balanced and informative analysis of serious policy issues (see Semetko, Scammell and Goddard later). Television devoted extensive coverage to the campaign. As a proportion of domestic news space, election stories were 14% of the tabloids, about 28% of the broadsheet press, but about 41% of broadcast news (*Guardian*). Yet the result of the flat election was that more viewers turned off the flagship BBC1 and ITV evening news. During the period of the official campaign, according to the Broadcaster's Audience Research Board (BARB), the audience for BBC1's 9 O'clock News dropped from an average of 6.3 million per night during the 1992 campaign down to 4.2 million this year, while ITN's News at Ten fell from around 6.8 million per night in the 1992 campaign down to about 5.6 million. Still, on the Election '97 specials, at the peak 12.7 million viewers were glued to the results (about 29.5% of the electorate). Between one to two million stayed switched on well into the early hours of the following morning and all the next day.

Did the campaign matter? Some commentators claimed that despite all the sound and fury of the official campaign, and the strenuous attempts by parties and the media to control the agenda, in the end this had little impact on the outcome, which was decided on Black Wednesday five years ago. In this regard in a model of punctuated equilibrium, the ERM fiasco, like the Falklands war before it, could be regarded as a decisive event which ratcheted public opinion into a new direction. Yet regarding the outcome as inevitable following Black Wednesday seems far too deterministic. Currency crises do not usually, by themselves, produce a change of government. As noted by Ivor Crewe, the opinion polls showed a glacial slide in Labour support from the start to the end of the campaign, with the Liberal Democrats the main beneficiaries. True, the campaign probably did not decide the outcome, given Labour's lead, but this evidence suggests it still mattered for votes. Ivor Crewe demonstrates that Labour support declined by seven points (from an average of 51.4% in the first two weeks of the campaign down to 44.4% on polling day), Liberal Democrat support climbed 4 points

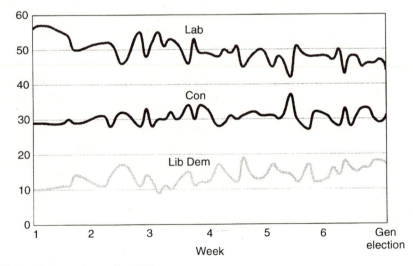

Figure 3. Campaign polls 1997
Source: All National Polls published 17 March–1 May 1997

(from 12.98 to 17.2% during the campaign), while the Conservatives rose by two points (from 29.8 to 31.5%) (see Crewe, Table 4 in this volume). Overall campaign swing was slightly higher than average, compared with many previous elections.[4] While Labour support was probably over-inflated at the beginning of this period, if the polls are believed to have their fingers on the nation's pulse this swing still indicates significant movement.

The effect of the campaign can also be estimated from the NOP/BBC exit poll when people were asked about the timing of their voting decision. Over half (57%) said they had decided how to vote before the election was called, while one quarter decided during the last week of the campaign, including one in ten who decided on election day. The Liberal Democrats were particularly strong among late deciders (see Kellner, Table 3) which is consistent with the slight swell in Liberal Democrat support very late in the opinion polls.

Electoral volatility

How many switched? Net volatility (the change in the distribution of votes between two elections) reached record levels. Across the whole country there was a 10.5% (Butler) swing from the Conservatives to Labour, the highest any party had experienced since 1945.[5] Moreover, this built on a series of earlier gains in elections since 1983, when a deeply-divided and left-wing Labour Party reached its nadir of support. In a series of steps, the swing towards Labour was 1.7% in 1987, and 2.1% in 1992. In this sense, 1997 was 'one more heave'. The cumulative effect of successive elections was to ratchet the pendulum against the Conservatives. The Con-Lab swing in this election was far greater than that achieved by Harold Wilson when he came to power in 1964 (3.0%), by Edward Heath in 1970 (4.7%), or even by Margaret Thatcher in 1979 (5.2%).

Moreover, rather than being uniform, the swing varied more greatly across the whole country than in most previous elections, although this variation was partly attributable to boundary revisions. The standard deviation of the Con-Lab swing was 3.4% in this election, higher than any election since 1983. A couple of seats bucked the trend: Bradford West, and Bethnal Green and Bow, swung by five per cent from Labour to the Conservatives, both contested by Asian Tory candidates with strong local appeal. In sharp contrast, at the other extreme, there were massive swings towards Labour (over 18%) in Harrow East, Crosby, Hastings and Rye, and Brent North, while another ten seats produced swings over 17%. Among Con-Lib seats, the Liberal Democrats experienced an impressive surge in support in some of their target seats, such as Sheffield Hallam, and Harrogate and Knaresborough, as well as retaining by-election gains in Eastleigh, and in Newbury.[6] The Pederson index summarises change in the share of the vote for all British parliamentary parties.[7] In 1992–97 this index was 12.3, the second highest recorded since the war (after 1970–74 which was notable for the surge in support for minor parties).

Yet net volatility is only loosely related to gross volatility, meaning the total amount of change that takes place between two points in time, as measured at the individual level by panel surveys or recalled vote. *Net* change represents the flow of the vote which produces each party's overall level of support, while *gross* change measures the electoral flux or 'churning' which occurs among voters see-sawing between parties. Gross volatility can be estimated from the NOP/BBC Exit Poll, conducted for among 17,073 voters as they left polling stations after casting their ballot on 1 May. We can compare reported vote in 1997 against recalled vote in 1992, an imperfect measure given the vagaries of memory but the best now available in the absence of panel surveys. This data suggests that about two-thirds of voters remained stable, consistently voting for the same party in both elections, while in contrast about a third switched from 1992–97 (see Kellner, Table 2). This degree of electoral stability is not dissimilar to estimates in previous elections as measured by BES panel surveys from 1964–92. Most importantly, if confirmed by later panel surveys, this suggests that the Labour landslide in seats was not caused by increased electoral volatility among voters.

Who switched? Almost three quarters (71%) of those who voted Conservative in 1992 continued to support the party in 1997 (see Kellner, Table 2). The haemorrhage of Tory support came from the 11% who reported switching to the Liberal Democrats, and, most remarkably, from 13% (or about two million Conservatives) who reported switching directly to Labour. The centre party is usually regarded as a 'turn-around station' or 'half-way house', for temporary defectors from the major parties. To a remarkable degree, many more voters in this election moved directly between the major parties, or rather from the Conservatives to Labour, than is usual in British elections.[8] In contrast in BES panel surveys of voters in pairs of elections from 1964 to 1992, less than five per cent of voters were ever recorded as switching directly between the major parties.

The Liberal Democratic vote proved softest, as is common, with two-thirds staying loyal. One fifth of Liberal Democrats shifted to Labour, a move which was not counterbalanced by the seven per cent of Labour voters who switched to the Liberal Democrats. This pattern in the exit poll is confirmed also at constituency level. The change in the Labour and Liberal Democratic vote was strongly intercorrelated (R = 0.63). The sharp fall in the Conservative vote was most strongly related to the surge in Labour support (R = 0.40), and more weakly correlated with the change in Liberal Democratic support (R = 0.21).

UK turnout declined significantly, from 77.7 to 71.5%, the lowest since 1935, for reasons which remain unclear. As discussed by David Denver and Gordon Hands, explanations commonly relate to the type of seat. Some expected that Conservative voters, disillusioned with the government, would be more likely to stay at home on polling day. Others predicted that Blair's shift towards the centre ground would produce disillusionment among traditional left-wing Labour voters. Denver and Hands found that turnout fell slightly more (-7.9%) in seats held in 1992 by Labour than in those held by the Conservatives (-5.8%). Participation was not strongly related to region, although the decline in turnout was about one per cent higher than average in the Midlands and North of England, and slightly lower in Scotland. Nor can this phenomenon plausibly be explained by the closeness of the local race: turnout fell almost equally across different types of marginal and safe seats. One clue is that the fall was significantly associated with the social characteristics of constituencies, since turnout declined most sharply among seats with a high concentration of manual workers and council house tenants. Nevertheless individual level survey data is needed to explore this puzzle more thoroughly.

Regional swings

What made the result even more damaging for the Conservatives was the pattern of tactical voting and regional swings. The Conservative and Unionist Party, which campaigned as the only party to maintain the Union of the United Kingdom, was annihilated outside England, left without a single MP in Scotland (for the first time ever), Wales (for the first time since 1906), and, of course, Northern Ireland. The North/South divide closed slightly in votes, for the second election in a row. This cleavage can be summarised most simply by comparing the proportion of Conservative support in the South minus Conservative support in the North.[9] The Index in Table 3 shows a gradual increase in the North/South divide from 1974 to 1987, when the cleavage peaked, after which the divide slightly closed again. The pattern in 1997 has returned to the geographic division evident in 1983.

The reason for the closure, as discussed by Ian McAllister in this volume, is that Conservative support plummeted most sharply in areas where the party had been remarkably strong in the Thatcher decade: in Greater London (-14.1), the South-East (-13.1), East Anglia (-12.3),

3. The North-South divide

	Con	Lab
1974 (Feb)	8.5	9.3
1974 (Oct)	11.9	8.4
1979	11.7	15.1
1983	14.0	13.5
1987	17.3	17.9
1992	15.8	15.8
1997	13.6	13.6

Note: The Conservative index measures the proportion of Conservative votes from the South minus Conservative support in the North. The Labour index follows the same pattern with North minus South. The South equals London, the South East, South West, East Anglia and Midlands. The North equals the remainder of Britain.

Source: Calculated by William Field.

and the East Midlands (−11.7) (see Figure 4; McAllister, Table 2). In contrast, disguised by the pattern of seat losses, in 1997 the Tories experienced the smallest swings against them in Scotland and Wales. The Conservatives were wiped out in these areas because they were already so vulnerable that even a relatively modest swing against them (7.5%) was sufficient to eradicate their Members in Scotland and Wales. The problem facing the Scottish Conservatives is not just in MPs: the

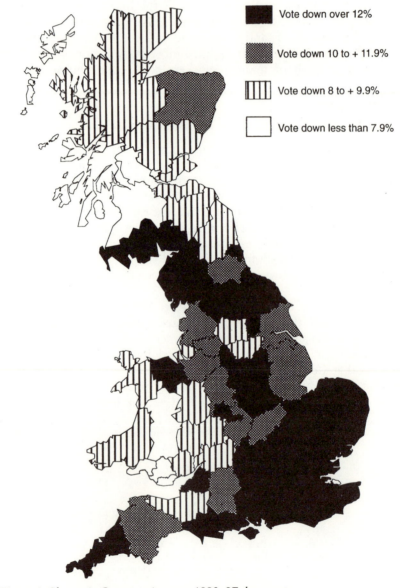

Vote down over 12%

Vote down 10 to + 11.9%

Vote down 8 to + 9.9%

Vote down less than 7.9%

Figure 4. Change in Conservative vote 1992–97, by county

grassroots base of the party has been washed away since the Conservatives no longer control any local councils, or have any MEPs, in Scotland.

In contrast, Labour made their greatest recovery in southern England
(see Figure 5). Labour dominated the nation's capital, winning an extra
twenty-five seats in Greater London, while the Liberal Democrats picked
up a swathe of five constituencies in the middle class suburbs of south
London. The Conservatives were reduced to eleven London seats,

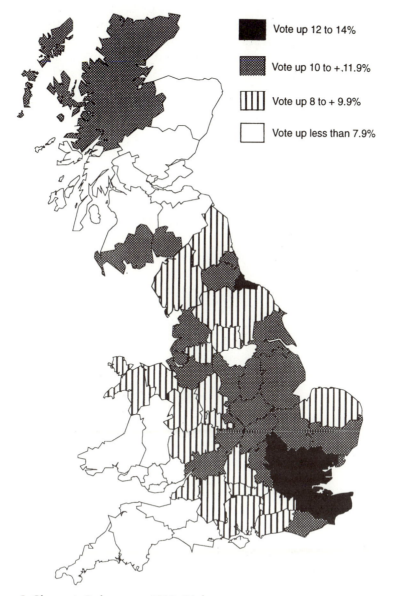

Vote up 12 to 14%

Vote up 10 to +.11.9%

Vote up 8 to + 9.9%

Vote up less than 7.9%

Figure 5. Change in Labour vote 1992–97, by county

mostly clustered in the stock-broker commuter belt on the Kent borders, as well as the affluent City, and Kensington and Chelsea. Winning seats across the whole country, Labour also took the majority of votes in their traditional heartland: Yorkshire and Humberside, the North West, the North, and Wales. Rather than piling up ever greater majorities in their rock-solid inner city seats of Glasgow and Merseyside, the change in Labour support was most effectively distributed: their smallest swing was in Wales and Scotland, both areas they already dominated. The Conservatives became the party, not just of England, but of Southern England: almost three-quarters of their MPs come from here. The only counties where the Conservatives enjoy a comfortable vote cushion, over 45% of the vote, are Surrey and West Sussex. The Liberal Democrats are breathing down their necks in the West Country, while in East Anglia the Conservatives are evenly balanced against Labour.

Tactical voting

What turned a substantial defeat for the Conservatives into an over-whelming rout was the closure of the ideological gap between Labour and the Liberal Democrats, and strategic campaigning by opposition

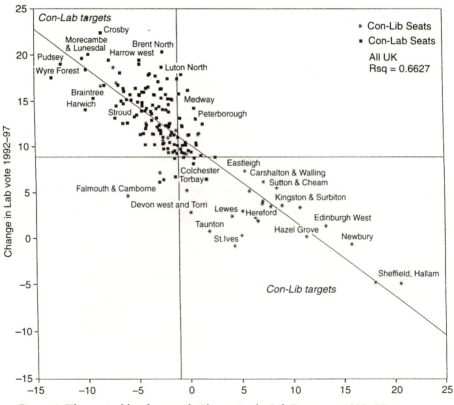

Figure 6. *The tactical battleground. Change in the Lib Dem vote 1992–97*

parties in their target marginals, producing tactical voting against the government on an unprecedented scale (see Figure 6). As Berrington suggests in this volume, there is absolutely nothing new about tactical voting, and indeed the 'wasted votes' argument against voting Liberal in the 1950s is a variant of this behaviour. Nevertheless the effect of tactical voting in 1997 was to concentrate the impact of the anti-Conservative tide.

As shown in Table 4, the electorate behaved differently according to the type of local contest. The fall in Conservative support was fairly uniform across different types of marginals. But in Conservative seats where Labour was in second place in 1992 (Con-Lab seats), Labour's share of the vote went up by 13% on average, while the Liberal Democrat share declined by about three per cent. In sharp contrast, in marginal Conservative seats where the Liberal Democrats were in second place in 1992 (Con-Lib seats), the Liberal Democrat vote increased by about two to three per cent, while the Labour share rose by less than average. This pattern is all the more remarkable given the boundary changes introduced since the 1992 election, which meant that many voters may have been unsure which party stood the best chance against the Conservative candidate.

Yet the distribution of marginals was clustered in certain areas like Greater London and the North West, and regional voting swings showed considerable variance, so we need to control for region to measure the impact of tactical voting. Table 5 estimates the difference between the change in the Labour and Liberal Democratic vote in all seats in a region, and in Con-Lab and Con-Lib seats. Compared with the regional mean, in Con-Lab seats Labour support was stronger than

4. Tactical voting by marginality

	Change in the vote, 1992–97		
	Con	Lab	Lib Dem
Con-Lab seats			
Very marginal	−12.7	12.2	−2.3
Fairly marginal	−11.5	12.2	−2.4
Semi-marginal	−12.3	13.2	−2.5
Fairly safe	−12.8	13.8	−3.9
Very safe	−13.2	13.3	−3.4
All Con-Lab	−12.7	13.0	−3.1
Con-Lib Dem seats			
Very marginal	−11.9	5.5	2.3
Fairly marginal	−9.5	3.6	2.8
Semi-marginal	−11.1	6.2	1.9
Fairly safe	−11.8	7.9	1.0
Very safe	−13.0	9.3	−0.3
All Con-Lib Dem	−12.4	8.3	0.4

Note: Seats are defined by the party in first and second place in the 1992 election, and the percentage majority, using the notional 1992 results under the new constituency boundaries. Very marginal = maj. 0.0–4.9; Fairly marginal = maj. 5.0–9.9; Semi-marginal = maj. 10.0–14.99; Fairly safe = maj. 15.0–19.9; Very safe = maj. 20.0+.

Source: British Parliamentary Constituencies, 1992–97.

5. Tactical voting by region

Region	Type of seat	Change in the vote, 1992–97	
		Lab	Lib Dem
South East	Con-Lab	2.6	−2.0
	Con-Lib	−1.6	1.1
East Anglia	Con-Lab	0.9	−0.5
	Con-Lib	−0.5	−0.2
London	Con-Lab	2.3	−0.7
	Con-Lib	−7.1	8.1
South West	Con-Lab	5.9	−4.0
	Con-Lib	−1.1	0.9
West Midlands	Con-Lab	1.5	−0.9
	Con-Lib	−3.0	2.8
East Midlands	Con-Lab	0.8	−0.9
	Con-Lib	1.2	−1.6
York & Humber	Con-Lab	4.1	−2.8
	Con-Lib	0.0	3.2
North West	Con-Lab	3.4	−2.1
	Con-Lib	−3.3	3.5
North	Con-Lab	3.9	−1.8
	Con-Lib	−2.6	4.3
Wales	Con-Lab	4.1	−1.3
	Con-Lib	−0.8	2.7
Scotland	Con-Lab	6.8	2.4
	Con-Lib	−2.1	9.3

Note: Change in the vote (1992–97) in Con-Lab and Con-Lib seats compared with the average change in the vote for all seats in the region.

Source: British Parliamentary Constituencies, 1992–97.

average, and the Liberal Democrats did less well than average, in every region except Scotland. Conversely, in Con-Lib seats, Liberal Democratic support rose by more than average, and Labour did less well than average, in all but two regions.

How many seats changed hands due to new tactical voting? The Con-Lab ('Butler') swing of the vote was 10.5%. If uniform across the country this should have produced about 391 Labour MPs, 211 Conservatives, and 29 Liberal Democrats, giving Blair a parliamentary majority of 122. Put in perspective this would have been a comfortable majority but still less than Mrs Thatcher enjoyed in 1983, and below Labour's historic landslide in 1945. The most striking feature of this election was that the variations in the swing probably lost the Conservatives 46 extra seats, of which 28 went to Labour and 18 to the Liberal Democrats, turning the government's defeat into the remarkable Labour landslide. Of these extra seats, about 24 may have fallen before the scythe of anti-government tactical voting, while half were probably lost due to other reasons like constituency campaigns.[10] In contrast, in 1992 an identical procedure suggests that about ten seats fell due to tactical voters.[11] Estimates by McAllister in this volume suggest that, after controlling for the social structure of seats, the effects of new tactical voting may have been even higher, although Berrington argues that the impact of this phenomenon has been exaggerated by some commentators.

There are disputes about the extent, and also the causes, of the growth in tactical voting. At least three plausible explanations are possible. Those focussing on the electorate suggest voters may have become more sophisticated in strategically identifying the party best positioned to defeat the Tories, and more willing to vote for their second-choice party. Alternatively, from a 'top-down' perspective Labour and the Liberal Democrats may have been more effective in concentrating campaign resources more heavily in their target marginals. Lastly, the closure of the ideological gap between the opposition parties, with Blair's move to steal Liberal Democrat clothes on the centre-left, may have paid electoral dividends. If there is less distance between parties, it is easier for voters to switch. Disentangling these factors remains a complex process, and we await individual-level panel data from the BES, and contextual information about constituency campaigns, to analyse this phenomenon further.

Social base of the vote

Another feature of change in this election is the social basis of the vote. At constituency level the Labour heartland has been inner city working-class areas, with all the multiple social problems associated with council estates, high unemployment and urban deprivation, a high concentration of Asian and black residents, and industrial decline. Irrespective of any social dealignment at the individual level, far from weakening in recent decades, many of these correlations at constituency level have strengthened over time. The gradual shrinkage of these areas, and the expansion of the more affluent suburban areas in southern England, strengthened the argument that Labour had to adapt to survive. Unless new Labour could expand beyond their traditional social base, by becoming a catch-all party, they faced defeat.

The evidence from the 1997 election is that new Labour has managed to widen its appeal beyond its core, like the Social Democrats in Sweden, yet also hold on to its traditional working class vote. As shown in Table 6, compared with the pattern under Harold Wilson in 1966, and under Neil Kinnock in 1992, Blair did better among constituencies with a high concentration of professional and managerial workers. While seats with many skilled non-manuals (C1s) swung sharply towards Thatcher in 1979, these areas shifted most strongly towards Labour in the 1990s. From 1979–97 weakening Labour support in working class seats indicates dealignment, particularly among the skilled working class (the C2s). In a similar trend, from 1966–79 Labour support strengthened in seats with high levels of council housing, but this association subsequently weakened in the 1990s. As we would expect, as a 'catch-all' party new Labour has triumphed by maintaining its traditional base and yet simultaneously widening its appeal to middle England.

Further confirmation of this pattern can be found at the individual

6. The social basis of Labour constituency support, 1966–97

	1966	1979	1992	1997
Professional	−.60	–	−.47	−.44
Managerial (a)	−.85	−.79	−.71	−.68
Skilled non-manual	−.39	−.57	.01	.03
Skilled manual	.57	.58	.44	.44
Semi-skilled manual	.49	.72	.57	.52
Unskilled manual	.60	.71	.57	.50
Owner occupied	−.51	−.60	−.47	−.49
Council house	.52	.71	.64	.58
Unemployed	.38	.71	.72	.73
Household no car	.65	.73	.76	.73
Retired	−.45	−.33	−.31	−.35
All non-white	.08	.28	.28	.30

Note: Correlation between constituency characteristics in the Census and percentage Labour vote. (a) 1979 professional and managerial.

Source: P. Norris, *Electoral Change Since 1945* (Blackwell, 1997).

level in the NOP/BBC exit poll, which can be compared against evidence from the equivalent poll in 1992 (See Kellner, Table 1). As a 'catch-all' party, Labour made gains across all social classes, although the shift was greatest among skilled non-manual workers (the 'C1s'), and also among semi-skilled manual workers (DEs). The net result is another ratchet down, and a sharp one, in class dealignment. The Alford Index, measuring Labour's share of the vote among non-manual workers minus its share among manual workers, dropped from 27 to 21 points, the lowest score since records began in 1945, and half the score of the mid-sixties. Most noticeably the decline in the Alford index over time shows a striking pattern of stepped shifts downwards: from 1966 to 1970, then from 1974 to 1979, before a further marked shift in 1992 to 1997. As argued elsewhere,[12] this strongly indicates that the explanation lies in the changing pattern of party competition, notably new Labour's shift towards the ideological middle ground with a classless appeal, rather than a steady secular slide due to long-term social trends.

Labour's support among council tenants remained solid and unchanged, but the swing to Labour was marked among owner occupiers, especially those with a mortgage. In the Thatcher years housing tenure proved one of the most significant indicators of party support but this relationship has weakened today. Perhaps the legacy of negative equity, and the end of the house price boom of the 1980s, made mortgage holders particularly bitter against the government which had so assiduously promoted the benefits of home ownership. As discussed later by Joni Lovenduski, the modest gender gap in 1992 closed in 1997, as more women (+ 11%) than men (+ 8%) shifted into the Blair camp. The familiar pattern of the gender-generation gap continued, however, with younger women more Labour than younger men, and the reversal of this pattern among the older generation. The general pattern by age group was striking: the strongest swing to Labour was monitored among the younger generation (+ 18%), (and first-time voters), while Labour made no gains among the over 65s.

The minor parties

Turning in more detail to the minor parties, in this election support for the Liberal Democrats fell from 17.8 to 16.8% of the UK vote. Nevertheless, like an under-fives birthday treat, all the opposition parties departed with seat prizes. As discussed by Hugh Berrington, the Liberal Democrats more than doubled their parliamentary strength from 1992–97, rising from twenty to forty-six MPs, their best result since 1929. They benefited from the fall in Conservative support while maintaining their share of the vote in Somerset and Devon, and increasing their support in Cornwall and Dorset. They captured eight seats in the West Country, often by wafer-thin margins, including Torbay, St Ives, Somerton and Frome, Weston-Super-Mare, Devon West and Torridge, Taunton. With fourteen seats, including Paddy Ashdown's Yeovil, the South West is the Liberal Democrats' area of greatest parliamentary strength.

Another swath of gains were made in the moderately affluent commuter belt of South West London, including Richmond Park, Kingston and Surbiton, Twickenham, Sutton and Cheam, and Carshalton and Wallington. Eight more Conservative seats were captured in the South East, notably in coastal areas including the Isle of Wight, with the largest electorate in the UK, along with Portsmouth South, Eastleigh, and close-by Winchester. The Liberal Democrats also consolidated their hold in Scotland, picking up Edinburgh West against Lord Douglas Hamilton, and West Aberdeenshire and Kincardine. Due to the distribution of their support in the vast rural tracts of the Borders, the Highlands and Islands, and the workings of the electoral system, the Liberal Democrats won ten seats in the region, despite getting a lower share of the Scottish vote (13%) than the Conservatives, who got none.

North of the Border, as discussed by Alice Brown, the Scottish Nationalists doubled from three to six MPs, with 22.1% of the Scottish vote. To their old seats of Angus (Andrew Walsh), Banff and Buchan (Alec Salmond), and Moray (Margaret Ewing), they took Galloway and Upper Nithsdale, and Tayside North from the Conservatives, and held Perth which Roseanna Cunningham won in a by-election in 1995. SNP support was particularly strong in the regions of Dumfries and Galloway, Tayside and Central, and Grampian. Meanwhile in North Wales, Plaid Cymru held on to Ynys Mons, Caernarvon, Merionnydd Nant Conwy, and Ceridigion, with 10.6% of the Welsh vote. Unlike the SNP, Plaid Cymru's support is strongly concentrated, with 37% of the vote in Gwynedd and 22% in Dyfed, but little outside their linguistic base. The Liberal Democrats performed well in the Welsh border region, holding the sprawling rural seats of Montgomeryshire, winning Brecon and Radnorshire, as well as Hereford next door in England, while

Labour predominance remained unchallenged in their heartland in South Wales.

In Northern Ireland, as O'Leary and Evans discuss, Sinn Fein achieved its most successful result in four decades with 16.1% of the vote in the region, and the capture of two seats. Gerry Adams swept to victory in West Belfast while Martin McGuiness took Mid Ulster. The Sinn Fein MPs will not sit at Westminster although their victory can be seen as highly symbolic, with potential consequences for the peace process. Sinn Fein got 39.9% of the nationalist vote against 60.1% for the SDLP, who have three MPs headed by John Hume. The Ulster Unionists, led by David Trimble, rose from nine to ten MPs, with the gain of West Tyrone, and they won 70.6% of the Unionist vote against 29.4% for the DUP, headed by the Reverend Ian Paisley.

Overall 1,678 candidates stood for the fringe parties or under an independent label, almost twice as many as in 1992. The most successful stood for the Referendum Party, funded by Sir James Goldsmith, which polled 811,829 votes overall, or three per cent. The party was most successful in the South West, South East and East Anglia, notably in two constituencies which could have been expected to have benefited from the cross-channel European link, namely Harwich, and Folkstone and Hythe, where the party picked up over eight per cent of the vote. The Conservatives lost 24 marginals where the Referendum vote was greater than the size of their 1992 majority, (19 to Labour and five to the Liberal Democrats). Nevertheless it is difficult to establish whether the Referendum Party actually made the difference in these seats, as some claimed, since according to the NOP/BBC exit poll, less than half the Referendum voters were ex-Tories.

The results for the new parliament

After eighteen years of Conservative predominance, the election blew a breath of fresh air into parliament, replacing the tired staleness of British political life. The combination of record retirements and record electoral upheavals meant that Westminster saw the entry of 259 new members, the highest number since the war. A younger generation transfused the Commons, with a third of the new members under forty, replacing some of the weary and divided old guard. Moreover the new cadre has exacerbated trends towards the professions, especially education: only nine of the new Labour intake (five per cent) are from a working-class occupation, compared with a third of all Labour MPs in 1945.[13]

As discussed later by Joni Lovenduski, women made substantial gains, 120 swept into the House (18.2%), including 102 on the Labour benches. This doubled female representation to bring Britain into line with other EU member states, although remaining below Scandinavia. There were 362 female candidates for the three main parties, or 18.8%, a slight increase on 1992. As Lovenduski argues, what produced the breakthrough to power was less the number than the type of seats which Labour women fought, since they were well-placed in the key marginals. The shift in votes for women and men standing in each party was identical: women candidates neither gained nor lost more support than average.

The popular label of 'Blair's babes' disguised the effective shift in power: five women were appointed as Secretaries of State, four became Ministers of State, another nine became Parliamentary Under-secretaries. Moreover women were not just appointed to 'women's ministries': Mo Mowlam was made Secretary of State for Northern Ireland, Margaret Beckett became President of the Board of Trade, Dawn Primarolo entered the Treasury, Ann Taylor became Leader of the House. In total, more than a fifth of the Labour government is female.

Ethnic minorities made slower progress, with the election of five Asian and four black Labour MPs, including Britain's first Muslim MP, Mohammad Sarwar, in Glasgow Govan.[14] The only Asian Conservative MP, Nirj Deva, lost his seat in Brentford and Isleworth, swept out on the general anti-Conservative London tide. As a result the number of minority MPs rose from five to nine, or 1.3% of the Commons. As discussed by Shamit Saggar in this volume, there were more Asian and black candidates than ever before—the number for the major parties rose from 24 to 44, but many faced hopeless seats. Whether minority candidates faced any electoral penalty because of their background is difficult to establish. Black and Asian Conservative candidates experienced a smaller than average fall in their vote (down—9.3%). As mentioned earlier, where two minority candidates fought each other the results were sometimes unexpected. Conservative Kabir Choudhury fighting Labour's Oona King in Bethnal Green and Bow, and Mohammed Riaz fighting Marsha Singh in Bradford West, even managed to gain positive swings against Labour. But on the other hand, Labour Asian and Black candidates generally saw a smaller than average rise in their share of the vote (5.1 instead of 9.7%) although Labour's candidates fighting seats in inner London experienced substantial swings in their favour (from 8 to 15%), in line with Labour's performance in the capital, including Paul Boateng in Brent South, Piara Khambra in Ealing Southall, Diane Abbott in Hackney North and Stoke Newington, and Bernie Grant in Tottenham. In general, Saggar concludes, racial politics played a limited role in the British campaign. This is in marked contrast to the politicisation of racial conflict evident in recent elections in countries like France and the United States. As Saggar suggests, whether this is because racial concerns were frozen out of the campaign as too divisive by the major parties, or because the concerns of minority voters were largely absorbed and integrated into the mainstream agenda, remains a matter of interpretation.

Turning to the government, the cabinet lost seven members, as well as dozens of junior ministers. Frontbench spokespersons suffered slightly above average Con-Lab swings against them (11.5%). The most notable head to roll was the Conservative leadership contender of the right and Defence Secretary, Michael Portillo, defeated in Enfield Southgate by a 16.8 swing to the young Labour challenger, Stephen Twigg. Others who lost included Treasury Chief Secretary William Waldegrave (Bristol West), Leader of the House Tony Newton (Braintree), Scottish Secretary Michael Forsyth (Stirling), Foreign Secretary Malcolm Rifkind (Edinburgh Pentlands), and President of the Board of Trade Ian Lang (Galloway and Upper Nithsdale). Other familiar faces leaving the Commons included the Vice-Chairman of the Conservative Party, Angela Rumbold (Mitcham and Morden), the flamboyant Eurosceptic Tony Marlow (Northampton North), leader of the 1922 Committee Sir Marcus Fox (Shipley) and former ministers Edwina Currie, Norman Lamont, David Mellor, Jonathan Aitken, Sir Rhodes Boyson and David Hunt.

Many Conservative members who had been involved in problems of sleaze, and who entered the election with a cloud hanging over their name, suffered above-average swings against them (11.9%), and 16 of the 23 who stood again lost. Piers Merchant clung on in Beckenham, despite being set up in a sexual scandal by the *Sun* at the start of the campaign, and Alan Clark survived despite (or because of?) his memoirs. But both MPs most heavily involved in the 'cash-for-questions' row, Michael Brown in Cleethorpes and Neil Hamilton in Tatton, lost heavily. Following a remarkable anti-sleaze campaign in the constituency, the BBC correspondent Martin Bell was returned from Tatton to Westminster as the first independent MP (without any party affiliation) since A.P. Herbert represented Oxford University almost half a century earlier.

Europe, an old wound dividing the Conservative Party, reopened dramatically in the third week of the campaign. The issue of membership of a single European currency had split the party throughout Major's term in office, and only the opt out clause negotiated at Maastricht kept the two wings together. The official line in the Tory manifesto was to 'wait and see' about the conditions of membership. If the government concluded that it would be in Britain's interest to join then there would be a referendum before becoming a member. Many in the Conservative party had tried to distance themselves from official party policy by taking a Eurosceptic line against the EMU in their candidate leaflets. The press made much of this, with the *Daily Mail* and *The Times* publishing long lists of eurosceptic MPs and advising voters to support them. In the end this came to naught: the known eurosceptics suffered identical swings against them as the rest of the party. The image of disunity which this reinforced in the eyes of the voters, however, probably deeply hurt the party. In the NOP/BBC exit poll, when asked whether each party was united or divided, two thirds saw the Conservatives as divided, while only a third thought the same of the Labour Party.

What will the new House of Commons be like? With such a large turnover we will have to wait to see how the House reacts when debating some of the key issues before Parliament, including devolution, constitutional reform, and Britain's membership of the EMU. Nevertheless to analyse the composition of the House we can look at political attitudes among new and old MPs drawing on the *British Representation Study 1997*, a survey of almost 1,000 parliamentary candidates and MPs from all the major parties conducted well before the official campaign opened. The survey, which achieved a response rate of 61%, includes replies from 261 Members elected to the new House of Commons from all the major parties, including 100 new Labour MPs. The survey includes a series of 11-point ideological scales, and candidates were asked to place themselves on a general left v. right scale, privatisation v. nationalisation, taxes v. spending, jobs v. prices, EU membership, and women's equality.[15]

As shown in Table 7, the results show three clear patterns. First, on most of these scales there is remarkably little difference between the Labour and Liberal Democrat Members, but the Conservatives are far to the right. This is clearest on the classic economic issues of privatisation versus nationalisation, and taxes versus spending, but the party cleavage is also evident on non-economic issues such as Europe and gender equality. On many of scales Labour and the Liberal Democrat MPs share a broadly similar consensus.

7. **Attitudes in the new House of Commons**

Scales	Labour MPs			Lib Dem MPs			Conservative MPs		
	Old	New	Diff	Old	New	Diff	Old	New	Diff
Left-Right	3.27	3.71	−.44	3.75	3.60	.15	4.64	4.78	−.14
Privatisation	4.79	5.06	−.27	6.00	5.72	.28	10.00	10.05	−.05
Taxes & spending	3.64	4.04	−.4	4.11	3.22	.89	8.11	8.78	−.67
Jobs/prices	2.07	2.67	−.6	3.66	3.81	−.15	7.07	7.86	−.79
European Union	4.08	3.95	.13	2.77	3.77	−1.00	8.50	9.63	−1.13
Women's equality	1.60	1.19	.41	1.66	1.22	.44	4.60	4.77	−.17
N.	81	100		9	22		31	18	

Note: These scales range from 1 (most leftwing) to 11 (most rightwing). A positive difference means a shifts to the left, a negative difference indicates a shift to the right.

Source: The British Representation Study 1997.

Secondly, if we turn to compare differences within parties, many commentators claim that the new Labour MPs, who swept to power with the Blairite centre-left, have very different values to old Labour. The survey does confirm that new Labour Members see themselves as slightly more rightwing than old Labour, and indeed they are slightly more rightwing on privatisation, taxation, and inflation. But on the non-economic agenda they are slightly more in favour of Britain's membership of the EU, and more egalitarian towards gender equality.

In general, however, the difference in attitudes between old and new Labour MPs are modest. As the party has moved centre-left, this tide seems to have swept most Labour politicians in the same direction.

Lastly, if we compare the Conservatives on the same basis, the most striking finding is that across all scales the new Conservatives are consistently more rightwing than the old Tories, and the gap is particularly marked on Europe. The survey includes only 18 new Conservatives, but these are sharply more eurosceptic. What this suggests is that some of the divisions within the party over the EU, far from being resolved by the election, may be exacerbated. The Conservative party is also particularly out of touch with the rest of the House on the issue of women's rights, perhaps reflecting the fact that the party contains so few women Members. The scales only tap into certain values but a broader comparison of MPs on a wide range of issues in the survey confirms this general picture: on many issues Labour and Liberal Democrat MPs share a common political agenda, while the Tories have established clear blue water between them and other parties.

The electoral system

Lastly, as Patrick Dunleavy and Helen Margetts demonstrate, the electoral system was critically important for the outcome. In this election the winner's bonus, and the penalties against the party in second place, operated with particular vengeance. With 43.3% of the (UK) vote, Labour won 63.6% of seats, producing a votes:seats ratio of 1.46. In contrast, with 30.7% of the vote, the Conservatives gained only 25.0% of all seats, producing a votes:seats ratio of 0.81. The size of the winner's bonus for Labour, and the penalty for the main party in second place, were larger than any since the war. In 1987, with a similar share of the vote to the Conservatives under Major, Labour won sixty more seats. What this meant in practice was that it took, on average, 113,987 votes to elect every Liberal Democrat MP, 58,127 votes to elect every Conservative MP, but 32,318 votes to elect every Labour one. This disproportionality was produced by certain factors: the size of the winner's bonus under the British system of first-past-the-post; the geographic distribution of party support; the effects of the anti-government tactical squeeze; and the disparities in the size of constituency electorates, which continue to benefit Labour despite the redistribution introduced by the Boundary Commission. In 1997 Conservative seats included on average about 5,000 more electors than Labour constituencies.

The result is that the Conservatives are confronting an Everest every bit as daunting as that facing Labour in 1983. If the Conservatives and Labour get exactly the same share of the vote (37%) in the next election, a uniform swing would produce 341 Labour MPs and 254 Conservative MPs, that is, an 87 seat winner's bonus for Blair. As Table 8 indicates, if we assume a uniform swing from Labour to the Conservatives, it would take a minimal swing of eight per cent to produce a hung

8. Projections of seat change with a uniform swing

Swing	Lab	Con	Lib Dem	Lab	Con	Lib Dem	Nat	Other	Par maj
		%					Win		
1.0	44.3	29.7	16.8	428	153	48	10	20	Lab 197
.0	43.3	30.7	16.8	419	165	46	10	20	Lab 179
1.0	42.3	31.7	16.8	412	175	42	10	20	Lab 165
2.0	41.3	32.7	16.8	402	186	41	10	20	Lab 145
3.0	40.3	33.7	16.8	392	198	39	10	20	Lab 125
4.0	39.3	34.7	16.8	373	219	37	10	20	Lab 87
5.0	38.3	35.7	16.8	358	236	34	11	20	Lab 57
6.0	37.3	36.7	16.8	344	251	33	11	20	Lab 30
6.3	37.0	37.0	16.8	341	254	33	11	20	Lab 23
7.0	36.3	37.7	16.8	334	262	32	11	20	Lab 9
8.0	35.3	38.7	16.8	320	278	31	11	20	–
9.0	34.3	39.7	16.8	309	290	29	11	20	–
10.0	33.3	40.7	16.8	294	305	29	11	20	–
11.0	32.3	41.7	16.8	279	320	28	11	20	–
11.6	31.7	42.3	16.8	270	331	27	11	20	Con 1
12.0	31.3	42.7	16.8	262	340	26	11	20	Con 21

Note: This assumes a uniform Con-Lab swing with no change in the vote for the other parties.

Source: British Parliamentary Constituencies, 1992–97.

parliament which would deprive Labour of their majority, and a vast swing of 11.6% for the Conservatives to regain an overall parliamentary majority. This size of swing has only ever been achieved this century by Labour in 1945 (11.8%), and by the National coalition government in 1931 (14.4%). Yet, although massive, a similar scepticism was always voiced about the size of the swing required for Labour to recover power, and the 1997 election demonstrates that nothing can be taken for granted. What the electorate giveth with one hand, they can always take away. But the Conservatives need to undertake a critical re-evaluation and reorganisation as fundamental as that experienced by the Labour Party in the last decade before they can hope to recover from this nadir.

Conclusions

Many elections are described as historic watersheds in British politics, often with exaggeration as the familiar pattern restores itself in subsequent contests. Nevertheless this election, more than most, seems to deserve the epithet. The result for the Labour Party is an outstanding testimony to the resilient ability of a social democratic party fundamentally to regenerate or reinvent itself, although it took fourteen years to recover from the ashes of 1983. In the concluding article Rose outlines many reasons why the Labour honeymoon may not last, but nevertheless in the immediate aftermath of the election Blair was setting new records (82% approval) as the most popular Prime Minister since opinion polling began in Britain fifty years ago. The result for the Conservatives is an opportunity to rethink their strategy, to reorganise their party from the grassroots up, and to re-energise themselves in opposition, under new leadership. The result for British democracy is a sense of a fresh wind blowing through government, with a renewed sense of the capacity of the system to change, which can only be healthy for the body politic.

I would like to thank William Field for generating the maps, Nick Moon at National Opinion Polls and Peter Horrocks at the BBC for early release of the NOP/BBC Exit Poll, Nick Bent for helping to enter the data for the British Parliamentary Constituency, 1992–97 database, and David Denver for helping to check the results data.

1   For an analysis of the impact of the currency crisis see H.C. Clarke, M.C. Stewart and P. Whiteley, 'Tory Trends: Party Identification and the Dynamics of Conservative Support Since 1992', *British Journal of Political Science*, 27 (1997).

2   D. Sanders, 'Economic Performance, Management Competence and the Outcome of the Next Election', *Political Studies*, 44 (1996).

3   'Media Content Analysis of National Press', *CARMA*, May 1997.

4   Similar changes from the earlier polls to election day have been estimated by Ivor Crewe for elections from 1959–92. These estimates suggest that the usual effect of the campaign is to produce a swing between 0.2 to 4.2%.

5   The Con-Lab (Butler) swing, used throughout this paper, is conventionally measured as the average of the percentage point Conservative increase minus the Labour decrease divided by two.

6   It is worth noting that the government normally recovers its by-election losses, but not this time as only Christchurch reverted home to the Tories.

7   The Pederson Index is measured by summing the change in the percentage vote for all parties and dividing by two.

8   Obviously the differences between recalled votes and panel surveys with voting choice recoded at each election means this provides an imprecise comparison over time, although if anything, recalled measures are more likely to under-estimate the degree of electoral change.

9   I am grateful to William Field for suggesting and calculating this measure.

10   There were eight seats which Labour gained from the Conservatives where the percentage point fall in the Liberal Democrat vote exceeded the regional average, and also exceeded the percentage size of the 1997 Labour majority: Harwich, Castle Point, Braintree, Milton Keynes North East, Harrow West, Romford, Kettering and Wellingborough. There were 16 seats which the Liberal Democrats gained from the Conservatives where the percentage point fall in the Labour vote exceeded the regional average, and also exceeded the percentage size of the 1997 Liberal Democrat majority: Colchester, Lewes, Winchester, Eastleigh, Twickenham, Richmond Park, Carshalton and Wallington, Sutton and Cheam, Kingston and Surbitan, Somerton and Frome, Torbay, Devon West and Torridge, Weston-Super-Mare, Taunton, Northavon, and Aberdeen West and Kincardine.

11   I. Crewe, P. Norris and R. Waller, 'The 1992 General Election', in P. Norris et al. (eds), *British Elections and Parties Yearbook 1992* (Harvester Wheatsheaf, 1992).

12   See P. Norris, *Electoral Change Since 1945* (Blackwell, 1997).

13   See P. Norris and J. Lovenduski, *Political Recruitment* (Cambridge University Press, 1995); C. Mellors and D. Darcy, 'Enter the Comprehensive Game', *Times Educational Supplement*, 9.5.97.

14   At the time of writing, Mohammad Sarwar's election remains under a cloud due to alleged irregularities in campaign financing.

15   The BRS 1997 was directed by Pippa Norris in collaboration with Joni Lovenduski, Anthony Heath, Roger Jowell and John Curtice. The BRS received replies from 999 candidates. The scales in the survey were used also in the British Election Study, 1997.

The Labour Campaign

BY DENNIS KAVANAGH*

THE LABOUR PARTY in 1997 is recognisable to the Kinnock-led party in 1992. But it contrasts sharply with the divided party that lost in 1979 or the 'democratised' one that failed so disastrously in 1983. Labour leaders learnt bitter lessons from the four successive election defeats between 1979 and 1992. Starting after the 1983 review, a series of incremental steps produced changes in policy—to a new centre ground defined largely by Thatcher—greater authority for the leader and for the parliamentary leadership vis à vis the party conference, and a greater reliance on modern communications based campaigning. The effect of the changes was a transformation in the structure and ethos of the Labour Party.

Labour in decline

The impact of the unexpected 1992 election defeat is crucial to understanding both the subsequent evolution of the Labour Party and its approach to the 1997 campaign. The defeat could easily have resulted in a repudiation of the modernising changes which Neil Kinnock had made, and a demand that Labour should move sharply to the left. The two years of John Smith's leadership were a victory for those who believed that the party needed to make only marginal changes to policy and only 'one more heave' for victory. By the time Smith died in May 1994, Labour had moved into a commanding lead in the opinion polls, thanks to the collapse of Conservative support following the exit from the ERM in September 1994 (see Whiteley in this volume). But apart from OMOV victory (see below) the party was substantially still the one that lost in 1992.

The party modernisers, the supporters of the policy and organisational changes made by Neil Kinnock, grew impatient with Smith. Their ranks included Tony Blair and Gordon Brown. They were aware of the analyses which showed that Labour's support was increasingly confined to the declining sectors of society—trade unions, the north of Britain, the council estates and the working class. The party had not gained over 40% of the vote since 1970. Its 'normal' or average share of the vote had slumped to one third of the electorate by 1992, way behind the Conservatives. They believed that unless Labour changed radically, it would win an election only in exceptional circumstances. Aspirational

* Professor of Politics at Liverpool University.

members of the working class turned away because they associated the party with holding back people with ambition and drive. The party appeared to be more interested in helping the poor and the disadvantaged than those who wanted to 'get on'. They liked Labour's social policies but would not trust it to run the economy. These sentiments were reported in post-election surveys and suggested that the party was still too much old Labour and had not modernised sufficiently.[1]

Kinnock's modernisation measures involved three steps. He reformed party institutions so as to empower the leadership and enable it to be more responsive to the electorate at large, rather than to the activists. He established a Shadow Communications Agency, drawn largely from the public relations industry, and gave it a key role in developing campaign strategy and promoting the party. Increasingly, Kinnock used this and such other leader-driven bodies as the campaign management team and the campaign strategy committee to bypass the NEC. The leadership also took powers to intervene in the selection of by-election candidates. Although plans to introduce one member one vote for selection and reselection of parliamentary candidates made only partial progress, by the time he stepped down it was already agreed that the trade union vote would be reduced to 70% at the annual conference.

A second step involved shifting the party's policies, in particular abandoning the electorally unattractive ones on defence, public ownership, the trade unions and Europe. This was largely achieved in the policy review in 1989. Although the party had accepted most of the Conservative's privatisation measures and virtually abandoned the policy of public ownership by 1992, Clause IV in the party constitution remained. Finally, Kinnock wanted to alter the party's image which in turn would grow out of the actions taken on policy and party institutions. By the 1992 election, however, he had achieved only limited progress on the last.[2]

New Labour

Tony Blair resumed the campaign for policy and structural changes, but also sought to change the ethos or culture of the party. His modernisation involved the creation, in effect, of a new party. Labour had to break out of its working class and trade union ghettos and lose its fear of change. The emphasis on the traditional values of redistribution and public ownership was replaced by the themes of equal opportunity and encouraging the free market, though tempering it with a sense of social responsibility. Labour had to come to terms with the social and cultural changes of the Thatcher years and a more individualistic and inquisitive society. It also had to rid itself of its tax and spend image.[3]

Blair pursured his agenda along various fronts. First, there was the drive to increase individual membership. Labour Party membership had steadily declined over the previous twenty years to a figure of some 280,000 in 1994. Under Blair it added 100,000 in two years and reached 420,000 by the time of the general election. A larger membership was a source of funds—so reducing the party's dependence on trade unions—and would restrict the opportunity for small groups of activists to impose their parliamentary candidates in run-down constituencies. The culture of local parties was already being transformed as the effect of OMOV (one member one vote) gave members greater influence over annual elections to the NEC constituency section and the selection of parliamentary candidates. Blair used the enlarged membership to force through policy changes (see below). Getting the approval of ordinary party members via ballots gave a new twist to the idea of party democracy. Traditionally, this has been exploited by party activists and the Labour left. Labour leaders now used ballots against the latter. It now had a computerised membership list, a feature of any effective organisation, which is used for direct mailing and fund-raising.

A second front involved finance. Modernisers were embarrassed at the party's close relationship and financial dependence on the trade unions. The party cultivated rich businessmen who made substantial donations, held regular dinner of the 'Thousand Club', and encouraged private funding of the offices of the party leader and other frontbenchers. Between 1986 and 1996 trade union funds as a proportion of party income declined from three quarters to one half.

A third area of change involved the unions. The 1993 party conference accepted a version of OMOV—so ending the unions' block vote at the annual party conference—and constituency party ballots to select parliamentary candidates and for the electoral college to elect the party leader and deputy leader. The conference also agreed to reduce the union share of the electoral college vote from 40% to one third, the same proportion as MPs and constituency parties and the union share of the conference vote to 50% when the party's individual membership reached 300,000. Blair kept the unions at arms' length, made clear that they could expect no special favours from a Labour government, and that the Conservatives' industrial relations legislation would remain in place.

A fourth element was decisive leadership. It has often been noted that Blair rose in the party without a background in the trade unions or the public sector and had not been a member of the factions that dominated the party in the 1970s and early 1980s. Educated at a private school and the son of a Conservative father he was in some respects an outsider, and impatient with the state of the party.[4] He told a meeting of Rupert Murdoch's News Corporation executives in July 1995 that the early 1980s were over, when, 'frankly [Labour] was unelectable'. Strong leadership, the party's private research suggested, would reassure voters that old Labour would be firmly under control. Blair insisted on party discipline and loyalty and rebuked shadow ministers who breached the party line. The NEC and party conference ceased to be alternative voices of the party but were clearly subordinate to the leader.

Indeed, in January 1997 the NEC approved changes which would emphasise the role of itself and conference as 'a partner' to a Labour government.[5] Running the party effectively was a way, the only way, that Blair could demonstrate his leadership credentials. When faced by potential opponents about his inexperience, he pointed to the changes he had achieved in changing the party.

Finally, Labour had to become a people's party, which meant embracing the middle class and prosperous working class. Appealing to the trade unions and the working class was no longer sufficient; both had shrunk dramatically in size since 1979 and Labour still could not get 50% of their voters. The Labour leadership openly cultivated the Liberal Democrats, businessmen (including addressing the CBI conference) the Conservative press (eventually resulting in the election endorsement of Blair by the best selling Sunday *News of the World* and best selling daily *Sun*). In a daring theft of Conservative rhetoric Blair proclaimed Labour as the 'one nation' party.

On policy Blair dispensed with the terms right and left. Labour was now the party of the centre. An example of his bold approach was seen in his determination to revoke Clause IV of the party constitution, which committed the party to public ownership. Labour no longer believed in public ownership—but it suited its opponents to say that it did and that it was hostile to the free market. The party should henceforth say what it meant and mean what it said. Blair launched the proposal at the 1994 party conference and it was carried overwhelmingly at a special conference in April 1995. The new clause welcomed the enterprise of the market and praised the rigour of competition, but wanted them to operate in a just society and an open democracy. Virtually all of the constituency parties balloted their memberships and they voted overwhelmingly for change. Opposition largely came from the trade unions which had not consulted their members. Blair had appealed directly to the members, over the heads of local activists and union leaders. The change and the manner of its achievement were presented as the symbols of a new Labour Party. For Blair they were also a vindication of his boldness and encouragement to carry on in a similar style.[6]

In 1996 a draft party manifesto was put to a ballot of members. Blair insisted on this step, in spite of opposition from the NEC. The manifesto confirmed that Labour accepted yet another instalment of the Conservative agenda. It accepted the internal market in the health service and allowed the grant maintained schools to retain many of their freedoms. The redistributive thrust of John Smith's 1992 shadow budget had gone; Labour no longer proposed to make increases in state pensions and child benefits, or to raise the top rate of income tax. The whole exercise clearly clipped the wings of the authority of conference over policy. Blair was offering the party a plebiscitary form of leadership. He was almost obsessive in speeches, interviews and soundbites in his use of the words 'new' and 'change'. His use of the term 'new Labour' suggested a rebirth of the party, one which now closely resembled the catchall party described by Kirchheimer over 30 years ago.[7] Among the features Kirchheimer identified in such a party were: a reduction in the party's ideological baggage; the greater authority and autonomy of the party leadership; a weakening of party/interest-group links; a down-grading of the role of extra-parliamentary bodies; the use of opinion polls, advertising and public relations to enhance the party's electoral appeal; and the adoption of policies and themes which would appeal to the electorate as a whole, rather than a segment of it.

Labour modernisers were of course inspired above all by an interest in winning the next election. Neil Kinnock reflected that when he had referred to the need to take account of public opinion his critics had dismissed this as mere 'electoralism'.[8] But they were also influenced by how the centre left parties in the United States and Australia had managed to win elections. They were impressed at how Bill Clinton had presented himself as a new Democrat in 1992, appropriating the language of 'renewal' and 'change', repudiating the tax and spending image of his party and appealing to the 'working middle class'. There were many personal links between the parties and these were reflected in Labour's campaign methods in the 1997 election. The Blair leadership was also impressed with the election successes of the Australian Labour Party under Hawke and Keating. Australia's Labour government prac-tised 'market socialism', reassuring business with privatisation and deregulation.

The terms 'old' and 'new' are stereotypes, as Eric Shaw has observed.[9] But they do express the essential contrasts between Labour in the 1970s and 1980's, and Labour post-1994. Old Labour favoured high and progressive taxation, high levels of public spending, Keynesian methods of achieving full employment, granted the trade unions both a dominant position in the party and partnership in economic policy and relied on government action over market forces. New Labour, however, accepted the case for low marginal rates of income tax, low inflation and levels of public spending and borrowing which would reassure financial markets and business. The role of the state should be to work with and not replace the market. It could do this by encouraging training and improving the infrastructure. Globalisation, or the growing freedom with which labour, capital and goods could cross borders, imposed limits on the possibility for Keynesian full employment policies in one nation. The failed Mitterand experiment in France in the early 1980s was a warning.

If the ending of the old Clause IV was a symbol of new Labour, so also was the state of the art media centre at Millbank Tower, which was established in 1995. This borrowed the idea of a 'war room', which would contain the key campaign personnel, from Clinton's 1992 campaign. It also contained a 'rebuttal unit', and a key seats task force which engaged in marathon telephone canvassing, both American imports. From early 1996 the American, Stan Greenberg, who had been President Clinton's pollster, also helped to frame questions and conduct regression analysis of the private polling. The professionalism evident in by-elections and in local elections showed that Labour had overtaken the Conservative Party as a campaigning organisation. Opinion polling was conducted regularly from late 1993 (the Conservatives started only in Autumn 1996) and Philip Gould and Deborah Mattinson, of Opinion Leader Research, mounted an ambitious focus group programme. Gordon Brown conducted campaign planning meetings almost daily from late 1994. When the campaign began the opinion polls showed an average lead of nearly 20%. The party's objective was simple: to defend a good part of that lead that it had built up over the previous three years.

The campaign

Much of the important work had been done beforehand. Labour strategists had been scarred by the circumstances of the 1992 election defeat, when they had failed to counter the tax charges of the Conservatives and were quite unprepared for the late swing away from the party. The Blair team was therefore always cautious about the large leads reported by the opinion polls. Perhaps as important as any positive message over the preceding months was Labour's protective strategy. The old weaknesses on income tax, trade unions, public spending and law and order had all been tackled. In January, Blair and Brown had pledged that a Labour government would not raise marginal rates of income tax in the life time of the next parliament. As Shadow Chancellor Gordon Brown had ruled out spending pledges from his colleagues and in January 1997 also announced that he would accept Conservative total public spending figure for the next two years. Labour advertising hammered relentlessly at the Conservative record on tax, reminding voters of the broken promises and the 22 tax increases. Labour had effectively killed tax as an issue before the campaign began. The party outscored the Conservatives in many indicators of perceived economic competence. Tony Blair had also been projected as a national leader. The polls showed that on a wide range of leadership criteria he easily led John Major. Finally, the national press had been 'squared'. The benefit was seen in the election when papers with two thirds of circulation supported Labour, compared to a third for the Conservatives (see Seymour-Ure in this volume). The City was so unconcerned by the prospect and then the fact of a Labour government that the stock market reached new record heights before and after the election. As Peter Mandelson said in a post-election interview: 'There was no reason left not to trust Labour, all the old 'ifs', 'buts' and 'maybes' had gone. We removed the target. Without new Labour the Conservatives might have won'.

Similarly the important work on targeting of voters had taken place over the preceding two years. In Millbank there was a task force on key seats. The party invested heavily in contacting the potential switch voters in the 90 seats which it would gain on a swing of six per cent or less. 'Soft' Conservatives or converts to Labour in these seats were identified by personal canvassing in 1994 and 1995 and then regularly contacted by telephone. These contacts provided much information about the political and social characteristics of such voters and were logged on computer. By October 1996, over 80% of them had been contacted. Focus group research sampled these voters as well as those in a dozen or so Pennine constituencies. Party posters were concentrated in key seats and advertisements in the regional press.

Labour had a clear idea of its message for the electorate. The manifesto, *New Labour: Because Britain Deserves Better*, restated the draft manifesto's five pledges: cutting class sizes to 30 or under for five, six and seven year olds, cutting waiting times for persistent young offenders; cutting waiting lists, removing 250,000 under 25 year olds from benefit and into work; and cutting VAT on heating to five per cent. The party's advertising offered reassurance, e.g. 'Labour will punish offenders'; 'Labour will not increase income tax' and attacked the government's record. Having effectively nullified the Conservative charges on tax and economic competence, the party fought on its social agenda of education, health and jobs. According to its 'war book' the campaign strategy focused on the future, Tony Blair's leadership and appealing to the many not the few. But the party was also determined to exploit popular fears of a fifth Tory term. Launching the pensions scare six days before polling day was an important part of this strategy. During the campaign Tony Blair gave four lectures on the economy, Europe, social class and education. He also held a dozen meetings with 'wavering' Conservatives to take questions.

The professionalism and discipline of Labour's campaign was recognised by the electorate. When voters were asked which party had fought the most effective campaign, three times as many mentioned Labour as the other parties. Labour also outscored the Conservatives when it came to activity in the constituencies. The party phoned two million voters, double the Conservative total and did even better in the key marginals. MORI found that Labour supporters were more confident in their allegiance and more active in trying to convert other voters. A quarter of Labour voters were so committed to the cause that they encouraged others to support the party, compared to only one tenth of Conservatives who did so. Whereas 12% of Labour supporters actively discouraged people from voting Conservative, only three per cent of Conservatives took a similar anti-Labour stance. The image of the Labour Party also improved greatly compared with 1992, although again it has to be stated that the big improvements long predated the 1997 election campaign. When asked whether the Conservative and Labour Parties were good for one class or good for all classes only one third saw the Conservatives appealing to all classes, compared to over two thirds who took a similar view of the Labour Party (see Kellner in this volume). The Conservatives were seen as divided by 84% of the public, compared to only 34% for Labour. The same BBC NOP exit poll found that Labour had greatly improved its position on trustworthiness to make the right decisions about the economy and income tax, and led the Conservatives comfortably on both. The story of the 1997 election campaign is partly about the massive erosion of trust in the Conservative Party, but also about a significant increase in trust for Tony Blair's Labour Party.

Conclusion

It is possible to argue that the election campaign did not change many votes. After all, Labour won by a landslide and over the previous four years had decisively outfought the Conservatives at local elections, by-elections and the European elections. It had also enjoyed commanding leads in the opinion polls since the Autumn of 1992. Conservative support collapsed after September 1992 and never recovered. In the 1994 European elections, Labour scored 44% of the votes compared to 28% for the Conservatives, pretty close to the 1997 result. In spite of presiding over an economic recovery, Conservative support was suppressed by a record of disunity, sleaze, embarrassing ministerial resignations, and broken promises. Labour had ample material for its slogan 'Enough is Enough'. If ever an election seemed to be in the bag, then it was 1997.

Such a verdict, however, misunderstands the nature of the Labour campaign. Labour began campaigning for the next general election almost from the time when Blair was elected leader; it was a permanent campaign. The campaign machine, themes and key policy decisions had all been established several months before the election began. In so far as the election went relatively smoothly this was a tribute to the work done beforehand. During and after the election campaign Conservative strategists, in interviews, were almost unanimous in admitting that they had not found an answer to Blair, or to new Labour.

The 1997 election is likely to be a watershed in modern campaigning, just like those of 1959 and 1979. It demonstrated the importance of technology for rapid rebuttal of opposition arguments and in targeting voters. It reinforced the importance of discipline, remaining focused on a simple message, fighting a long campaign, and using focus groups to shape the style, language and demeanour of party leaders. The early days of the Labour government suggested that the party would translate many of these lessons from campaigning into government.

1 G. Radice, *Southern Discomfort* (Fabian Society, 1992).
2 P. Seyd, 'Labour: The Great Transformation' in A. King (ed.), *Britain at the Polls* (Chatham House, 1993).

3   P. Mandelson and R. Liddle, *The Blair Revolution: Can Labour Deliver?* (Faber, 1996).

4   J. Sopel, *Tony Blair* (Michael Joseph, 1995) and J. Rentoul, *Tony Blair* (Little, Brown and Co., 1995).

5   *Labour into Power: A Framework for Partnership* (Labour Party, 1997).

6   D. Butler and D. Kavanagh, *The British General Election of 1997* (Macmillan, 1997).

7   O. Kirchheimer, 'The Transformation of Western European Party Systems' in J. La Palombara and M. Weiner (eds), *Political Parties and Political Development* (Princeton University Press, 1966).

8   N. Kinnock, 'The Labour Party' in *Twentieth Century British History* (Oxford University Press, 1994).

9   E. Shaw, *The Labour Party Since 1945* (Blackwell 1996).

The Conservative Campaign

BY PAUL WHITELEY*

WITH THE benefit of hindsight the Conservative defeat had the air of inevitability about it, for the reasons described by Pippa Norris in the introductory essay. However, as always, this is only apparent with the benefit of hindsight. The eve-of-poll forecast by the panel of election experts organised by the Reuters news agency in London predicted on average a Labour majority of 92, and most commentators were startled by the size of the majority when the final outcome of the election became known. Could it have been different? The short answer to that question is no, since we will argue in this paper that a different Conservative campaign would not have significantly altered the electoral outcome.

When discussing the campaign, it is important to distinguish between the official version of six weeks duration, which we shall refer to as the 'short campaign' and the pre-election period or the 'long campaign' of a year or more which preceded it.[1] A different short campaign by the Conservatives might have reduced the losses somewhat, but it would not have significantly changed the election result. A similar point can be made about the long campaign; a different campaign strategy by the Conservatives could have turned a Labour landslide into a more modest victory on 1 May 1997. But, as we shall argue below, the fate of the Conservative government was essentially settled in September 1992, shortly after their fourth election victory in a row. In a real sense the Conservatives won an election and then lost another election in the same year. Only a major political shock could have turned things around after that, and this did not happen.

To support this thesis and to assess the importance of the campaign in general, it is necessary to have a clear theoretical model of the determinants of the electoral behaviour. We need to know what motivates voters before can we explain and account for both the actual election result, and any alternative hypothetical or 'virtual' election results which might have occurred if events had turned out differently. Such a model highlights those factors which could have changed electoral support for the Conservatives, if the government had made different choices, or if events had worked out differently.

The paper is divided into three sections. Firstly, we develop and test a model of the determinants of Conservative electoral support, which is

---

* Professor of Politics at Sheffield University.

used to explain trends in voting behaviour during the inter-election period and in the long campaign. This model can then be used to consider what might have happened if things had worked out differently. This is followed by a second section which discusses Conservative tactics and strategy during the short campaign, and considers their impact on the final outcome. In the final section we consider conclusions about the overall effectiveness of the Conservative campaign.

The origins of defeat and the long campaign

The literature on voting behaviour is voluminous, but there is enough of a consensus in the field to discern a 'standard model' which can be applied to Britain. This standard model suggests that voting behaviour in Britain is directly influenced by four classes of variables: party identification, issue-perceptions, leadership evaluations and political events or 'shocks'. Party identification, or voters' long-term psychological attachments to one or other of the political parties, provides the 'ballast' to the system, which prevent loyally attached voters from abandoning their preferred party when times become hard. Issue perceptions clearly drive vote intentions, but there is some controversy about which issues matter in this regard. In this paper we focus on economic issues, since these are consistently the most salient in surveys of issue perceptions.[2] Thirdly, leadership evaluations were for some years a relatively neglected aspect of the study of voting behaviour in Britain, partly because Butler and Stokes played down their significance in their original analysis. But recent research shows that the popularity of the prime minister and leader of the opposition have a major influence on voting intentions.[3] Evaluations of political leaders play a vitally important part in explaining voting support. These variables directly influence the vote, but are in turn influenced by other factors, notably demographic variables such as social class, age, sex and the like. The direct influence of such demographic variables on voting behaviour is very weak, once the effect of partisanship, issues and leadership evaluations are taken into account.[4]

The standard model is not so well defined that there is universal agreement about which issues should be included in the specification, or precisely how leadership evaluations should be measured. Thus in the popularity function literature, which uses time series analysis of poll data to model electoral trends, the focus has been exclusively on economic issues.[5] In contrast, in the literature on voting behaviour which stresses the importance of values and ideologies,[6] issues such as social welfare, health and education are thought to play an important role in addition to evaluations of the economy. Equally, while there is a broad consensus about the measurement of partisanship, there are significant differences over the theoretical meaning of this measure.

A final class of variables is also relevant for dynamic versions of the vote model, which involve estimating political support over time. These are political 'shocks', or events which influence the electorate at any one point of time, some of which may persist for quite a while. Earlier work, for example, showed that the Falklands war of 1982 made a significant contribution to the Conservative election victory of 1983.[7] It has also been suggested that Britain's ejection from the European Monetary system on 'Black Wednesday' in September 1992 had a long-term influence on Conservative election prospects.[8] As we shall argue below, this event was crucial to understanding the evolution of Conservative support during the inter-election period. With this theoretical framework in mind we can estimate a vote function, in which Conservative vote depends upon these four classes of variables. The vote function uses monthly observations of the measures taken from the Gallup polls, from the start of 1992 up to April of 1997. The model we are estimating is known as an error correction model, and we begin by briefly outlining the meaning of this type of model.

An error correction model of time series variables involves incorporating both short-term and long-term relationships between variables into the model at the same time. Short-term relationships between variables are captured by measuring the variables in differenced or in change form. Thus the dependent variable in the model is the change in support for the Conservatives in the polls between successive months, and the independent variables are also measured in a similar way. It is also methodologically quite important to ensure that the variables in a time series model are stationary, that is, they fluctuate around a constant mean over time and do not contain long term trends which increase or decrease. This is because recent econometric work suggests that if variables are non-stationary, having trend increases or decreases in their values, there is a strong likelihood of making misleading or spurious inferences about the effects in the model. This is why the variables are modelled in differenced form, since this ensures that they are stationary.

Long-term relationships in the model are measured by an error correction term. This can be done if series *cointegrate*. Simply stated, two or more series cointegrate, if they are in a state of long-term equilibrium. If, for example, Conservative vote intentions, Conservative party identification and voters' evaluations of John Major's leadership all move together in a long-run equilibrium, then a political shock which affects Conservative voting support, but not partisanship or leadership evaluations, will have only a temporary influence on voting intentions. This is because voting support will be quickly pulled back to its original level by the influence of partisanship and by perceptions of John Major's leadership. The latter two variables, in effect, restore the equilibrium, or in the terminology of time series modelling, *correct the error* in the voting series caused by the political shock.

It turns out that there was such an equilibrium relationship between party identification, leadership evaluations and voting intentions for the Conservatives during the period 1992 to 1997. This can be seen in

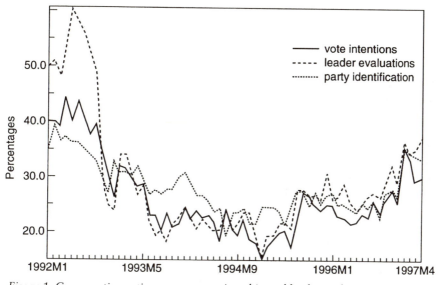

*Figure 1. Conservative voting support, partisanship and leader evaluations,
January 1992–April 1997*

Figure 1 which shows that the three variables closely track each other
over time. This inference is confirmed by some statistical tests.[9] Thus
we are able to model both the short-run and long-run relationships
between the series at the same time, which as we see below had
important implications for Conservative support during the long campaign. The short run effects are measured by changes in the variables
and the long run effects by deviations from an equilibrium measured by
the error correction model.

The model of Conservative voting support contains indicators of the
four classes of variables discussed earlier. Voting intentions, party
identification and prime ministerial approval are measured by means of
standard Gallup questions, which are reproduced in Table 1. Issue
perceptions focus on both the objective and subjective economies and
include six different measures. The objective economy relates to variables like inflation, unemployment and interest rates, and the subjective
economy to variables such as *perceptions* of unemployment and inflation, which are a different thing. The objective economy of employment
and economic growth can be doing well, at a time when the subjective
economy of economic perceptions is doing badly. Some commentators
have suggested that the state of the objective economy had little or no
influence on Conservative support, because the economy was doing
reasonably well at a time which produced an unprecedented defeat for
the incumbent Conservatives. However, as we shall see below, this
interpretation is incorrect. Our results show that both the objective and
subjective economies played a major role in explaining the election
results, both in the short run, but more significantly in the long run.

The model contains five different dummy variables which are all designed to measure the impact of key political events on short-term Conservative support during the estimation period. Black Wednesday has been referred to already, and this was the starting point of political difficulties for John Major's new government. 'Mad Cow' disease refers to the period during the spring of 1996 when the issue of BSE affecting cattle dominated the headlines and provoked a conflict with the European Union. The Maastricht vote variable refers to the Parliamentary vote on the terms of the Maastricht treaty in June 1995 which provoked great backbench dissension in the Parliamentary Conservative party, and which inflamed the disputes over Europe which continued up until election day. Tony Blair won the Labour party leadership in July 1994 and his instant popularity was an immediate setback for John Major's government, and so this is included as a potential influence on Conservative support. Finally, the sleaze issue is measured by a dummy variable scoring one in March 1997 at the start of the short campaign, when a series of sleaze allegations overtook the Conservative campaign. These are discussed more fully below.

Table 1 contains estimates of the voting intention model. The first model, A, contains all the indicators, and the second model, B, is the most parsimonious version with non-significant variables deleted. It can be seen that in model A, Conservative party identification and prime ministerial approval are both highly significant predictors of voting intentions. Thus a ten per cent change in party identification produces an approximate three per cent change in voting intentions, and a ten per cent change in prime ministerial approval produces just under a four per cent change in voting intentions. Party loyalty and leadership evaluations are both very important short term influences on Conservative voting support. The error correction mechanism coefficient captures the long-term equilibrium relationship referred to earlier. As mentioned earlier, it measures how rapidly a shift from an equilibrium between the three variables will be restored after a shock or a change in the short-term perturbs this equilibrium. The estimates show that 73% of the effect of a short term shock to voting intentions is corrected by this relationship within a month of its occurrence.[10] The magnitude of this coefficient indicates how closely Conservative voting intentions were influenced by the performance of John Major and also by party identification. It can be seen that interest rates were highly significant short term influences on voting intentions, as were perceptions of unemployment as the most serious problem facing the country. None of the other measures in model A are significant, although the model has a reasonably good fit, with an R^2 of 0.65.[11]

Model B is the most parsimonious version and contains only the six variables which were statistically significant. The model shows that Conservative party identification and prime ministerial approval are both highly significant predictors of changes in support. In addition,

1 The dynamic model of Conservative vote intentions 1992M1 to 1997M4

Dependent variable: Δ Conservative vote intentions

Predictor Variables	A	B
Constant	−0.37	−0.43
ΔConservative party identification	0.29***	0.31***
ΔPrime Ministerial approval	0.38***	0.35***
Error correction mechanism (t-1)	−0.73***	−0.76***
ΔUnemployment	−2.66	−2.77*
ΔInflation	0.12	–
ΔInterest rates	−2.63***	−3.09***
ΔPerceptions of unemployment as most serious problem	−0.11**	−0.12***
ΔPerceptions of inflation as most serious problem	−0.03	–
ΔPersonal prospective economic evaluations	−0.01	–
Black Wednesday	1.80	–
Mad cow disease crisis	−0.78	–
Maastricht vote crisis	−0.64	–
Tony Blair wins Labour leadership	−0.13	–
Sleaze issue	−2.30	–

A: $R^2 = 0.65$; DWS=2.13; $F = 9.16$***; Normality test = 0.45; Heteroskedasticity test = 0.29.

B: $R^2 = 0.71$; DWS=2.01; $F = 23.0$***; Normality test=0.32; Heteroskedasticity test=0.49.

Note: *** $p < 0.01$; ** $p < 0.05$; * $p < 0.10$; Δ—means difference of variable i.e. $X_t - X_{t-1}$; n=64. Survey variables taken from the following questions: *voting intention* ('If there were a General Election tomorrow, which party would you support?' and 'Which party would you be most inclined to vote for?', % Conservative); *party identification* ('Generally speaking do you think of yourself as Conservative, Labour, Liberal Democrat, or what?', % Conservative); *leadership evaluation* ('Are you satisfied or dissatisfied with John Major as Prime Minister?', % satisfied); *perceptions of unemployment* ('What would you say is the most urgent problem facing the country at the present time?', % answering 'unemployment'); *perceptions of inflation* ('What would you say is the most urgent problem facing the country at the present time?', % answering 'inflation'); *personal prospective evaluations* ('How do you think the financial situation of your household will change over the next 12 months?', % answering 'better' minus % answering 'worse'). *Error correction measure*: the residuals of the regression of party identification and leadership evaluations on voting intentions. *Unemployment*: % of workforce unemployed; *Inflation*: % change in 'All item' index of retail prices'; *Interest rate*: base rate (source: *Economic Trends*). *Black Wednesday* (1 in September 1992, 0 otherwise); *Mad cow disease* (−1 in June 1996, 0 otherwise); *Maastricht vote crisis* (1 in June 1993, 0 otherwise); *Tony Blair leadership* (1 in August 1994, 0 otherwise); *Sleaze issue* (1 in March 1997, 0 otherwise).

unemployment, interest rates and perceptions of the importance of unemployment as the most serious problem facing the country are also significant. Thus two measure of the state of the objective economy, and one measure of the subjective economy influenced short term changes in voting support during the long campaign. The coefficients in model B suggest that a rise in interest rates of one per cent had the effect of reducing Conservative voting intentions by about three per cent, which is roughly the same as the effect of a rise in unemployment of the same magnitude. In contrast a one per cent increase in voters' perceptions of unemployment as the most serious problem facing the country reduced Conservative voting intentions by just over 0.10%. Again the goodness of fit of model B is good, with an R^2 of 0.71, and it appears to be statistically well behaved.

Up to this point, the evidence shows that the objective and subjective economies had an important influence on short term Conservative support in the run-up to the election campaign. But this presents something of a paradox, since interest rates were low and unemployment was falling in the period prior to the election. If the economy was important, and in the case of the objective economy performing reasonably well, why did the Conservatives lose? The reason for this lies in the long-term equilibrium relationship captured by the error correction mechanism. To see this it is necessary to focus on the influence of Black Wednesday, or Britain's ejection from the European Monetary System, in September 1992. At first sight it appears that Black Wednesday had no effect on voting intentions, since it is not statistically significant in the model. However, this variable only measures the direct short-term effects of the crisis on changes in support during the five year period. What the crisis did do, was to profoundly influence all three aspects of Conservative support at the same time in late 1992 and early 1993, which as was pointed out earlier, are in a long term equilibrium with each other. The crisis had the effect of pushing Conservative support into a new long-term equilibrium, *which then became self-sustaining*.

John Major repeatedly launched new political initiatives from 1993 onwards, in order to try to regain lost political support. These might have influenced his own standing with the voters in the short run, but any such favourable changes from his point of view were quickly eliminated by the equilibrium relationships in the model. In effect, partisanship and voting support quickly cancelled out any temporary improvements in his leadership evaluations. To put this another way, the Conservatives needed a political initiative big enough to move all three variables in tandem, if they were to regain their former position of popularity. Smaller initiatives were of little use, since their effects were rapidly removed by the error correction mechanism. They needed a positive shock to the system to counteract the huge negative shock imparted by Black Wednesday, and this never arrived.

The remarkable fall in voting intentions, partisanship and leadership evaluations after Black Wednesday which is seen in Figure 1 indicates that far from being a small influence on the vote, the economy played a decisive role in the outcome of the 1997 general election. The crisis meant that the Conservatives lost their reputation for competence in the management of the economy, and this drastically affected all the key factors underpinning their popularity. If, for example, the crisis had only affected John Major's standing, the Conservatives might have recovered quickly by replacing their leader, or by achieving policy successes, or by simply waiting until the error correction mechanism restored equilibrium. But the crisis removed all three pillars of Conservative support at one go, and this stalled the recovery in that support for years after it had occurred. This is an example of a 're-equilibrating' political shock of a type which occurs infrequently, but which can profoundly influence the fortunes of a governing or opposition party. There was a modest recovery in these variables in early 1997, but it was not enough to make a difference to the outcome of the election. This relationship also has implications for the strategy which the Conservatives pursued during the short campaign. They were wrong to emphasize John Major's leadership as the key campaign theme, since his image had been fatally damaged. Instead they should have concentrated on the message of an improving economy, and had they not been constantly side-tracked by political divisions and accusations of sleaze, this might have been possible. Unfortunately as events unfolded during the short campaign, this became impossible.

The short campaign — from defeat to meltdown

The most appropriate adage to apply to the short campaign is 'nothing succeeds like success, and nothing fails like failure'. The Conservatives entered the short campaign with a big deficit in the polls, which made them look like losers from the beginning. A coherent campaign strategy which emphasised the economy could have made up some lost ground, although they were unlikely to have won with such a deficit. But they had a chance of avoiding a meltdown, given that many voters started the short campaign uncertain as to how to vote. In the event the Conservative campaign started disastrously and never really recovered. They were never able to articulate a clear message, or to pursue a coherent strategy, and this served to reinforce voter doubts about their competence and effectiveness.

Their short campaign which began immediately before the election was initiated by floating some radical policy ideas, particularly in relation to pensions reform, which were aimed at deflecting the criticism that they were stale, and had no new ideas to offer the voters. However, all this did was create hostages to fortune, and gave Labour the opportunity to go 'negative' on the pensions issue in the last week of the campaign.

As the campaign evolved the Conservatives were unsure about whether to campaign negatively with an all out attack on Labour, or alternatively to try to highlight the positive achievements of the government, particularly in relation to the economy. They were confused about how to deal with Tony Blair and new Labour, characterising them as 'New Danger' one minute, and then the next arguing that Labour were merely Conservative clones who the voters should reject in preference for the real thing. Chancellor Kenneth Clarke clearly wanted to play up the economic good news, but many Tories on the right wanted to focus on what they perceived as the iniquities of the European Union. The end result of this was that the message was muddled. The Wirral South by-election fought in late February 1997 was a portent of things to come. The Labour vote share in the by-election was 52.6%, up from 34.6% in the 1992 general election, with a swing of 17.2% to Labour (*Daily Telegraph*, 1.3.97). Despite this John Major could no longer delay calling the general election, and he may well have miscalculated by openly stating after the by-election that 'if opinion doesn't change, then we are going to have a Labour government' (*Guardian*, 1.3.97). The speech was designed to rally Conservative sympathizers, but it probably reinforced their expectations of a Labour win.

The official campaign was launched on March 15th, making the short campaign an unusually long one of six weeks. The aim was to give the government the longest time possible to catch up with Labour. Unfortunately for the government, the campaign opened badly with a Gallup poll published in the *Daily Telegraph*, the house journal of Conservative activists, which gave Labour a 28 point lead (18.3.97). The *Sun* then added to the difficulties by switching sides and announcing that it was going to support Labour. Few things could have been more calculated to demoralize grassroots party activists, or convince wavering voters that the Conservatives could not win. To make matter worse, the first days of the campaign were dominated by political sleaze stories involving sex scandals and bribery allegations among backbench Conservative MPs. These produced the premature retirement of two backbenchers, Allan Stewart, following allegations of an extramarital affair, and Tim Smith, who admitted accepting £25,000 from Mohammed Al Fayed, the owner of Harrods, in exchange for political services. In addition there was pressure on two others, Neil Hamilton and Piers Merchant, to step down as well. In the event Neil Hamilton lost his very safe Conservative seat to the television journalist Martin Bell, who stood as an independent candidate with the support of Labour and the Liberal Democrats.

It had been widely thought that in the 1992 election the Conservative campaign on Labour's tax plans played an important part in securing the Conservative victory. Thus early attempts were made by the Conservatives to raise the tax issue. This took the form of attacks on Labour's spending plans, highlighting their tax implications, but also the promise of an £800 million tax reduction package designed to ease the local tax bills for small firms across the country (*Guardian*, 9.4.97). John Major followed up these tax promises with the claim that 'an average family is now around £1,100 a year better off than when they voted at the last election' (*Guardian*, 10.4.97). Yet unlike in 1992, Labour was well prepared to deal with the tax issue, and it countered the attack with two different tactics. Firstly, it made very limited tax commitments, and one of these, a windfall tax on the profits of privatised utilities, was popular among voters because of public concerns about profiteering in these industries. Secondly, Labour frontbenchers repeatedly claimed that there had been twenty-two tax rises under the Conservatives since 1992, and that these were equivalent to 7p in the pound on the basic rate of income tax. The authoritative Institute for Fiscal Studies concluded that the average family was 2.6 per cent worse off as a result of tax and benefits changes between April 1992 and the election (*Guardian*, 10.4.97). Thus while Labour exaggerated the size of the tax increases under the Conservatives, the government's record on taxation was nonetheless rather poor. Given that the Conservatives could not claim with any credibility to have made average tax payers better off, this removed the tax issue as an effective weapon for the duration of the campaign.

Another issue raised by Tory strategists was trade union influence over the Labour party, something which had worked quite well for them in previous elections. This was linked to the poster campaign before the election which had depicted Tony Blair with 'Demon Eyes'. The campaign resumed during the election with another poster depicting the British Lion in tears at the prospect of a Labour government. This aspect of the campaign failed for three reasons: firstly, because voters did not like it; in a Gallup survey carried out just before the election, voters were asked: 'Do you personally approve or disapprove of the Conservative party poster depicting Tony Blair with demonic red eyes?'; some 73% disapproved, and only nine per cent approved (*Gallup Political Index*, 1996, no 433). The second reason for the failure was that the issue of trade union power had lost a lot of its earlier potency in British politics. The responses to a Gallup survey published in September 1996, showed this. Electors were asked: 'Do you think that trade unions are becoming too powerful, are not powerful enough, or are about right?'. Some 16% of electors thought that trade unions were too powerful, 23% thought that they were not powerful enough, and 52% thought that trade union power was about right (*Gallup Political Index*, 1996, No. 433). This was in sharp contrast to the 1979 election in which trade union power had played a major role in bringing down Labour. The third reason was that Tony Blair also moved rather quickly to confront the criticism that new Labour was in the pockets of the trade unions. On BBC Radio 2's Jimmy Young programme on 10 April, the Labour leader was asked how he would respond to any Labour supporters demanding a pay back for their votes, and he replied 'People will not be able to threaten or bully any government that I lead' (*Guardian*, 11.4.97). This message was further reinforced by the launch of Labour's 'Business Manifesto' in the second week of the campaign, which stressed that there would be no return to 1970s type trade union power.

A third issue where Tory strategists felt Labour to be vulnerable was Britain's relationship with the European Union. John Major sought to undermine the 'Business Manifesto' by drawing attention to Labour's plans to sign up to the social chapter and the working time directive. He accused Tony Blair of opening the gates to a wide range of new regulations from Brussels which the British Parliament would be unable to change. 'Changing from the red flag to the white flag is no bargain for Britain in Europe', he said (*Daily Telegraph*, 12.4.97). But the issue of Europe was a double-edged sword for the Conservatives, since it drew attention to their own divisions. By the second week of the campaign it became clear that many Conservative candidates were defying the party line of 'wait and see' on the question of Britain joining the single European currency, and opposing monetary union in principle in their own election addresses. The *Daily Telegraph* on Thursday, 17 April reported that as many as 84 Conservative candidates planned to oppose monetary union in principle and only six supported it, with the rest being eurosceptics to varying degrees.

The pressure on John Major to revise the policy on monetary union became so great that he abandoned a prepared party political broadcast on 16 April and spoke directly to camera for more than four minutes about relationships with Europe. In the broadcast he begged euroscep-tics not to 'tie my hands in dealing with my European colleagues' (*Guardian*, 17.4.97), an argument which merely drew attention to the deep divisions within the party, and to his own inability to deal with them. Although attempts were made in the third week of the campaign to move away from the issue of Europe, it still continued to dog the Conservative campaign. Within hours of the Prime Minister's broadcast, a junior minister, Eric Forth, issued an election leaflet opposing any further transfer of power from Britain to Europe, a thinly veiled message of opposition to monetary union, and a challenge to John Major's earlier assertion that ministers not supporting the government line would be sacked. Despite this Forth remained in his post. Subsequently, Kenneth Clarke and Michael Howard openly contradicted each other about whether Britain could survive as a nation state if it joined the monetary union. Thus the Conservatives never really overcame their divisions on Europe.

A fourth issue which appeared very important to John Major was devolution to Scotland and Wales, which he characterised in apocalyptic terms as being a threat to the unity of the United Kingdom. In a speech to Scottish Conservatives he accused Tony Blair of breaking up the United Kingdom: 'Through thick and thin, the Union between Scotland and England has lasted for nearly 300 years. Yet for purely party advantage the Labour leader wants to throw it away' (*Daily Telegraph*, 4.4.97). The problem with this from an electoral point of view, was that the devolution issue is largely invisible to voters in England. It did not figure at all in the list of most urgent problems facing the country in the April 1997 Gallup survey (*Gallup Political Index*, 1997, No. 440). In Scotland the issue was salient, but among Scots voters there was overwhelming support for devolution. Thus John Major appeared to believe that an issue which was irrelevant to English voters, and on which most Scots disagreed with the Tory policy, could be a vote winner.

By the final week of the campaign private polls were telling the Conservatives that the election was lost, and when Edwina Curry, the flamboyant former minister, predicted a Labour landslide, defeat stared the Conservatives in the face. The headline of the *Sunday Telegraph* in

the last week of the campaign summed up the Conservative predica-
ment, when it said 'It's all over, admit top Tory aides' (27.4.97). One
contributory factor to the landslide was the weakness of the Conservative campaign on the ground. The party organisation had been declining
for many years,[12] but the huge losses of local councillors in the years
preceding the election had made this much worse (see Rallings and
Thrasher, in this volume). The national swing to Labour in the election
was 10.5%, but it was 12.1% in the 80 most marginal seats. Similarly,
there was clear evidence of tactical voting, although this was rather
mixed. Both tactical voting and differential swings in the marginals are
evidence of the effect of local campaigns on the vote (see McAllister, in
this volume), and they showed that the Conservatives suffered from
their lack of party activists at the grassroots level.

Conclusions

The model of the dynamics of public opinion which underlies this paper
is that of a 'punctuated equilibrium'. That is, public support for a
political party moves in equilibrium with other important variables over
time, and this equilibrium is buffeted all the time by exogenous
economic and political shocks of various kinds. Periodically and rarely,
however, a really major shock occurs which shifts the political equilibrium to a semi-permanent new level. The winter of discontent in the
dying months of the 1974–1979 Labour government, was one example
of this, as was the Falklands war for Mrs Thatcher's government. Black
Wednesday was also an example of this type of shock, in that it
fundamentally changed the way that the electorate regarded the Conservative government. Thus the basic problem for the Conservatives
was that they were very badly damaged by the loss of their reputation
as effective economic managers shortly after the 1992 general election,
and they were never able to overturn that image despite an improving
record on the economy in the run-up to the 1997 general election. The
fact that this loss of reputation profoundly influenced long term party
loyalties and images of John Major as well as voting intentions made
the task of recovering that reputation much harder, since all three
variables had to recover if an improvement was to be sustained. This
did not happen during the period of the long campaign, partly because
nothing occurred to cancel out the significance of the early setback, but
also because divisions in the party, political failures like the BSE crisis,
and political sleaze nullified the attempts by John Major to climb back.

As a consequence the Conservatives started the short campaign with
a deficit in support which was unprecedented, and the poor handling of
the campaign in comparison with Labour made things worse. An
electoral win was unlikely following the short campaign, even if things
had gone well. But their lack of focus, internal divisions and their
inability to concentrate on their strengths, as well as a very effective
Labour campaign turned the defeat into a landslide. In fact there was a

pernicious feedback process at work towards the end of the campaign—
actors perceived that their party could not win, and began to focus on
the post-election situation, which meant assigning blame for the defeat,
arguing about policy in public, and in the case of the leading frontbench
spokespersons, positioning themselves for the inevitable leadership
contest. This made things worse, from the point of view of the
effectiveness of the campaign.

The only consolation for the Conservatives is that we are in a period
of unprecedented and growing electoral volatility, and this may allow
them to recover lost ground by the time of the next election. But they
have a big mountain to climb and a lot of work to do to rethink policies
and organisation if they are to stand any sort of chance of winning in
the future.

Research for this paper was supported by the US National Science Foundation (grant #SES-9309018). My thanks go to Harold Clarke of the University of North Texas and Marianne Stewart of the University of Texas at Dallas for their help with this project.

1   See W.L. Miller, H.D. Clarke, M. Harrop, L. LeDuc and P.F. Whiteley, *How Voters Change: The 1987 British Election Campaign in Perspective* (Oxford University Press, 1990), where this distinction was first introduced.

2   In the *Gallup Political Index* a question asking voters about the most important issue facing the country shows that the economy, particularly unemployment and inflation are easily the most salient issues in the minds of voters, something which has been true for decades.

3   See H.D. Clarke and M.C. Stewart, 'Economic Evaluations, Prime Ministerial Approval and Governing Party Support: Rival Models Reconsidered', *British Journal of Political Science*, 25/1995.

4   See P. Whiteley, 'Predicting the Labour Vote in 1983; Social Backgrounds versus Subjective Evaluations', *Political Studies*, 34/1986.

5   See H. Norpoth, *Confidence Regained* (University of Michigan Press, 1992), for a review of this literature applied to Britain.

6   See E. Scarborough, *Political Ideology and Voting* (Oxford University Press, 1984) and R. Rose and I. McAllister, *Voters Begin to Choose* (London: Sage, 1986).

7   H.D. Clarke, W. Mishler and P.F. Whiteley, 'Recapturing the Falklands: Models of Conservative Popularity 1979–1983', *British Journal of Political Science*, 20/1990.

8   D. Sanders, 'Economic Performance, Management Competence and the Outcome of the Next General Election', *Political Studies*, 44/1996.

9   This involves regressing Conservative vote intentions on party identification and leadership evaluations and then testing to see if the residuals of this model are stationary. A Dickey-Fuller test of the residuals shows that we can accept the hypothesis that they are stationary at the 0.01 level. Intuitively, this means that they move together in tandem over time and do not drift apart to any significant extent.

10   The coefficient is negative because a deviation from the equilibrium between the three variables is rapidly corrected, and hence has a negative impact on changes in voting support.

11   The various diagnostic tests indicate that the model is statistically well behaved and there is no autocorrelation or heteroskedasticity in the residuals.

12   See P.F. Whiteley, P. Seyd and J. Richardson, *True Blues: The Politics of Conservative Party Membership* (Clarendon Press, 1994), in which a prediction is made that the Conservative membership would fall to below 100,000 by the end of the century if nothing was done to turn it around.

The Liberal Democrat Campaign

BY HUGH BERRINGTON* WITH ROD HAGUE†

THE Liberal Democrat Party was barely nine years old when Mr Major called the election. When the party was formed in 1988, through the merger of the old Liberal Party and the SDP, it seemed that its midwife had been bitterness rather than hope, with some in both parties rejecting the union. The new party suffered heavily in its first big test, the European elections of 1989, its share of the vote falling to six per cent, far behind the Greens. Under its new leader, Paddy Ashdown, the party picked itself up, recovered in time for the local elections of 1990, and then proceeded to win three by-elections from the Conservatives, two of them in what had hitherto been safe seats. The result of the 1992 general election, though far better than might have been expected two or three years before, was a disappointment for the Liberal Democrats. The opinion polls pointed to a close finish, and with it the likelihood of a hung parliament, in which the new party would hold the balance of power; Liberal Democrat support, after lagging well behind the 1987 vote for the Alliance, rose gradually during the campaign and on election eve most polls put them at 20%. The Conservatives, however, won with an overall majority big enough to enable them to govern without allies, tacit or open, until a few months before the 1997 election; and it seemed that the Liberal Democrats had slipped back during the last day or two of the contest, gaining only 18% of the vote in Great Britain.

The Conservatives, however, did not have long to enjoy the pleasures of victory. Enforced withdrawal from the Exchange Rate Mechanism in September 1992, only five months after John Major's election triumph, provoked a sharp fall in the government's popularity. The Liberals were at first the most conspicuous beneficiaries of this change in the electoral climate. Whilst Labour obtained a comfortable lead in the opinion polls, the Liberals won some remarkable by-election victories. Newbury, where the Liberal Democrats were a good second in the general election, saw a huge swing of 28%, with the tiny Labour vote squeezed almost to vanishing point; soon afterwards, Christchurch, with a majority of 40% and one of the safest Conservative seats in the country went to the Liberal Democrats with a swing, unprecedented since the war, of 35%. In 1994, Eastleigh, where the Liberals had also come second at the

* Professor of Politics (Emeritus) at Newcastle University.
† Senior Lecturer in Politics at Newcastle University.

general election, saw another victory with a swing of 21%; perhaps ominously, however, this by-election saw a rise in the Labour vote.

The by-election euphoria for the Liberal Democrats came to an end in 1994 with a continued erosion of their poll rating. John Smith died in May, and Labour elected Tony Blair as leader. According to the Gallup 9000, the Conservatives had already fallen to the 25% level by late 1993; Liberal Democrat support, still running at 22% in March–May 1994 fell to under 17% in August, and declined to 14% by the end of the year.[1] The party won the Littleborough and Saddleworth by-election in the summer of 1995 coming from a fairly close second. Labour, however, which had run a poor third in 1992, came within 2,000 votes of taking the seat. Apart from one seat in Scotland, where the Nationalists were the main challengers to the Conservatives, the remaining by-elections during the parliament all took place in seats where Labour had come second in 1992. Labour then won these seats by big margins.

The Liberal Democrats, like Labour, scored well in the local elections held in May of each year. In 1993, the Conservatives lost control of every county in England except for Buckinghamshire; Labour and the Liberal Democrats shared the spoils, the latter taking Cornwall, Somerset and the Isle of Wight. Moreover, Liberal Democrats often achieved strong representation in many counties where no party was in overall control. The same pattern was repeated in the district council elections held in 1994, 1995 and 1996. By the end of this period, the Liberal Democrats had displaced the Conservatives as the second party in local government, whether this was measured by the number of councillors elected, or the number of authorities controlled by the party. Nevertheless, the opinion polls registered a slow and continuing decline in the party's rating so that according to some polls, the party was down almost to 10%,[2] when on 17 March the Prime Minister announced the date of the general election. Yet the party, if weak in the opinion polls, was in other ways stronger than in 1992. Membership had risen by around 12% between the start of the 1992 campaign and the beginning of that in 1997, and stood at a little over 100,000. Financially, the party was less stretched than it had been five years before. Central party expenditure, including that spent by the national party on local campaigns, more than doubled to about £3 million, the money being spent over a longer period than in 1992.[3]

The Liberals and their successors had long had to wrestle with the problems created by their own electoral progress. Liberal Democrats, and the Liberals before them, had raised their parliamentary representation from six in 1959 to 26 by the end of the 1992 parliament, largely by capturing seats from the Conservatives. After 1970, Liberals found themselves coming second in a fluctuating, but over the longer term, growing number of Conservative constituencies; one ingredient of victory was the squeezing of the small Labour vote in such places, and a call on such electors to vote tactically, for the Liberal Democrats, to defeat the Conservative incumbent. The Liberals, in short, turned the wasted vote argument on its head. Thus in 1987, the Alliance came second in 261 constituencies, 223 of which were represented by Conservatives.[4] However, such constituencies, by definition, also contained numerous Conservatives; often, it was arithmetically impossible for Liberals to win such seats merely by cannibalising the Labour vote. They had to take votes from the Conservatives as well. A vote gained from Labour reduced the Conservative majority by one; a vote taken from the Conservatives reduced the majority by two. In their bid to attract Labour votes, Liberal Democrat candidates had to avoid alienating those former Conservatives whose support was essential to winning.

The relationship with Labour was one of the prime questions exercising the new Liberal Democrat party. Equidistance from the two main parties had been the attitude of the party since it was formed in 1988. Indeed, Mrs Thatcher's fall and the advent of John Major to the leadership of the Conservative party, in late 1990, had raised the possibility of Liberal Democrats and Conservatives working together in a hung parliament.[5] The result of the general election put an end to such speculation and Paddy Ashdown set the scene for a change in attitudes to Labour, in a speech at Chard as early as May 1992.

The Labour and Liberal Democrat gains, in the county council elections of 1993, broadened the way to collaboration in the council chamber, continuing and expanding a development already visible before the election. After the 1993 county elections many more councils were hung, with no one party having an overall majority, and Labour groups on county councils up and down the land, found themselves co-operating with Liberal Democrats, against the common Conservative enemy. This collaboration reached its highest pitch in Berkshire, where the two parties had a joint administration. Labour's National Executive were not enthusiastic about such highly formalised cooperation, but accepted the proposal and approved more limited and specific arrangements in seven other counties along with two districts.[6] The result was to breed a culture of cooperation between the parties and to give the notion of working together, in the pursuit of common agenda, a new respectability.[7] Nevertheless, both parties were wary of pacts at national level and both proceeded to adopt parliamentary candidates in all constituencies in Great Britain. However, though Liberal Democrats and Labour might fight one another in the constituencies, this did not preclude cooperation on particular issues. In Scotland, Liberal Democrats and Labour worked together in the Scottish Constitutional Convention to agree on proposals for devolution; for the UK as a whole Labour and Liberal Democrats committed themselves to a joint approach to constitutional reform. Such collaboration before a general election was almost unprecedented; there were rumbles within the Liberal Democrat Party that the party was coming too close to Labour and there were fears that the party's independence and identity might be compromised.

It was a Liberal Democrat MP, Simon Hughes who first raised the issue that dominated the first fortnight of the campaign, obtruded, at intervals, in the remaining month of the contest, and probably worked to the advantage of both opposition parties. The issue was sleaze. Following admissions by the lobbyist, Ian Greer, about MPs receiving money for advocacy, the Parliamentary Commissioner for Standards, Sir Gordon Downey began an investigation into the conduct of 25 MPs, all but four of them Conservatives. The investigation was already far advanced when Mr Major announced that the general election would be held on 1 May. The House would be prorogued on Friday, 21 March and Parliament dissolved on the 8 April. The effect of proroguing Parliament was to stop the Commons Standards and Privileges Committee from any further action on Sir Gordon's report; there seemed a sinister implication in that the date for prorogation had in itself no implications for the date of dissolution, and prorogation so long before dissolution had not happened since 1918. The leadership of both the main opposition parties then took up the issue. The committee then brought forward part of the report, which exonerated 15 of the 25 MPs, but publication of the meat of the report was delayed, including sections on the behaviour of two former junior Ministers, Tim Smith and Neil Hamilton, until after the election. Tim Smith then resigned as candidate for the safe seat of Beaconsfield, but Neil Hamilton, backed by the local Conservative Association at Tatton in Cheshire, refused to stand down. The Labour and Liberal Democrat candidates gave way, so that a jointly supported Independent, Martin Bell, the veteran BBC television reporter, could fight Neil Hamilton on the issue of sleaze. This was a rare example of electoral cooperation between the two parties and it helped to ensure that the issue of sleaze, even if it ceded the dominance it had had in the fortnight following the announcement of the election, remained prominent until the end of the campaign. On this the two opposition parties were united against the Conservatives.

The two weeks between Mr Major's announcement and Easter Monday saw some early skirmishing between the parties, but the party manifestos were not published until after Easter, with the Liberal Democrat manifesto 'Make The Difference' the last to appear. The party's attack on the approach of the two big parties, 'Punch and Judy politics', set the tone of the manifesto and of the party's campaign. The centre-piece was a promise, inherited from the 1992 election, to spend £2 billion more on education, to be paid for by increasing income tax by a penny. Both Labour and the Conservatives had pledged not to raise rates of income tax, the Conservatives, it seemed on grounds of conviction, Labour in a bid to pre-empt any Conservative attempt to exploit public fears of higher taxes under Labour. Labour's caution placed it, ideologically, to the right of the Liberal Democrats. Perhaps more important, electorally, the Liberal Democrats were able to present themselves as the party of honesty, the party that was prepared to tell the people that the better social services they yearned for could only achieved if people paid more taxes. The Liberal Democrats were able to portray both Labour and the Conservatives as stale, timid, unwilling to come clean with the electorate.

The Liberal Democrats began their campaign almost wholly dependent on the national television networks, and radio, for the nationwide propagation of their message. 1997 was distinctive in that, measured by daily newspaper circulation, a majority of the press rejected the Conservatives; they turned, however, not to the Liberal Democrats, who were not favoured with any endorsement from this source, but to Labour.[8] Moreover, in presenting favourable reports on the parties, the national dailies concentrated overwhelmingly on the two big players. BBC1 and ITN's News at Ten, especially the latter, were much more even-handed. In their treatment of personalities, the media gave scant attention to any Liberal Democrat personalities apart from Paddy Ashdown, who in turn attracted only about a third of the coverage given to either Tony Blair or John Major.[9] Liberal Democrat propaganda itself focused heavily on the party leader. One party election broadcast was devoted to the life and character of Paddy Ashdown, recalling Hugh Hudson's famous election broadcast on Neil Kinnock in 1987. Education, the health service, law and order figured prominently in the other broadcasts; the party strove to contrast its own honesty (as shown in its pledge to increase taxation to pay for selective expansion in the public services) and sense of principle with Labour's trimming and evasion. Above all, the party's message was to juxtapose its own concern for the real issues worrying voters with the name-calling and negativism of the Punch and Judy politics of the two big parties.

The Liberal Democrats also stressed the programme of constitutional reform, much of it agreed with Labour. Their manifesto promised to turn the House of Lords into a predominantly elected second chamber to represent, 'the nations and regions of the UK'. It pledged the incorporation of the European Convention on Human Rights into UK law, a Freedom of Information Act, and a clean-up of the funding of political parties. Labour had not endorsed proportional representation but had promised a referendum; not surprisingly, 'Make The Difference' explicitly promised to bring in PR, for all elections, but mindful, however, of the charges that this issue had lost the party votes in the last few days of the 1992 campaign, the party laid little emphasis on this feature. In Scotland the manifesto promised to set up a Home Rule Parliament (elected by PR as agreed by the Scottish Constitutional Convention) and in Wales to set up a Welsh Senedd.[10] In terms of the long-term implications for the governance of the UK, the proposals for Scottish devolution, and for a referendum on PR, are potentially the most far-reaching. Whilst Tony Blair has little enthusiasm for proportional representation, and Labour are likely to split on this question, a referendum at least puts the issue on Westminster's agenda; moreover, even if the cause of PR fails at the referendum the example of a Scottish Parliament, elected by PR, is likely to keep the issue near the forefront of public controversy.

The low poll rating the party had at the outset of the campaign threatened a serious setback, if not disaster, when the votes were counted. The party slowly inched its way forward; Gallup showed the party at a low point of ten per cent at the outset of the campaign. Unevenly, the party's ratings began to rise, following the precedent of most past elections, until on election day, the press reported figures ranging from 14% to 18%.[11] The closing days of the campaign were marked by public optimism about the outcome. The improvement in the party's opinion poll standing was not the only source of this hopefulness for the party's ratings remained low by the standards of the eighties. The best that the party seemed to hope for in terms of the popular vote was to maintain the level of 18% attained in 1992. Liberal Democrat hopes, however, were based less on the aggregate vote than on the tally of constituencies to be gained. The party's strategy of targeting the party's better prospects, and tactical voting, it was held, might deliver a substantial block of seats, that given the normal workings of first-past-the-post, would have been denied to the party.

The target seats

Targeting and tactical voting have been adduced as the keys to the party's remarkable achievement in more than doubling their representation in parliament, despite a slight fall in their share of the national vote. Paddy Ashdown appointed Lord Holme as chairman of the team to run the party's election campaign, and one of the major tasks of this committee was to oversee the targeting of winnable seats. Targeting involves the selective allocation of resources and of time, both from the voluntary arm of the party and its leading figures. The operation, however, seems to have been rather fluid with the criteria changing (especially in the light of local election results), the list of seats being altered from time to time as new evidence emerged, and some constituencies having a nominal position on the list. No definitive list of target seats has yet been released, and even the numbers cited (34 at the lowest, and 70 at the highest) vary from source to source. On the face of it, targeting paid off; later, we shall see that the party was less successful, in terms of increasing the Liberal Democrat share of the poll, in the seats where it had come closest to victory in 1992, possibly the most heavily targeted. The question that must be asked is how much the improvement here, and the bigger increase attained in some of apparently rather less promising seats owed to the policy of targeting; most of the targeted constituencies were, almost by definition, marginal seats where there was likely to be a powerful squeeze on the Labour vote. The fate of the party's candidates in some of the three-way marginals suggests that forces independent of the efforts of the Liberal Democrats determined the outcome in some constituencies.

Opinion poll data

Aggregate data has major limitations; surveys may throw further light on electoral change. We have two sources of survey information about changes from 1992 to 1997—the opinion polls themselves and the exit polls conducted on election day. Johnston and Pattie have used Gallup's figures over the fifteen month period to early March 1997, to make estimates of the flow of the vote.[12] Their evidence suggests that about three and a half million voters supported Liberal Democrat candidates at both elections—i.e. 59% of their 1992 voters. Almost 900,000 defected to Labour whilst fewer than 200,000 switched to the Conservatives. In turn, the Liberal Democrats gained almost as many votes from, as they lost to, the two big parties. Whereas, however, most of those who deserted went to Labour, nearly three-quarters of their new supporters came from the Conservatives. The remaining quarter, three hundred and twenty thousand, had voted Labour in 1992. We cannot however, identify tactical voters by reference to the party they backed in 1992. Some of the Conservatives might have preferred to go right over to Labour but voted tactically, because of the local situation. In short, some of these ex-Conservatives were really Labour supporters casting a tactical vote for the Liberal Democrats. But even allowing for this factor, the extent of new tactical voting for the Liberal Democrats (and Labour) in the country as a whole cannot have been very big. Even if we assume that half of the Liberal Democrats' losses to, and gains from, the two main parties were inspired by tactical calculations, we can find only just over a million electors—around three per cent of the total. Of course, such an estimate relates only to new tactical voters; we simply do not know how many of the three and a half millions who voted Liberal Democrat in both 1992 and 1997 did so for tactical considerations; nor indeed, how many of the 17.3 million who stayed loyal to one of the two main parties did so.

Like the Conservatives, the Liberal Democrats lost more from 1992 supporters who abstained in (or had died by) 1997, than they gained from those too young to vote in 1992, or who had not voted then but did so in 1997. Differential abstention, and the balance of numbers between young voters and those who had died, cost them nearly 600,000 votes or just under a thousand in every constituency. Again, note that some of these first-time voters would have voted tactically. The BBC/NOP Exit Poll sheds light on the social make-up of the party's electoral support; in class terms, as measured by the market research classification, Liberal Democrats closely resembled Conservatives. In each case, about 70% of their voters were classed as ABC1.[13] In educational terms, Liberal Democrat voters were distinctive; 24% of them had a university degree or its equivalent, compared with 17% of Labour voters and 15% of Conservatives, which calls to mind the finding of Heath et al., in 1983 that within the salaried middle-class, there was a division based on educational background with voters for the Liberal/SDP Alliance having higher formal educational qualifications than Conservative supporters.[14] Liberal Democrats, too, tended to make up their minds later in deciding how to vote. Almost two-thirds reported that they had decided how to vote since the election was called, more than half as many again as of voters for the two big parties. Indeed, 40% said that they had made their choice either within the last week or on election day itself. This finding is consistent with the rise in Liberal Democrat support during the later stages of the campaign, and is consistent with earlier evidence about the behaviour of Liberal Democrats, and before them, the Liberals.

Tactical voting

Tactical voting shares with targeting the credit for the major Liberal Democrat advance of 1997. Indeed, it is hard to separate the two. In trying to assess the effects of tactical voting, we have again, to rely on analysis of aggregate data. There is nothing new in tactical voting. The 'wasted vote' cry has plagued the Liberals for decades and the Conservatives had over the years exploited it with particular vigour. Indeed, over time electors accustomed to voting tactically, because of the weakness of their most-preferred party's local position may come to think of themselves as normal supporters of the 'second best' party. However, what turned the 'wasted vote' slogan from a near universal liability for the Liberal Democrats to a local asset in a growing number of seats, was their pushing Labour into third place in numerous constituencies. This first became evident in the election of February 1974, when the Liberals polled 19% of the national vote and elected 14 MPs—then a postwar record. Less noticed was the number of seats in which they came second. In 1983, the Liberal-SDP Alliance reached a new peak; although winning only 23 seats they polled 26% of the vote in Great Britain, just two per cent behind Labour. This was reflected in the number of seats in which they came second. Labour's limited recovery in 1987, and 1992, saw a falling-off from this figure but even in 1992, after boundary revision, there were still estimated to be 158 of this kind.[15]

In some constituencies, Labour voters, recognising the weakness of their party locally and keen to ensure the defeat of the sitting Conservative Member (or his replacement) would vote Liberal Democrat. In others, Conservative supporters might vote Liberal Democrat to prevent Labours winning the seat. In fact, there were far more seats where the Liberal Democrats ran second to the Conservatives than there were where they were runners-up to Labour. Tactical voting meant, in practice, recruiting those who would otherwise vote Labour and persuading them to support the Liberal Democrats, in those constituencies where Labour had finished third (or lower) in 1992. In 1992, the results, as previously suggested, already embodied a degree of tactical voting. Indeed, the vote for all three parties probably contains layers of tactical votes, often now indistinguishable from genuine choices, laid down at successive elections. With aggregate data analysis, it is possible to make estimates of the extent of *new* tactical voting.

Following the extensive boundary changes, 1997 was bad for the Liberal Democrats in general, and not conducive to tactical voting.[16] Rational tactical voting depends on an accurate knowledge of which candidate is best placed to beat the least preferred party. Boundary changes make it more difficult to find a clear, unambiguous guide to the state of the parties. In unchanged constituencies, the outcome last time is likely to be the best indicator, though even here, changes in the distribution of party support as manifested, for example in local council elections, may blur the diagnosis. Where there have been major changes there is likely to be much less awareness of the true state of the parties. The BBC/ITN list of constituencies with their notional 1992 majorities is not likely to be well-known, and the parties themselves will take advantage of this ambiguity to press their own claim to be the party best-placed to defeat the outgoing Member.

The tactical vote is the vote that dare not speak its name. Tactical voting is not easy for a party to organise nationally. No party can publicly write off its chances and abandon its candidate and the party activists in a constituency. A party can, and indeed does, call on supporters of third parties, who have no chance of winning a particular constituency, to transfer their support to them. It can hardly tell its own voters to do the same in hopeless seats. Tactical voting, as a party stratagem, has often to be hidden behind the mists of obfuscation. When questioned on the BBC radio Election Call programme Mr Ashdown seemed to dismiss tactical voting: 'What is politics about? What are elections about? Elections are about voting for what you believe in. I am inviting people to vote Liberal Democrat and that's the only way you get the things only we now stand for.'[17] Like a country which disowns its spies, if caught, a party leader has to deny tactical voting. Campaigns for reciprocal tactical voting, therefore, have to be led in the constituencies, without overt encouragement from the centre. What is retained in the centre is loosened in the constituencies. For its part, Labour, although the beneficiary of tactical voting in some constituencies, would not countenance any local arrangements of this sort. The party summarily expelled ten activists in Lewes who had called on voters to support the Liberal Democrat candidate, who, apparently benefiting from significant tactical voting went on to win the seat.

Let us look first at the evidence for the existence of tactical voting: the most obvious statistic here lies in different degrees of change in constituencies with different patterns of candidature, a point already alluded to in the discussion of targeting. If tactical voting has occurred on a significant scale, the results in seats where Labour ran second in 1992 (the Con-Labs) should show a bigger rise in the Labour share of the poll and a smaller rise, or even a fall, in the Liberal Democrat share, than in seats where the Liberal Democrats had been runners-up in 1992 to the Conservatives. Moreover this difference should have been sharper, other things being equal, in marginal seats (where tactical voting was most likely to make a difference to the outcome) than in safe seats (see Table 1). In the Con-Lab seats, the Labour vote rose sharply, almost regardless of marginality, whereas support for the Liberal Democrats fell significantly. That the latter fell less in the marginals can be explained by Liberal Democrat voting in these seats having already been acutely squeezed. In the Con-Lib seats, Labour rose by nearly five points less than in the Con-Labs where it was the main challenger; the Liberal Democrat share rose, albeit by less than half a per cent; the influence of marginality on Labour's share comes out clearly. In the most marginal Con-Lib constituencies, Labour increased its share by less than six per cent, but in the safest by more than nine per cent. The Liberal Democrats mustered another 2.3% in their most marginal hopefuls, but actually fell a little in the safest seats. Numerous potential Labour voters, it seems, were constrained by the pattern of competition, and voted for the Liberal Democrats in the latter's best prospects.

1. **Voting results. Change in Labour and Lib Dem share of vote in different categories of constituencies**

Conservative held 1992 (Great Britain)	Con-Lab		Con-Lib	
	Lab	Lib Dem	Lab	Lib Dem
All	+13.0	−3.0 (181)	+8.2	+0.4 (158)
Very marginal	+12.3	−2.3 (30)	+5.5	+2.3 (7)
Very safe	+13.3	−3.5 (76)	+9.3	−0.3 (103)

Con-Lab = Conservative 1st, Labour 2nd 1992. Con-Lib = Conservative 1st, Liberal Democrat 2nd 1992. Very marginal = seats held in 1992 by up to 5%; Very safe = seats held in 1992 by more than 20%. (Four intervening categories of marginality omitted.)

So far, the case for tactical voting having occurred has been well-supported by the evidence from the detailed results. However, some commentators seem to have exaggerated the degree of tactical voting which took place. There were 65 seats in England where the Liberal Democrats had come second in 1992, and were within 25% of the Conservative total.[18] Those won by the Liberal Democrats are labelled Lib Dem gains, those not gained the Lib Dem possibles; there were a further 88 constituencies where the Liberal Democrats achieved second place, but were more than 25% behind the victorious Conservatives. Here they were too far away to nourish any realistic hopes of victory (though one of these seats, Kingston and Surbiton, did actually fall by 56 votes.) Let us compare the changes in the Con-Lib seats actually won by the Liberal Democrats, with these in the Con-Lib seats held by the Conservatives, where the Conservatives in 1992 had run up to 25%

2. Voting results. Changes in Labour and Lib Dem share of votes

Con-Lib seats (England)

Lib Dem gains		Lib Dem possibles		Lib Dem forlorn hopes	
Lab	Lib Dem	Lab	Lib Dems	Lab	Lib Dem
+3.5	+5.8	+9.5	+2.5	+9.3	−0.4
(26)		(39)		(87)	

Lib Dem gains = all English seats gained by Lib Dems in 1997 regardless of previous marginality level; Lib Dem possibles = all other English Lib Con seats vulnerable to a swing of 12.5% after 1992; Lib Dem forlorn hopes = all other English Lib Con seats.

ahead, and with those in the Forlorn Hopes (see Table 2). The first column in Table 2 focuses attention, not on the marginality of the seat after 1992, but on actual success in 1997; this brings home the importance of tactical voting in the seats the Liberal Democrats won from the Conservatives. Here, in contrast to its massive rise in almost every other kind of seat, Labour registered an increase of less than four per cent, whilst the Liberal Democrats put on a rise of nearly six per cent. Column 2 brings home the extent to which the Liberal Democrats failed in their possibles; here we can see little sign of tactical voting; even though having run third in these seats in 1992, Labour still rose by over nine per cent, whilst the Liberal Democrat vote fell substantially. In the forlorn hopes, by definition even more forlorn for Labour than for the Liberal Democrats, Labour rose by over nine per cent, whilst the Liberal Democrats actually lost a little ground.

The figures in Table 3 take the argument further; in what were statistically the most vulnerable seats, the rise in the Labour vote actually outstripped the Liberal Democrat increase. What is striking is how poorly the Liberal Democrats performed in some of what, on the evidence of 1992, were their best constituencies.[19] The Liberal Democrats won all of these constituencies, but in three of them (Isle of Wight, Portsmouth South, and Somerton and Frome) their share in fact dropped with Labour's share actually rising by between six and eleven per cent. This is hardly evidence for extensive new tactical voting; in other seats, notably Hazel Grove, there is a clear indication of voters being swayed by the local pattern of contest, but the overall impression is that of a party gaining seats, not because of its own appeal, but because of the sharp decline in support for one of the other parties, namely the Conservatives. The Liberal Democrats gained their most marginal seats almost by default.

3. Voting results. Changes in party share of vote (England only)

Liberal democrat gains

	Con %	Lab %	Lib Dem %	N
Probables	−10.8	+4.1	+2.3	11
Good prospects	−12.0	+4.0	+5.5	7
Outside chances	−16.0	+2.2	+11.5	8

Probables = Con Lib seats vulnerable to a 5% swing after 1992; Good prospects = Con Lib seats vulnerable to a swing of between 5.1% and 7.5% after 1992; Outside chances = Con Lib seats vulnerable to a swing of more than 7.5% after 1992.

Among the good prospects, the Conservatives did a little worse, Labour the same and the Liberal Democrats better than in the probables, though even here, Torbay, won by 12 votes, showed a small drop in the Liberal Democrat share. Paradoxically, the Liberal Democrats made their most striking advance among the seats they gained in the eight outside chances (including Kingston and Surbiton). The Conservative share of the vote dropped by 16%, whilst Labour rose by a mere two per cent, and the Liberal Democrats put on nearly 12%.[20] Of course, outside chances could never have become gains without exceptional vote changes; but the figures do raise the question as to why Liberal support was so sluggish in its best seats. They must also question the efficiency of targeting.

There was a diversity of response to the tactical situation which does not lend itself to simple explanations. Amongst the Con Lib seats, the Liberal Democrats did somewhat worse in the 39 English sets which were vulnerable to a swing of 12.5% and which the party failed to win, than in the 87 'forlorn hopes'; their gains consisted of a number of highly marginal seats where the party struggled to victory and another group of less marginal seats, the 'good prospects', where the party seems to have made considerably bigger tactical conversions, together with several unexpected wins, the 'outside chances'. Why voters chose to behave tactically, on a big scale, in some constituencies but not in others apparently similar or even better suited tactical voting, is a question that must occupy both students of elections and party strategists. So far, no satisfactory answer seems to have been given.

There remains another category, the three-way marginals in which the Liberal Democrats had run second in 1992, with relatively strong support for a third-placed Labour candidate. Statistically, on the evidence of the 1992 results, the Liberal Democrats were better-placed than Labour to attract tactical votes. Labour's success in these seats has already been hinted at in the discussion of targeting. In seats such as Conwy, where the Conservatives had led the Liberal Democrats by nearly a thousand votes in 1992, and Labour by nearly 3,500 the Liberal Democrats should have been well-placed to squeeze the considerable Labour vote. In fact, Labour won the seat, adding an extra nine per cent to its share, whilst the Liberal Democrat vote remained static. In Falmouth and Camborne, where there had been a similar pattern in 1992, Labour again came from third place to take the seat; here, however, Liberal Democrat support fell by six per cent and their candidate dropped to third place. In such seats, Labour had been a strong rival for second place in 1992; but as Hastings shows, there were others where Labour had finished a weak third in five years before and yet overtook a strongly placed second Liberal Democrat in 1997 to take the seat. Thus, the notional result in Hastings and Rye in 1992, showed the Conservatives ahead with 48%, the Liberal Democrats in second place with 35% and Labour, trailing badly with less than 16%. Labour more than doubled their share to win on an 18% swing with the Liberal Democrats falling back to third place with a drop of seven per cent in their share of the poll. Likewise, in Bristol West Labour, third behind the Liberal Democrats in 1992, added nearly 12% to their vote in 1997, ousting William Waldegrave, and relegating the Liberal Democrats to third place.

To cite these examples, is not to say that voters were not voting tactically, in their lights: tactical voting depends ultimately, as indeed do all political choices on perceptions and not on objective reality. Sometimes, too, objective reality may offer ambiguous or inconsistent cues; the closeness of the result in 1992 is only one indicator of who, among the opposition parties, is best placed to win. Local council elections, which have the merit of offering a more up to date map of the constituency electorate may tell a different story. Labour's success in the Hastings local elections hardly squared with the weakness reflected in the 1992 general election outcome. However, there remains the problem that the lack of generally accepted criteria for tactical voting, limits its utility for the parties themselves, and somewhat qualifies its value in appraising election outcomes.

Conclusion

The recovery of the centre in British politics has happened unevenly, even jerkily, over the last 25 years. Yet it is indisputable that this recovery now has a firmness, a solidity that the Liberal revivals of the Grimond era did not have. However vulnerable some of the gains of 1997 may appear, the party has a core strength, a sense of permanence that the party of Jo Grimond and Jeremy Thorpe did not have. Perhaps the most telling point about the weakness of the party in the fifties, is not that the party boasted only six MPs, but that in 1955, for example, only one of these had had to face both Conservative and Labour opposition. The 46 seats it holds today, all won in competition with both main parties, include eight held by absolute majorities (as a comparison the Conservatives can claim only 14).[21] More significant is that its support is now more unequally spread over the country than it used to be. Time was when the old Liberals could count on 5,000 votes in almost every seat, but be top in no more than a handful. The standard deviation of the Liberal Democratic vote share reached the high point of 10.2 in 1992, and today stands at 10.9; the figure for the Conservatives at 12.2 remains higher than for the Liberal Democrats, but not that much so. In the distribution of its vote the Conservative Party has looked increasingly fragile in recent years; the example of Canadian meltdown is not one to be lightly ignored.

Since the time of Jo Grimond, leader of the Liberals for the ten years from 1956, the rhetoric of the Liberals and their successors has dwelt on a realignment of the Left. In its extreme form, this realignment has assumed the replacement of Labour by the Liberals, or the Alliance, or the Liberal Democrats.[22] What has been clear from the electoral evidence is that a resurgence of the Liberals is likely to be achieved at the expense of the Conservatives. Indeed, what has been remarkable has been the reluctance of commentators and politicians to address this likelihood. Whatever happens to the two-party system, under first-past-the-post the future of Labour is assured. With a standard deviation of its vote share at 17.9 it will have, as far ahead as we can see, its industrial strongholds, which, as in 1983, will return Labour MPs in their scores even in the worst days. The future of the Liberal Democrats seems to depend on the 1997 revolution in voting behaviour being sustained. Part at least of the Liberal Democrat success rested not on tactical voting, not on targeting, but on the refusal of millions of erstwhile Conservatives to come out and vote Tory again. The massive decline of the Conservative vote is the central feature of the 1997 election; the possible revival of the Conservative Party is the biggest threat the Liberal Democrats have to face.

I would like to thank Ron Johnston and Charles Pattie for their ready assistance and permission to cite from unpublished findings; Dennis Kavanagh for his helpfulness in providing sources and information, and John Curtice for sharing with me his views on aspects of the Liberal Democratic advance.

1   Gallup Political and Economic Index 1993 and 1994.
2   Gallup Poll (*Daily Telegraph*, 19.3.97).
3   Private information.
4   J. Curtice and M. Steed, 'Appendix 2: The Results Analysed' in D. Butler and D. Kavanagh (eds), *The British General Election of 1992* (Macmillan 1992) p. 334.
5   *The Times*, 15.3.91.
6   *Independent*, (14.8.93).
7   See for example Peter Kellner (*Sunday Times*, 30.5.93).
8   P. Golding, D. Deacon and M. Billig, 1997 election study (*Guardian*, 5.5.97).
9   See n. 8.
10 Liberal Party Manifesto, 'Make the Difference'.
11 See *Daily Telegraph*, *The Times*, *Guardian* and *Independent*, 1.5.97.
12 C.J. Pattie and R.J. Johnston, private communication and letter to *The Times*, 15.5.97. I am most grateful to Dr Pattie and Professor Johnston.
13 BBC/NOP Exit Poll, 1.5.97.
14 Heath et al., *How Britain Votes* (Pergamon, 1985).
15 British Parliamentary Constituencies 1992–1997 database.
16 Apart from tactical voting Liberals would have suffered because so many of their incumbent seats seem to depend on the personal appeal of the Member. The effect of boundary revision will be to reduce the number of electors who know their constituency MP. Party is likely to have a greater pull than personality, the party image more than local service.
17 *Independent*, 29.4.97.
18 British Parliamentary Constituencies 1992–1997 database.
19 These and other figures are derived from the author's calculations of data in British Parliamentary Constituencies 1992–1997 database.
20 See n. 19.
21 See n. 19.
22 See for example, Ian Wrigglesworth in an interview with the *Independent*, 17.8.88.

The Opinion Polls: Confidence Restored?

BY IVOR CREWE*

THE STORY of the opinion polls in the 1997 election begins on 9 April 1992, the day John Major won the election and made fools of the polling industry. In 1992 the four final polls, published on election day, showed the Conservative and Labour parties level pegging, as the polls had been doing throughout the campaign. NOP and MORI put Labour slightly ahead, ICM declared a dead heat and Gallup put the Conservatives ahead by a mere half per cent; the average of the four was a Labour lead of 0.9%. Everything pointed to a hung parliament and a coalition government. In the event the Conservatives won with an overall majority of 21 seats, 7.6% ahead of Labour in the popular vote. In their forecast of the lead, the polls were out by over eight points, having underestimated the actual Conservative vote by four percentage points and overestimated the actual Labour vote by four percentage points. Even the BBC and ITN exit polls, which could not have been distorted by any last minute swing, underestimated the Conservative lead by three to four points.

Opinion polls had been wrong before, notably in 1970 when the Conservatives under Edward Heath won by three per cent and 30 seats, even though three of the four final polls forecast a clear Labour victory. But in 1970 the polls completed their interviewing three days before the election and thus failed to detect a late swing to the Conservatives. In 1992 the interviewing continued right up to the eve of election and the margin of error was much greater. Despite the growing sophistication of the polling industry, 1992 was the worst disaster in its fifty year history. It cast a five year shadow on political polls and haunted the parties, the media and the polling organisations throughout the 1997 campaign.

In the light of this legacy, this article explores what went wrong with the polls in 1992, how the companies adjusted their methods as a result, and how the media covered poll stories during the 1997 campaign. It concludes that although the polls undoubtedly improved on their disastrous performance in 1992, their record remained distinctly patchy, and the polling industry's initial complacency after the election was unjustified. Moreover the growth of non-uniform constituency swings, as a result of tactical voting and other factors, makes the use of polls as a guide not just to vote share, but also to seat share, much more hazardous than before.

* Vice Chancellor of the University of Essex and Professor of Government.

The polls' failure in 1992

What went wrong in 1992? The Market Research Society's post-mortem, conducted by a panel of academics and pollsters,[1] identified three main causes, which contributed in roughly equal proportions to the polls' error. The first was a small swing to the Conservatives on the eve and day of the election itself. In the 1992 election the electorate was exceptionally volatile, torn between a Conservative government with a poor record and a Labour opposition it did not trust: fully 21% changed their mind during the campaign, compared with 19%, 15% and 13% in the three previous elections. Before-and-after panel surveys showed that in the 36 hours up to election day some who declared they would abstain actually voted, and vice versa; some 'don't knows' made up their minds; and some 'firmly' for one party changed parties. All these last minute shifts helped the Conservatives.[2]

The second culprit was faulty sample design. Almost all the polls adopted a 'quota' sample: interviewers were instructed to interview a pre-set number of people according to their age, gender, social class and employment status such that the overall sample would be socially representative of the electorate as a whole. Quota samples are frowned upon by the purists, but if properly designed and executed they are the most practical basis for conducting polls and have a good track record. In 1992, however, they suffered from two flaws. Firstly, the selection of quota variables was unsatisfactory. Ideally, the variables should correlate with party preferences, in order to maximise the political representativeness of the sample, and should be easy for interviewers to apply. But gender and age are usually only weakly related to voting. Social class correlates with voting much more strongly, but is a poorly defined concept and notoriously difficult for busy interviewers to apply accurately to voters. Interviewers tended to mis-assign respondents up the social scale, including too many working class and thus Labour voters in their quotas. Secondly, the national social benchmarks used by the polling companies to set quotas (and weight their raw results) had not kept pace with socio-demographic changes in the electorate—the growing ranks of the elderly, fewer council tenants, an expanding middle class—and thus were biased in Labour's favour.[3]

The third contributory factor to the polls' debacle was the 'spiral of silence', the term coined by the German social researcher, Elizabeth Noelle-Neumann, for people's tendency to remain silent or evasive about their own views when they sense a hostile climate of opinion around them.[4] There was an anti-Conservative edge to the 1992 campaign: even the Conservative media derided the Conservative campaign as lacklustre (as did Mrs Thatcher) while Labour was portrayed as taking the moral high ground on taxes and spending. In opinion polls 'silence' takes the form of declining to answer the 'how will you vote?' question, or responding 'don't know' or refusing to be interviewed at all. These 'silent' respondents were excluded from the opinion poll results on the assumption that in their politics they were similar to more forthcoming respondents and, if they turned out, would vote for the parties in the same proportions. Their answers to other questions, however, revealed that the majority had voted Conservative in 1987, preferred Major to Kinnock as prime minister and thought the Conservatives to be better at managing the economy. They were, in the main, closet Conservatives.

Cooking to taste: the pollsters change the recipes

The 1992 debacle inevitably shook the confidence of the parties and the media in the validity of conventional polls. In April 1993, BBC Television, bruised by predicting a hung parliament in its election night programme, issued new producers' guidelines which ruled out the commissioning of exit polls or the compiling of 'polls of polls' 'until we are satisfied that polling methodology is more robust' and restricted the reporting of polls published in the press.[5] The *Independent* immediately abandoned regular polling and did not change heart until immediately before the 1997 campaign. The political parties occasionally undertook private polls but relied more heavily than before on the semi-structured discussions of small 'focus groups'. Most of the broadsheets, however, continued to invest in a monthly poll, while pressing their polling organisation to improve its techniques in order to avoid another embarrassment.

In 1993 and 1994, each of the major polling companies changed its methods, but each did so differently. Each tried to perfect the alchemy that would convert the rough stone of a raw poll into the gold of a perfect forecast. MORI and ICM drew up more elaborate quotas, adding politically sensitive characteristics such as housing tenure and, in MORI's case, car ownership to the standard variables of age, sex and work status; Gallup and NOP, however, stuck to a traditional quota design.[6] MORI and NOP took pains to update their estimates of the proportion of the electorate falling into each quota, by cross-checking the 1991 Census data against more recent national surveys such as the labour force, family expenditure, general household and national readership surveys. NOP went furthest, by making an allowance for the social difference between the total adult population and the electorate that resulted from differential non-registration. This was because those least likely to register, even though eligible, are all Labour-voting groups: the young, the unemployed, frequent changers of address and black Caribbeans.

All four companies sought to adjust for any residual unrepresentativeness in their sample by weighting their raw data to their quota controls, a traditional feature of opinion polling. In addition, three of them (MORI was the exception) weighted the answer to their vote intention question so that recalled vote in 1992 came into line with the actual result in 1992. They differed, however, in their application of this weighting. Throughout the 1992–97 period, respondents' recall of their 1992 vote produced a Labour lead, typically of 5–7%, even though the Conservatives actually won by eight per cent. This recall bias arose for three reasons. It owed a little to the death of elderly (and predominantly Conservative) voters since 1992. It owed more to faulty memory: about one out of five respondents confused the previous general election with a more recent local or European election or they projected their current voting intentions (which after October 1992 were more likely to be Labour than Conservative) back onto their past vote. Liberal voters in 1992—many of them fleeting or tactical Liberals—were particularly prone to misremember their electoral past and to claim to have voted Labour. But apparent recall bias could also have arisen from a 'spiral of silence': if 1992 Conservatives were more likely to refuse to be interviewed at all, the sample as a whole would contain too many Labour supporters. Gallup weighted back to the actual 1992 result (an eight percent Conservative lead); NOP, on the other hand, decided to weight to how a perfectly representative sample would recall having voted in 1992, which it estimated to be an equal balance between Conservative and Labour; ICM plumped for an intermediate position of a five per cent Conservative lead, without offering a rationale.

All four polling companies tried to address the problem of 'shy Tories'. ICM, pollsters for the *Guardian*, was the pioneer.[7] In 1993 it experimented with a 'secret ballot' which respondents dropped into a mock ballot box so that they did not have to tell the interviewer face to face how they intended to vote, and with the allocation of 60% of 'non-disclosers' (i.e. those answering the vote intention question with 'don't know', 'won't vote' or a refusal) to the party they recalled voting for in 1992 (*Guardian* 9.12.93, *Guardian* 6.7.94). Uniquely among the polling companies, its vote intention question named the parties, which appears to have boosted the figure for Liberal Democrat support. All these changes reduced the Labour lead obtained by the conventional polling methods, although the impact of the secret-ballot was variable and gradually diminished. In July 1994, ICM switched from face-to-face to telephone interviewing, thus dropping the secret-ballot technique. Telephone interviewing precludes the need for geographically clustered samples and thus reduces sampling error; it allows interviewers to return to initial non-contacts more than once, an advantage in view of the apparent tendency for Conservatives to predominate among those difficult to contact;[8] and with 90% of the electorate available by telephone the bias arising from non-ownership is small and adjustable.

MORI immediately followed suit in their regular outlet, *The Times*, by allocating all their non-disclosers to the party they recalled voting for in 1992.[9] Four months later, Gallup, the pollster of long-standing for the *Telegraph* newspapers, changed its approach. It weighted its raw data according to recall of vote in 1992 and it reallocated its non-disclosers on the basis of which party leader they preferred as prime minister and which party they considered better at handling the economy: respondents favouring the same party in both answers were allocated to that party. NOP, which began regular polling for the *Sunday Times* from July 1995 reallocated its non-disclosers according to their answers to questions on their party identification and their perception of the parties' economic competence.[10]

These experiments produced encouraging results at a trial run in the European elections of June 1994 (see Table 1). Three polling companies published their 'unadjusted' and 'adjusted' results after the voting on 9 June and before the count on 12 June. In each case the adjusted poll recorded a higher Conservative and lower Labour vote than the unadjusted. On average the unadjusted polls overestimated Labour's lead over the Conservatives by seven percentage points, a discrepancy close to that in 1992, whereas the adjusted polls were almost spot on for both parties. All the polls overestimated the Liberal Democrats' support and underestimated that for minor parties, although this may have been due to late swings (in various directions) between the fieldwork and the actual election as well as to the effects of turnout, which was considerably lower than the polls forecast. More troublesome but unnoticed was NOP's unadjusted poll for the Labour party which was just as accurate as the adjusted polls.[11]

1. Final polls for European elections, June 1994: standard and super-adjusted

| | | Standard | | | | Super-adjusted | | | |
	Fieldwork	Cons	Lab	Lib Dem	Lab lead	Cons	Lab	Lib Dem	Lab lead
Gallup	1–7 June	24.5	49.5	18	25	28	44	19.5	16
ICM	6 June	27	45	22	18	29	43	20	14
MORI	2–6 June	23	51	20	28	27	47	20	20
Mean		25	48.5	20	23.5	28	44.5	20	16.5
Actual result	9 June	28	44	16.5	16.5	28	4.0	16.5	16.5
Discrepancy		−3	+4.5	+3.5	+7	0	+0.5	+3.5	0

Thereafter Gallup, ICM and MORI published what they called 'adjusted' as well as 'unadjusted' polls. More accurate terms would have been 'super-adjusted' and 'adjusted' since both versions of the poll fine-tuned the raw data; indeed long before 1992, published polls were weighted to be socially representative of the electorate, some used recalled vote to weight to the previous election result and all excluded non-disclosers, itself a form of correction. This article uses the terms 'standard' and 'super-adjusted' to distinguish the conventional poll from those which allocated non-disclosers to a party.

The apparent success of the pollsters' new recipes at the European elections was qualified by another awkward fact: the magnitude of the adjustment made by different formulae varied considerably. Table 2 shows that in the thirty-month period from July 1994 to January 1997 the adjustments made by ICM and Gallup cut Labour's lead by an

2. The impact of adjustments by the polling companies, July 1994–January 1997

Polling organisation	Number of polls	% Lab lead over Con		Change in Lab lead (% points)
		Standard	Super-adjusted	
Gallup	(21)	33.7	24.3	−9.4
ICM	(28)	27.8	17.7	−10.1
MORI	(32)	27.6	22.2	−5.4
NOP	(16)	26.4	21.7	−4.7
Mean (unweighted)		28.9	21.5	−7.4

average of 9–10 percentage points whereas those made by MORI and NOP made a difference of only four to five points. They could not all be correct. Over the same period Labour's average lead in the super-adjusted polls varied from 18 percentage points in ICM and 22 points in MORI and NOP, up to 24 points in Gallup. These differences were perplexingly unrelated, moreover, to the ingredients of the recipe: of the two heavy adjusters, ICM interviewed by telephone and used politically sensitive quotas whereas Gallup did not; of the two lighter adjusters, NOP reallocated non-disclosers according to their answers to political questions whereas MORI reallocated them according to recall of 1992 vote. It was clear that some of the recipes were wrong but it was not clear which — or why.

Two polling organisations changed their formulae shortly before the election. In January 1997 Gallup switched to telephone interviewing. Concerned about the consistently larger Labour leads in its polls than in others (see Table 2) — a pattern that began before 1992 but was initially less pronounced — it concluded that its interviewers were systematically going too 'down market' within their quotas when selecting respondents and discovered that telephone polling brought Gallup's figures much closer to the average of other polling organisations (*Daily Telegraph* 17.1.97). At the same time it switched from asking 'if there were a general election tomorrow, which party would you *support*?' to 'which party would you *vote for*?' (author's italics). It retained its method of allocating a vote intention to non-disclosers, but dropped the weighting of recalled 1992 vote to the 1992 result. The change of approach had a clear effect: the Labour lead (24%) in its (super-adjusted) snapshot poll in late November 1996 was five points higher than the average in other polls taken at that time, whereas the Labour lead in its mid-January poll (18%) matched the average for all January polls. In March 1997, immediately prior to the campaign, and encouraged by the accuracy of its conventional, standard poll early in the February 1997 Wirral South by-election campaign, MORI decided against assigning voting intentions to non-disclosers (*Mail on Sunday*, 9.2.97). This time, it decided, there were very few closet Conservatives lurking behind the 'don't know' column; and, after all, conventional standard polls had served well in the 1970s and 1980s; 1992 was a 'one-off'.

The polling organisations therefore entered the 1997 campaign with a wider range of approaches than at any time since the war. The potential for conflicting messages during the campaign, and the attendant likelihood that opinion polls and their methods would themselves turn into a campaign issue, as had occurred in previous elections, was greater than ever. In the event opinion polls had a somewhat lower than expected profile.

The opinion polls in the 1997 campaign

Opinion polls were the permanent backcloth of the 1997 campaign but they did not play centre stage under the spotlight as they had in each of the three previous elections. The amount of polling, which had steadily increased since 1974 and had reached saturation levels by 1992 fell back sharply to 1974 levels. In 1992 an average of two national polls were published each day (57 polls in a 29 day campaign); in 1997 the average was one poll a day (44 polls in a 45-day campaign).[12] Polls also found considerably fewer outlets than in 1992. Although the broadsheets published a weekly poll, the tabloids confined themselves to 'feature story' polls of special groups such as first-time voters or to special constituencies such as Tatton and Basildon or dispensed with polling altogether.[13] Television was conspicuously abstemious; ITN commissioned a panel of voters in six marginal seats and one or two programmes broadcast feature polls on, for example, 'Thatcher's children' and Asian voters; but otherwise, quite unlike 1992 and 1987, they restricted themselves to reporting the broadsheet polls. Except for polls of Scotland, of which there were fifteen in three different Scottish newspapers during the campaign, other types of polls were also in less

3. The growth of opinion polls in general election campaigns, 1945–1997

Election year	Number of national polls in campaign	Number of different agencies conducting polls	Number of different newspapers/TV programmes commissioning polls
1945	1	1	1
1950	11	2	2
1951	n/a	3	3
1955	n/a	2	2
1959	20	2	4
1964	23	4	4
1966	26	4	8
1970	25	5	6
1974 (Feb)	25	6	9
1974 (Oct)	27	6	11
1979	26	5	8
1983	46	6	14
1987	54	7	15
1992	57	7	18
1997	44	5	13

Note: (a) The number of polls excludes election-day surveys and private polling by the parties, as well as regional and local surveys. (b) Gallup produced a daily 'rolling' poll, in which one third of the sample was replaced each day, for the *Daily Telegraph* and *Sunday Telegraph*. Every third Gallup poll is included in the total. (c) Some of the different newspapers are owned by the same company.

demand in 1992. The national press published almost no polls in any other region and relatively few single-constituency polls. In 1987 at least 78 single constituency polls in 52 seats were commissioned;[14] in the national media in 1997 there appear to have been no more than 29 single constituency polls in 26 seats, including an ICM/*Observer* poll of sixteen Conservative seats vulnerable to tactical voting published on the Sunday before polling day.

The media commissioned fewer polls than in 1987 or 1992. They also gave them less coverage. The BBC, sticking to the producer guidelines, never led the news with a poll story although Peter Snow was given the time to provide detailed analysis, accompanied by fancy graphics of polls of polls, despite the earlier prohibition. ITN's *News At Ten* behaved likewise. The newspapers rarely devoted its lead story to a poll even when they were reporting their own; more often the front page carried a capsule summary while the main report was confined to an inside page. About a fifth of all front page lead stories in the national press were devoted to the polls in 1987 (20%) and 1992 (18%); in 1997 the proportion dropped to a mere four per cent.

The ebbing of the poll frenzy probably owed less to their tarnished reputation than to the apparent certainty of the outcome from the very start of the campaign. The polls pointed to a runaway Labour victory with almost tedious persistence. Every national poll but one gave Labour a double-digit lead that ranged from comfortable to massive, the exception being ICM's for the *Guardian* on 23 April which reported a five per cent lead. Conservative support seemed firmly stuck at about 31%, presumably its core: of the 43 polls, 33 put the Conservatives in the 29–33% range and all but two within the 28–34% range. The 24 daily rolling Gallup polls in the *Daily/Sunday Telegraph* barely rolled at all: Conservative support never strayed beyond the 29 to 33% range and Labour support stayed within the similarly narrow band of 48 to 53%. Had the gap between the two parties been smaller, sampling error and rogue polls might have occasionally suggested a hung parliament or even a narrow Conservative victory; and apparent contradictions between the national and local polls, or between safe and marginal seats, or between vote intentions and other measures of party preference might have hinted that the horse-race headlines were not telling the full story. Any ambiguity of this kind would have injected some excitement into the campaign and led to more polls and more extensive media coverage. However, Labour's perpetually large leads were reinforced by its superiority on almost every other measure of party support. Tony Blair was consistently preferred to John Major by margins ranging from 7 to 24% (except in the ICM/*Guardian* 'rogue' poll when he lagged by one per cent)[15] and Labour comfortably led the Conservatives on all issues other than taxes and Europe, where its lead was narrow. Polls in London, Scotland and single constituencies confirmed the national picture. From the very beginning of the campaign, therefore, the press

4. The opinion polls and the 1997 election

Date of fieldwork (and number of polls)	Polling organisation	Outlet	Lab majority	Con	Lab	Lib Dem	Other
Pre-campaign polls							
January (4)			23.3	29.3	52.6	12.2	6.0
February (4)			23.8	29.2	53.0	11.9	6.0
early March (9)			24.4	28.8	53.2	12.0	6.1
Campaign polls							
Weeks 1 and 2 (6)							
17–30 Mar			21.6	29.8	51.4	12.9	5.9
Week 3 (9)							
31 Mar–6 Apr			21.2	30.6	51.8	11.7	5.9
Week 4 (9)							
7–13 Apr			18.2	30.9	49.1	14.0	5.9
Week 5 (7)							
14–20 Apr			14.7	32.3	47.0	14.3	6.3
(6)*			[16.3]	[31.5]	[47.8]	[14.3]	[6.3]
Week 6							
21–27 Apr			18.5	30.1	48.6	14.5	6.8
Final (forecast) polls****							
27–29 Apr	Harris	Independent	17	31	48	15	6
29 Apr	NOP	Reuters	22	28	50	14	8
29 Apr	MORI	Times	20	28	48	16	8
29–30 Apr	ICM	Guardian	10	33	43	18	5
30 Apr	Gallup	D Telegraph	14	33	47	14	6
30 Apr	MORI	E Standard**	18	29	47	19	5
Exit polls							
1 May	NOP	BBC	18	29	47	18	6
1 May	MORI	ITN***	16	30	46	18	6
Forecast poll mean			16.8	30.3	47.2	16.0	6.3
Exit poll mean			17.0	29.5	46.5	18.0	6.0
Actual result (GB)			12.9	31.5	44.4	17.2	6.9

* Excludes the 'rogue' ICM/*Guardian* poll published on 23 April.   ** Telephone poll.   *** Extrapolated on the basis of uniform national swing from a sample drawn from marginal constituencies only. Comparisons with the other polls should be cautious.   **** Excludes Gallup poll for Channel 4 News on 30 April. See fn. 22.

could do little on most days other than report the near certainty of a Labour victory and the distinct possibility of a Labour landslide.

The incessant chorus declaiming an impregnable Labour lead contained one discordant voice. Despite their different recipes, Gallup, Harris, MORI and NOP produced remarkably close, as well as constant, figures of party support, when averaged across the campaign (see Table 5). All four put the Labour lead at between 19 and 21%, placing the Conservatives at 30–31%, Labour at 50–51% and the Liberal Democrats at 12–14%.[16] ICM was the outlier. In its polls Labour's lead

5. Comparison of the vote intention figures between the different polling organisations: the campaign polls 1997

Polling organisation (Number of polls)	Labour lead	Con	Lab	Lib-Dem	Other
Mean					
Gallup (12)	19.0	31.3	50.3	12.1	6.3
Harris (6)	20.5	30.0	50.5	13.3	6.0
ICM (9)	12.9	32.9	45.8	16.0	5.1
MORI (10)	20.9	29.5	50.4	13.8	6.3
NOP (5)	20.0	30.0	50.0	14.0	6.0

was much lower — 13% on average. (Exclude the rogue poll lead of five per cent and the average is 14%, still much lower than in the other polls.) Compared with other polls, ICM consistently reported a much lower Labour vote (46%) and slightly higher support for the Conservatives (33%) and Liberal Democrats (16%). ICM differed from its competitors by combining all the techniques for identifying closet Conservatives: telephone polling *plus* politically sensitive quotas *plus* allocating non-disclosers to a party *plus* reweighting to a five point Conservative lead. Perhaps it had over-egged the pudding. The proof would be in the tasting of the actual result: perhaps ICM would bask in lonely splendour.

The media and the polls in the campaign

The media made the most of what few news opportunities the polls gave them. It suited the partisan press on both sides, for political as well as news-value reasons, to find evidence of Conservative recovery: Conservative newspapers wanted to maintain morale, Labour newspapers wanted to banish complacency. Both sides suspected anyway that Labour's huge lead in the polls was exaggerated and insecure. Their scepticism was reinforced by academics and the City. The weekly forecast of a Reuters' panel of academic specialists always discounted the polls heavily: ten days before polling, the panel forecast a nine point lead for Labour when the polls were averaging a 16-point lead, and three days before polling it forecast a ten point lead when the polls were suggesting an 18-point lead.[17] Similarly, spread-betting on the election result in the City reflected expectations of an 8–10 point majority.[18] All manner of reason could be found for discounting the polls: the figures were wholly unprecedented; the Conservatives usually put on a last-minute spurt; the state of the economy would trump all other issues on the day; the closet Conservatives, undetected by the polls, would indulge their secret desires in the privacy of the polling booth; above all, the polls were wrong last time and could be wrong again. Each of these points could be countered by logic or evidence[19] but the newspapers, desperate to turn a Labour walkover into a real contest, seized on any evidence that the gap was closing.

There was, in fact, real evidence of a progressive decline in the Labour lead. Table 4 shows that it fell from 22% in the pre-Easter fortnight, when sleaze dominated the headlines, to 21% in week three, 18% in week four and 16% in week five (if the rogue ICM/*Guardian* poll is ignored) before recovering slightly in week six. This was too glacial for good news copy. Instead reporters gave too much credence to haphazard evidence from small 'focus groups' of floating voters that Conservative waverers were returning to the fold[20] and grasped at the more dramatic falls in the Labour lead that intermittently and inevitably arose when sampling error added a surge to the gentle ebbing of Labour's lead.

'TORIES CLOSE POLL GAP' was the headline for the *Guardian*'s lead story on 2 April. On closer inspection the Labour lead in the ICM poll had slipped from 18% in late February (immediately after its Wirral South by-election triumph) to 14% in late March, having been 16% in late January: the three months' polls were in fact perfectly consistent with an unchanged lead of about 16% across the whole period. Somewhat more justified was *The Times'* lead story headline on 10 April 'LABOUR POLL LEAD SLASHED BY THE TORIES': its MORI poll reported a Labour lead of 15, down 12 points from a heady 27-point lead a week earlier, although the article forbore to mention that the previous week's poll had been exceptionally favourable to Labour and out of line with others. 'The general election came alive for the first time last night . . .', the story began, 'the Conservatives have started to make big inroads into Labour's commanding lead'. This bold assertion sat oddly with an acknowledgement later in the article that a Gallup poll in that day's *Daily Telegraph* had increased the Labour lead from 21 to 23 points. The prize for hype, however, was won by the *Sunday Telegraph* of 13 April whose front page headline 'LABOUR NOSEDIVES IN NEW POLL' referred to a fall in Labour's lead from 20 to 16 points in Gallup's rolling poll, the product of a one point rise in Conservative support and a three point drop in Labour support. Next to the article was a textbook case of a misleading graph: an elongated vertical axis represented Labour's percentage point lead while a truncated horizontal axis represented the years 1994–1997. Starting with Labour's 40-point lead in December 1994 (when Gallup polls were designed differently) a red line plunged down the graph to its 16 point lead that day. On the next page, under the storyline 'VOTERS DOUBTS BEGIN TO TURN TIDE FOR TORIES', Dr David Carlton, its in-house academic commentator, found a straw to clutch: 'On 12 June 1970, a *Daily Mail* poll showed Labour with a 12.4% lead. Six days later it had fallen to 4.1%. The second poll was on election day, when the Conservatives swept to power with a lead over Labour of 3.4%. This time, with 18 days to go, today's Gallup findings demonstrate the potential volatility of the electorate'. But there was nothing in the polls to suggest that voters were particularly volatile.

The most dramatic opportunity to claim that the election outcome was wide open arrived on 23 April when the *Guardian* published its weekly ICM poll: compared with the previous week, the Conservatives were six percentage points up and Labour three points down: the Labour lead had plummeted nine points to a mere five per cent — on the border of a hung parliament. Up to that point the smallest Labour lead in the campaign had been 12 points; indeed, this was the smallest Labour lead reported by any national poll since October 1992. Under a 'POLL SHOCK FOR LABOUR' headline, the *Guardian's* story exclaimed 'The general election was thrown wide open last night as Labour's huge lead over the Conservatives in most opinion polls was breached by a dramatic shift since John Major stepped up his eurosceptic campaign rhetoric. Today's Guardian/ ICM survey ... [has] opened up the possibility of a stunning Tory victory against the odds in eight days' time'. The *Guardian* was convinced that the Conservatives were rallying strongly as a result of the Conservative candidates' rebellion the previous week on their party's policy on the single currency and John Major's bold attempt to make an issue out of Europe. It was persuaded by leaks that ICM's private polls for the Conservatives that weekend showed euroscepticism to be playing well to floating voters and by the fall in the Labour lead in the NOP and Gallup polls of the previous few days. However, it virtually ignored the awkward fact that that same day's Gallup/*Daily Telegraph* rolling poll, conducted during the same time as ICM's, reported a five point leap in Labour's lead to 21 points. Other papers too could not resist the story: 'LABOUR LEAD COLLAPSES IN POLLS', shrieked the *Daily Mail*; 'NOW ITS A FIGHT TO THE DEATH', declaimed the *Independent*. The *Daily Telegraph* downplayed its own Gallup poll, preferring the politically more congenial news from ICM: 'LABOUR LEAD COLLAPSES IN NEW POLL' with a lead story which incongruously surrounded a capsule graphic of the Gallup poll's 21-point Labour lead. It was left to the inside pages of the broadsheets to explain how the two polls could be so far apart.[21] Almost certainly both polls were affected in different directions by abnormal sampling error but in ICM's case it reinforced ICM's regular tendency to produce smaller Labour leads than other polls did.

The performance of the polls

On 1 May the polling organisations published their final, forecast polls, in some trepidation. A repetition of the 1992 fiasco would have done irreparable damage to not only to political polls but to market surveys in general. The six forecasts[22] (see Table 4) ranged from the ICM/ *Guardian* ten point Labour lead to the NOP/Reuters 22-point Labour lead — the widest range of forecasts in the history of polling. The slightly different recipes had produced very different dishes. Even allowing for the conventional three per cent sampling error — six per cent on the party gap — some of them had to be wrong. The two exit polls — NOP's for the BBC and MORI's for ITN — came in the middle of the range, forecasting Labour leads of 18 and 16 points respectively.

The true test of a poll's accuracy is the mean of the difference between each party's percentage share of the vote (counting 'other' parties as a single party) and the poll's forecast of that share. By that yardstick ICM was the runaway winner, with a mean score of 1.25, followed by Harris/*Independent* and Gallup/*Daily Telegraph* (2.0 in each case), MORI (2.5 for both its polls) and NOP (3.5). ICM was also astonishingly accurate in Scotland with a mean difference score of a mere 0.25.[23]

But according to the Association of Professional Opinion Polling Organisations (APOPO), representing the five main polling companies, all of them were right. The day after the election they crowed:

The 1997 British general election is as much a test of the pollsters as of the parties. In 1992, the forecast of the share of the vote for each party by each of the pollsters ... was wider of the actual result than ever before. As a result, throughout this election campaign, the publication of nearly every poll was accompanied by carping that the polls could not possibly be right, that they had again under estimated the Conservative share, and it was 'inconceivable' that Labour could win by the margins indicated.

Not so in the 1997 general election.

Yesterday the five polling organisations [Gallup, Harris, ICM, MORI and NOP] got the average share of the vote for each party within the usually accepted plus or minus three per cent sampling tolerance.[24]

This understandable self-promotion was taken at face value by the media: 'POLLSTERS CAN FEEL SELF-SATISFIED' approved the *Independent* (3.5.97); 'POLLSTERS RESTORE TARNISHED REPUTATION' enthused the *Guardian* (3.5.97).[25] The polls undoubtedly improved on their disastrous 1992 performance but by historical and statistical standards their performance was patchy in a number of ways:

6. Accuracy of the final forecast polls in general elections, 1945–97

Year	Outgoing government	Number of forecast polls	Deviation of mean estimate from share of vote (GB)				Mean error per party	Mean error on gap between first and second party
			Con	Lab	Lib	Others		
1945	Coalition	1	+2	−2	+1	−1	1.5	−4
1950	Labour	2	+1	−2	+2	–	1.3	−3
1951	Labour	3	+2	−4	+1	+1	2.3	−6
1955	Con	2	+1	+1	−1	−1	1.0	–
1959	Con	3	–	−1	–	–	0.3	+1
1964	Con	4	+1	+1	−1	–	1.0	–
1966	Lab	3	−1	+3	−1	–	1.3	4
1970	Lab	5	−2	+4	−1	−1	2.0	−6
1974 (Feb)	Con	6	–	−2	+2	–	1.0	+2
1974 (Oct)	Lab	5	−2	+3	–	−1	1.5	+5
1979	Lab	5	–	+1	–	–	0.3	−1
1983	Con	7	+3	−2	–	−1	1.5	+5
1987	Con	7	−1	+2	−2	–	1.3	−3
1992	Con	4	−4	+4	+1	−1	3.0	−9
1997	Con	6	−1	+3	−1	−1	2.0	+4

Note: A final poll is defined for 1959–97 as any published on polling day and for earlier elections as any described as such. Fieldwork dates vary slightly but for elections since February 1974 are usually the Tuesday and/or Wednesday immediately before election day.

(1) As Table 6 shows, the mean error of 2.0 in the six final polls was the third largest since 1945, exceeded only by 1992 (3.0) and 1951 (2.3, when the absence of Liberal candidates in most seats made the polls' task more difficult) and equalled in the other postwar poll embarrassment of 1970. Between February 1974 (when Liberals for the first time contested most seats) and 1987 the mean error was always below 2.0. By historical standards 1997 was a relatively poor year.

(2) Five of the six final polls (six of the seven, if the Gallup/Channel Four is included) and both exit polls overestimated the Labour vote, in three cases by more than the accepted three per cent sampling error and in three further cases by close to it. The probability that sampling error was responsible for overestimates of such consistency and magnitude is extremely remote. (It is worth remembering that the probability of a three per cent sampling error is much less than the probability of a one per cent sampling error.) An eve-of-election swing (probably tactical) from Labour to the Liberal Democrats may have been a small contributory factor but cannot be the main explanation: both exit polls, which are immune to late swing, also overestimated the Labour vote.[26] The polls may have partly dealt with the 'closet Conservative' problem of 1992 but they had evidently not licked the other half of the problem, the 'lost Labour voters'.

(3) Six of the eight final/exit polls (seven out of nine if the Gallup/Channel 4 poll is included) underestimated the Conservative vote, albeit by smaller margins and within accepted sampling error. *Pace* APOPO's claims this falls short of finally cracking the 'closet Conservative' problem. It was simply not true to claim, as one pollster did, that there were no 'silent Tories' in 1997.[27]

(4) As a result of exaggerating the Labour vote and understating the Conservative vote five of the six final polls and both exit polls (ICM, again, was the exception) overestimated the Labour lead. The mean difference between the forecast and actual gap of 3.9 percentage points may fall within accepted sampling error; but seven of the fifteen postwar elections have been won by a smaller margin.

The contribution of new methods to ICM's success is unclear. The two most successful polls (ICM and Gallup) both adopted telephone polling after 1992 but the MORI/*Evening Standard* poll, which was five points adrift on the party lead, also used telephone interviewing. ICM and Gallup super-adjusted their standard vote intention figures, but so did NOP, the least accurate of the final polls. Moreover, although the super-adjustment typically reduced Labour's lead it did not do so much: by an average of three points for ICM, three points for NOP and two points for Gallup.[28] Had ICM dispensed with super-adjustments and reported its standard figures it would have remained the polling company reporting the lowest Labour leads and would have shared the honour of the most accurate final forecast with Gallup.[29] More important perhaps, was ICM's weighting of the recalled 1992 vote to a five point Conservative lead as a means of compensating for the assumed predominance of Conservatives among those refusing to be interviewed at all — a practice which went further than other polling organisations did. Only more detailed analysis will tell.

Confidence restored?

In 1992, and to a lesser extent the two earlier elections, the impact of the opinion polls on the election was an important question. In 1997 it was the reverse: the polls had little effect on the timing, course or result of the election, but the election had an impact on the polls. In fact, the pollsters were lucky. In a landslide they are bound to pick the winner. Had the party gap been six points or less—as it has in nine out of the fifteen postwar elections—the 12-point spread in the forecasts would have ensured that at least one and probably more of the final polls would have backed the wrong party. They also benefited, quite accidentally, from the non-uniformity of the constituency swings. Landslide Labour majorities of 170 to 220 were projected by applying uniform national swing to the campaign polls and the final forecasts of all but ICM, suggesting 17 to 22-point Labour leads.[30] On a uniform national swing Labour's actual lead of 13 points would have produced an overall majority of about 130 rather than the 179 that transpired. The polls were associated with the correct forecast of the Labour majority but for the wrong reason.

The accuracy of polls should be judged primarily by the closeness of their voting projections to the actual result. But polls are valued, not for themselves, but for their ability to predict the share of seats in the new Parliament, and ultimately therefore the party in government. Many polling companies publish the vote share and also project the consequences for seats. The decline of uniform constituency swing, due to tactical voting and other factors, has been documented by many contributors throughout this volume. This means that even if polls provide an accurate guide to the national vote, the task of projecting the results for seats has become far harder. This pattern seems likely to encourage the growth of more polls of marginal seats in the next general election, although in the past their track record has often been hazardous due to problems of sample size and the definition of marginality.

In 1997, therefore, the performance of the polls was creditable but far from brilliant. The widespread overestimate of the Labour vote, repeating a pattern found in 1992 and 1987, pinpoints a problem for the polling organisations to address with as much energy as they addressed the issue of 'closet Conservatives'. Lost Labour voters may matter more next time, if the contest is closer or many Labour supporters are disillusioned with the government. More tactical voting by an increasingly sophisticated electorate may confound predictions based on uniform swing. The polls may not be as fortunate in 2002.

1   Market Research Society, *The Opinion Polls and the 1992 General Election*, July 1994. The panel was chaired by David Butler.

2   *The Opinion Polls and the 1992 General Election*, p. 12.

3   *The Opinion Polls and the 1992 General Election*, p. 31.

4   E. Noelle-Neumann, *The Spiral of Silence* (University of Chicago Press, 1984).

5   See I. Crewe, 'The Last Exit Poll', *Guardian*, 22.11.93.

6   However, NOP weighted their raw data to housing and car ownership in addition to their quota controls.

7   See N. Sparrow, 'Improving Polling Techniques Following the 1992 General Election', *Journal of the Market Research Society*, 1993; and N. Sparrow and J. Turner, 'Messages from the Spiral of Silence: Developing More Accurate Market Information in a More Uncertain Political Climate', *Journal of the Market Research Society*, 1995.

8   R. Jowell et al, 'The 1992 British Election: The Failure of the Polls', *Public Opinion Quarterly*, 1994.

9   See MORI, 'Voting Intention', *British Public Opinion*, August 1994. MORI noted that 'whereas the adjustment method seems to be justified in the current political situation and would have improved the record of the polls at the 1992 election, at each of the previous three elections it would have made MORI's prediction worse rather than better'.

10 Letter from Nick Moon of NOP to author, November 1996. Non-disclosers were reallocated according to the matrix of these questions and the vote intention question in the poll as a whole.

11 *The Opinion Polls and the 1992 General Election*, p. 106.

12 This number includes a third of the Gallup's daily rolling polls in the *Daily/Sunday Telegraph*, which replaced one third of the sample each day.

13 The *Daily Mirror* and *Sunday Mirror* were minor exceptions, sharing MORI polls with the *Independent on Sunday*.

14 See R. Waller, 'Constituency polling in the 1987 election' in I. Crewe and M. Harrop (eds), *Political Communications: The General Election Campaign of 1987* (Cambridge University Press, 1989), p. 239.

15 See BBC, 'Best prime minister', *Election 97* website (www.bbc.co.uk/election 97/polls/bestpm.htm).

16 For each polling organisation the standard deviations were always larger for Labour (on average 2.4) than for the Conservatives (1.4), which suggests that it was the measure of Labour not Conservative support that was least reliable. Figures for means and standard deviations are very similar if the base is extended to before the campaign to all polls conducted since the beginning of 1997.

17 Reuters' press release, 23 April 1997 and 30 April 1997.

18 For example, the IG-Index 'price' for the Labour party (i.e. the average of the spread), which reflected the weight of betting, ranged from 368 to 374 seats during the campaign until the final two days when it rose to 382. On the assumption of a national uniform swing, this was consistent with Labour leads of 8 to 10 percentage points. Data collected by the author.

19 Precedents get broken; neither the Conservatives nor the party in office normally gain significant support during the campaign itself; the state of the economy had had no impact in the run up to the election; the polling organisations were making adjustments for closet Conservatives; the magnitude of the polls' error in 1992 was much smaller than Labour's lead.

20 A notable example was 'Tories close gap on Labour as voters confound the polls' in the *Independent* of 21 April, a double-page spread of quotes from members of focus groups of former Conservative voters in six marginal constituencies who had earlier indicated that they might switch. Careful analysis showed that the proportion saying they had definitely decided to switch was much in line with the proportion of Conservative switchers identified in the national polls. See also the *Guardian*'s weekly feature articles on voters in the marginal constituencies of Stevenage and Leeds North East, which regularly called the polls into doubt.

21 See A. King, 'Why the Election Surveys are Polls Apart', *Daily Telegraph*, 23.4.97 and P. Riddell, 'Diverse Results May be Telling Statistical Truth', *The Times*, 24.4.97.

22 In addition, a Gallup poll for Channel Four's News At Ten broadcast on 30 April put the standing of the parties at Conservative 30%, Labour 48%, Liberal Democrat 16% and Others 6%. This poll is excluded from the analysis because no further details were published.

23 The standing of the parties (with their actual vote in brackets) in ICM's final poll for *The Scotsman* was Conservative 18 (18), Labour 46 (46), Liberal Democrat 13 (13) and SNP 21 (22). The poll was conducted on 25–27 April. The NOP/*Sunday Times in Scotland* poll had a mean difference score of 2.5 and the Systems 3/*Glasgow Herald* poll a score of 4. Unlike ICM, both overestimated the Labour lead by 8 points, as a result of being 4 points adrift for both parties.

24 APOPO (Association of Professional Opinion Polling Organisations), 'General Election '97 Result', press release, 2.5.97.

25 For a more sceptical view, see 'Not right', *The Economist*, 10.5.97.

26 This switching was reported in MORI's telephone call-back of 1000 respondents for part of its election-day poll for the *Evening Standard*.

27 B. Worcester, 'They Got it Right This Time', *New Statesman*, May 1997 special edition. It is worth

noting that MORI, which decided against allocating non-disclosers to a party, underestimated the Conservative vote by 3 and 4 points in its two final polls.

28 Unpublished data kindly provided by Bob Wybrow of Gallup and Nick Moon of NOP.

29 The standard ('unadjusted' in ICM's terminology) figures in ICM's final poll were: Conservative 30%, Labour 46%, Liberal Democrat 19%, Others five per cent—a mean error of 2.0.

30 Gallup had a stroke of fortune. Throughout the campaign it put Labour ahead by between 16 and 23 points. Its final forecast of a 14-point lead, 4 points down from the previous day, was the most accurate forecast of the gap (although not of the parties' share of the vote) and was probably the product of sampling error and its decision to confine its forecast to respondents who claimed to be 'certain to vote'.

Editorial Opinion in the National Press

BY COLIN SEYMOUR-URE*

NEVER BEFORE has Labour enjoyed the majority support of the national daily press in a general election. Six out of ten national dailies gave the party their largely unqualified support. This was twice the previous highest number. Five out of nine Sunday papers, too, endorsed Labour. In the political history of the press, this was an historic moment every bit as significant as the size of Labour's majority, which sent commentators groping to the early nineteenth century. The modern daily press is not that old. Indeed it is much the same age as the Labour party, and it is a nice touch that Lord Rothermere, owner of the Conservative *Daily Mail* and great-nephew of its founder in 1896, Lord Northcliffe, announced in May 1997 that he would henceforth be sitting on the Labour benches in the House of Lords. In what follows, the focus is upon papers' leading articles, or editorials.[1] These are the definitive corporate view (anonymous, even if it is also the view of the proprietor), and they generally feed through into a paper's broader political coverage. Beyond that, they deserve scrutiny in 1997 for a number of special reasons.

Firstly, papers' partisan preferences had already begun to shift in the 1992 election, when four out of eleven dailies had heavily qualified partisanship or none. With Britain's ignominious ejection from the European monetary system on Black Wednesday—in September 1992—a drumroll of criticism began to rumble round John Major's government and his own leadership. 'NOW WE'VE ALL BEEN SCREWED BY THE GOVERNMENT', headlined the *Sun* in its inimitable way on the morning after Black Wednesday. The pro-Labour *Daily Mirror* described John Major as a political pygmy, with the leadership of a lizard and the status of a performing flea. More sinister in the longer term, the Conservative *Daily Mail* warned that Major's 'flip-flop government' was in danger of becoming no more than a joke. The entire daily press lined up against the government, to a greater or less extent, with only the *Daily Express* staying solidly loyal. Next year, when the government survived a debate on the Maastricht Treaty in July only by resorting to a vote of confidence, only the *Daily Telegraph*, *Daily Express* and *Financial Times* gave Major much comfort. As the ill-conceived 'back to basics' policy crumbled in the winter of 1993–94 ('mired in sleaze' in the *Daily Telegraph*'s words), Major's leadership

---

* Professor of Government and former Dean of Social Sciences at the University of Kent at Canterbury.

came under increasing threat. 'WHAT FOOLS WE ALL WERE' (that is, to elect Major), said the *Sun* in January 1994. When Major put his leadership on the line in July 1995, all the national press, with the exception again of the *Daily Express*, agreed that it was time for him to go (though not necessarily to be replaced by his challenger, John Redwood). When the long awaited report by Lord Justice Scott on the 'arms to Iraq' affair was published in February 1996—a benchmark of ministerial probity and competence—many papers rubbished it but almost all accepted that ministers had been at fault. As the government smashed records of unpopularity in the opinion polls during these years, papers had a long time to get used to the prospect of a Tory defeat. How would they position themselves in the formal campaign?

There was special interest in the intentions of Rupert Murdoch's Tory *Sun*. The paper's casual (and retracted) claim that 'IT's THE SUN WOT WON IT' in 1992 was often repeated in discussions about the electoral influence of the press.[2] Would the *Sun*, as seemed increasingly possible, go Labour? Lord Rothermere hinted that even the *Mail* titles might go Labour. Such possibilities were newly important because of the increasing concentration of the press within larger media conglomerates. When Labour last won a landslide in 1945, the national press included much the same number of titles, but each was in separate ownership and all were limited to print media. Legislation in the Thatcher and Major governments, ironically, facilitated multiple TV franchise ownership and cross-media concentration. By 1997, only the Canadian Conrad Black's *Telegraph* titles were not in a group with British TV interests. There were limits on market share which prevented Murdoch, notably, from owning terrestrial ITV stations in addition to his existing newspapers. But media became during the Thatcher era a significant and increasingly integrated economic sector and an inescapable area of government policy. Proprietors with editorial support in their gift had a more direct interest than before in the policy outcomes of the general election.

Changes of newspaper ownership since the 1992 election added spice to this mix. The two *Independent* titles, short of capital in the competitive broadsheet market, where Murdoch conducted a damaging price war, fell into the hands of the Labour Mirror group. The *Observer* was bought by the likeminded *Guardian* in 1993. But the two *Express* titles and their low circulation tabloid stablemate, the *Daily Star*, came under the control in 1996 of a lifelong Labour supporter, Lord Hollick. Hollick had been made a peer by Neil Kinnock. His MAI group controlled the Meridian and Anglia TV franchises, and the *Express* purchases created another new multi-media conglomerate. The *Express* titles were Conservative to the core, but whom would the papers back in 1997?

Changes of ownership were fewer than of editors. Only one national editor, Richard Lambert of the *Financial Times*, had been in post for the 1992 election. In 1992, by contrast, seven daily editors and three Sunday editors had been in post for the 1987 election. Half the editors in 1997 had been in the chair for about two years or less. In 1992 three heavyweights—Peter Preston of the *Guardian*, Sir David English of the *Daily Mail* and Kelvin MacKenzie of the *Sun*—had an average of sixteen years in post. In 1997, the editorial voice would be of comparative inexperience and youth (average age: forty-three).

It is worth mentioning, lastly, that papers' attitudes to the political parties between 1992 and 1997 came under far greater scrutiny than before by their media peers. Editorialists, especially on the *Telegraph*, *Mail* and Murdoch titles, knew that their sentences would be combed for clues and nuances, often by specialists writing for the media supplements. These flourished in the 1990s. Editors themselves became less anonymous, through profiles and diary items. Personalities and party affiliations among editors and senior political writers thus became a matter of comment, like that of politicians themselves. In this sense, editorial partisanship became something of an issue in politics.

The scale of change

Basic information about the ownership, circulation and party support of the daily and Sunday press in the 1997 election is given in Table 1. Labour has had the support of as many as three national dailies only once in fourteen general elections from 1945 to 1992. This was in 1964, when the party won by a whisker. The papers were the *Daily Mirror*, the old Labour *Daily Herald* (then lately relaunched as the *Sun*) and the *Guardian*. Normally, Labour had just two supporters, since the *Guardian* is required by the terms of its trust ownership to maintain, in practice, a radical liberal commitment, which has seen it change its support eight times from 1945 to 1992. No other paper has changed more than three times and the majority have never changed at all. So in 1997 Labour did three times better than usual, measured by the number of daily papers supporting the party. Most people, too, read a paper which supported the same party as they did themselves.

Measured by circulation, the picture looks different. Labour's two historic stalwarts had mass circulations. In 1945, when Labour won a majority of 146 seats (with 48% of the votes), the *Daily Mirror* and *Daily Herald* comprised 35% of total circulation. In 1964, those two plus the *Guardian* made up 42% of circulation, while the party won 44% of the votes and a majority of four. In October 1974 the *Sun*, by now a tabloid under Murdoch's ownership, wanted a coalition, and Labour therefore had the whole or partial support of papers comprising half the total circulation. But from then on, Labour's support went downhill. The low point was in 1983, when only the *Daily Mirror* supported Labour wholeheartedly. The party had 22% of circulation and 28% of the vote. The support in 1997 placed Labour for the first time in a position of disproportionately high circulation (familiar to the

Conservatives): 62% of circulation and 44% of the vote, compared with the Conservatives' 33% of circulation and 31% of the vote. The Liberal Democrats suffered as always from the dominance of a national press. In most of Europe there would be a regional daily paper penetrating, say, the South-West more strongly than any metropolitan paper. Here, the Lib-Dems were tossed the odd sweet, but most of the time they were editorially ignored.

The shift of support to Labour looks a little less dramatic when put in the context of the 1992 election, since two of the new supporters were already uncommitted then (the *Daily Star* and the *Independent*). Moreover, the *Financial Times* had declared in 1992 for a non-Conservative majority, and its support for Labour in 1997 was equivocal. In 1997 too, *The Times* abandoned the Conservatives but stopped short of endorsing Labour: it favoured eurosceptics and cheerfully said it was supporting candidates from six different parties. This leaves just one straight conversion from Conservative to Labour in 1997: the *Sun*. It was only the second unqualified U-turn since 1945. The first was also by the *Sun*, which abandoned its Labour roots in February 1974 and turned Tory. This makes two U-turns out of a possible 150 or so (if every daily paper, that is, had changed at every election). The party loyalty of the national press may waver, but the streams flow almost always in the same directions.

When and why did papers commit themselves?

The *Sun* came out for Labour on Tuesday, 18 March, the day after the Prime Minister announced the date of the election. But less than ever was this, for most papers, a campaign which began when it was announced. *The Times* and *Daily Telegraph*, for example, had started positioning themselves in the new year. On 17 January, *The Times* remarked that 'it would be surprising if the details of Mr Major's manifesto did not please us more than that of Mr Blair'—but went on to concede that Blair 'may yet quietly claim the 'Conservative' title'. Three days later the *Daily Telegraph* too pondered the prospect of new Labour before backing away for fear of the possibly resurgent Old. For the campaign proper, the *Daily Telegraph* published a supplement on 18 March, with a signed editorial and a profile of its election team. The *Independent* started billing its election coverage almost immediately but then, incongruously, produced a further announcement a week or two later. In general, papers stepped up their attention after the Spring Bank Holiday and the publication of the party manifestos, which was about the time when a campaign of normal length would have begun.

Papers' attitudes to partisanship are influenced by several factors, including their history, readership and ownership. The *Mail*, *Telegraph* and *Express* titles have always been Conservative. Their party loyalty has been tempered by the views of their proprietors, notably Lord Northcliffe and (for the *Express* group) Lord Beaverbrook. Over time,

1. National Daily and Sunday Press: Ownership, Circulation and Partisanship

Paper (Controlling owner)	Editor (Date of appoint.)	Circulation ('000s) April 1997 (April 1992)	Preferred Winner (1992 in brackets)	% Readers intending to vote (actual result in brackets)			
Daily Papers:				Conservative (31%)	Labour (44%)	Lib–Dem (17%)	Others (7%)
Daily Mail (Associated Newspapers; Lord Rothermere)	P. Dacre (July 1992)	2,151 (1,675)	Conservative (same)	49	29	14	8
Daily Mirror (Mirror Group)	P. Morgan (September 1995)	3,084 (2,903)	Labour (same)	14	72	11	3
Daily Star (MAI/United; Lord Hollick)	P. Walker (September 1994)	648 (806)	Labour (implicitly Conservative)	17	66	12	5
Daily Telegraph (Hollinger; C. Black)	C. Moore (October 1995)	1,134 (1,038)	Conservative (same)	57	20	17	6
Express (MAI/United; Lord Hollick)	R. Addis (November 1995)	1,220 (1,525)	Conservative (same)	49	29	16	6
Financial Times (Pearson; Lord Blakenham)	R. Lambert (January 1991)	307 (290)	Labour (not a Conservative majority)	48	29	19	4
Guardian (Scott Trust)	A. Rusbridger (February 1995)	401 (429)	Labour (Lab; more Lib Dems)	8	67	22	3
Independent (Mirror Group)	A. Marr (May 1996)	251 (390)	Labour (uncommitted)	16	47	30	7
Sun (News International; R. Murdoch)	S. Higgins (January 1994)	3,842 (3,571)	Labour (Conservative)	30	52	12	6
The Times (News International; R. Murdoch)	P. Stothard (June 1992)	719 (386)	Eurosceptic (Conservative)	42	28	25	5

Total Circulation pro-Conservative: 4,504 (33%)
Total Circulation pro-Labour: 8,533 (62%)
Total Circulation 13,757

Sunday Papers:

Express on Sunday (MAI/United; Lord Hollick)	R. Addis (September 1996)	1,159 (1,666)	Conservative (same)	53	27	14	6
Independent on Sunday (Mirror Group)	R. Boycott (September 1996)	276 (402)	Labour (not a Conservative majority)	14	48	32	6
Mail on Sunday (Associated Newspapers; Lord Rothermere)	J. Holborow (July 1992)	2,112 (1,941)	Conservative (same)	49	28	15	8
News of the World (News International; R. Murdoch)	P. Hall (September 1995)	4,365 (4,768)	Labour (Conservative)	28	55	11	6
Observer (Scott Trust)	W. Hutton (March 1996)	454 (541)	Labour (same)	11	63	22	4
People (Mirror Group)	L. Gould (September 1996)	1,978 (2,165)	Labour (same)	21	62	11	6
Sunday Mirror (Mirror Group)	B. Rowe (September 1996)	2,238 (2,774)	Labour (same)	18	67	12	3
Sunday Telegraph (Hollinger; C. Black)	D. Lawson (October 1995)	909 (558)	Conservative (same)	56	19	17	8
Sunday Times (News International; R. Murdoch)	J. Witherow (May 1994)	1,310 (1,167)	Conservative (same)	43	30	21	6

Total Circulation pro-Conservative (%): 5,490 (37%)
Total Circulation pro-Labour (%): 9,311 (63%)
Total Circulation: 14,801

Note: Circulation figures from ABC. They are rounded. *Daily Mirror* includes Scottish *Daily Record*, except in Voting Intention figures. Voting Intention figures copyright *MORI*. Fieldwork: 21 March to 29 April 1997. Figures excluded people who said they would not vote (7%), were undecided (9%) or refused to name a party (3%). Percentages are rounded and may not sum to 100.

readers have tended to share their papers' political views, although the correspondence has not been close. The direction of influence, too, is famously unclear. Papers thus have a possible commercial interest in the consequences of changing their partisanship. This used to give a frisson to the *Sun*'s support of the Conservative party. Most of its readers came from the social classes Labour has historically regarded as its natural constituency. In the Thatcher era, the paper thus epitomised Labour's popular failure. With Labour bouncing back, could Rupert Murdoch afford to go on supporting the Conservatives? Alternatively, if the *Sun* changed, would it lose irritated readers to the more traditionally Labour *Daily Mirror*? What would be the role of the proprietor in a decision about partisanship anyway?

These factors influenced the way papers declared themselves. They were the subject of speculation in the case of the *Sun*, both before and after its declaration on 18 May. The editor, Stuart Higgins, explained the timing later in terms of a campaigning role: 'There was no point in coming out at the last minute. If we were going to play a part in getting something done . . ., then we would do it in the way the *Sun* does everything: wholeheartedly, big and bold, unconditionally.'[3] No one doubted that the decision had been handed down by Rupert Murdoch — about a month earlier, according to 'insiders' quoted in the *Daily Telegraph* (19.3.97). This did not mean the editor and the political editor, Trevor Kavanagh, were not consulted: Murdoch obviously listens to their briefings with care. But neither of these two was said to be happy with the decision. As to circulation, irate readers phoned in their hundreds and sales fell by 204,000 in April. Higgins said Murdoch expected to lose 100,000 but he claimed in mid-May that the longer term loss would be no more than 30,000. The prospect of having stuck with the Conservatives when there was a Labour landslide, however, struck Higgins as much worse: 'It would have been a complete nightmare, going against everything we think the *Sun* stands for, i.e. popular opinion' (*Guardian*, 19.5.97).

The *Sun*'s commercial motive, then, was plain. How far Murdoch also had a media policy motive could only be inferred. One need not be a cynic to assume he did. His media empire would be at risk from controls on concentration and cross-ownership, including the coming digital TV systems, even if the union-bashing disputes which made Murdoch a demon to the old left were a thing of the past. His tabloid papers would also be hit by privacy legislation, a possibility put on ice by John Major in the year before the election. Tony Blair was said not to have done a deal but certainly to have indicated that if Murdoch behaved responsibly, his British interests would not be damaged. The most public display of courtship between Blair and Murdoch was Blair's flight to a resort island off the Australian Barrier Reef in 1995, to address Murdoch executives. But Blair, Murdoch and respective senior colleagues met several times in London before and after. At a different

level, Blair's press advisers regularly placed articles in Murdoch publications. As the election drew near, Conservative counter-pressure
included interventions both by Margaret Thatcher and John Major.

How did the *Sun* explain its conversion? Its full-page headline on 18
March was 'THE SUN BACKS BLAIR'. Underneath were the words, 'Give
change a chance'. Those two sentences summed it up: Blair, not Labour,
and time for a change. The Tories had 'all the right policies but all the
wrong faces'. Major was 'a decent man who does his best' but was no
leader. Labour must be given a chance to prove they were trustworthy.
If they were not, 'our attack on them will be ferocious'. In particular,
the paper was concerned about Europe and would watch with care, to
see if Blair stood out against a single currency and kept his promise to
have 'no truck with a federal superstate'. A content analysis of the
article (115 sq.ins.) shows that three-fifths was about policy issues and
two-fifths about competence and management style. The balance
between discussion of Labour and of the Conservatives was exactly the
same. Within the parties, however, 87% of the Conservative content
was about the party and only 13% about John Major; while nearly
60% of the Labour share was about Tony Blair and only 40% about
the party. Breaking down the content about the leaders further, there
was more about Major's style and personality than his policies, but as
much about Blair's policies as about his style (and little about his
personality). The content was largely negative both about the Conservative party and John Major personally. It was overwhelmingly and
predictably positive about Tony Blair but evenly balanced about his
party.

The *Sun*'s conversion was headline news in the *Daily Mail* and
Financial Times and on the front page of most others. The *Daily Mirror*
ignored it but made a joke next day about 'supporting Major', who
turned out to be a racehorse. Compared with all this, the partisanship
of other papers scarcely caused a ripple. Loyalist papers—the *Daily
Mirror*, *Daily Telegraph* and *Daily Mail*, barely broke their stride when
the election was finally announced. One or two were coy. 'When polling
day is near, we shall declare a preference', said *The Times* on 18 March.
It wanted to see how each party stood up to what it called 'the people's
test' in the campaign. The *Daily Express* talked in similar language on
the same day, as did the *Daily Star* rather more briefly. The *Independent*
admitted in a long signed editorial on 2 April that 'we are all biased.
But this is one newspaper whose central bias is towards reason and
fairness, not a single party manifesto'. Not until 30 April could we be
entirely clear what this meant: top priority to getting rid of the Tories
and in most constituencies a vote for 'Tony Blair and his talented
leadership team'.

Papers varied also in whether they thought their readers should care
much anyway. The *Financial Times* said bluntly on 29 April that it had
'no party affiliations, and its readers make up their own minds about

how they vote'. Its own economic opinions and support for an outward-looking Europe made it naturally Conservative in elections. 'But there have been exceptions. 1997 is one of them'. The *Independent* said its founders in 1986 had felt strongly that the papers 'should not presume to tell its readers how to vote' (30.4.97). The *Guardian* and *The Times* both gave little historical disquisitions when summing up their views. In two full columns on 29 April, relieved by a small line drawing of Big Ben and headed 'PRINCIPLE NOT PARTY', *The Times* ranged over its history (it was founded in 1784). This, it claimed, stressed the import-ance of the individual MP, of policy over party, of strong, unconven-tional leaders, and of a willingness to abstain. Since both parties were divided on the future of Europe, 'the fulcrum of public policy', it would support eurosceptics. But, the paper added, it never assumed its readers took its advice: it had too much respect for them. The *Guardian*, after reminding readers on 30 April of its history of independence, remarked that it had, 'at various times since the war, endorsed all three of the main alternatives on offer'. The choice this time was relatively simple: a big Labour majority, with tactical voting for Liberal Democrats where that was the best chance of displacing a Conservative.

In general, the impression left by the run of editorials is that they were ritualistic. The campaign had a formal beginning and end. The parties published manifestos, the politicians went through their hustings hoops, with the broadcasters in attendance. Everyone had known the election could not be later than about now. The result was not in doubt. So editorialists played along. But although the tap of electoral politics had gushed for a few weeks, the flow of controversy had barely stopped since Black Wednesday. British politics may not have become 'a permanent campaign'. But for the press, during much of the 1992–97 Parliament it must have seemed so.

Editorial topics

If those were papers' general attitudes, what did they choose for particular comment? Table 2 provides a summary. The topics are ranked in aggregate order. The progress of the campaign, the parties' records and their manifestos are by far the largest category and are difficult to break down in detail. After that, sleaze and Europe stand out. Nothing else provoked nearly as much comment. The individual subjects are a mixture of traditional policy areas (employment, the economy, health), issues thrown up by the campaign (TV debates between the leaders, Labour's plans for the national lottery, and—most prominently—sleaze) and the leadership qualities of the rival leaders.

The question of leadership cut across several of the other categories, and the table gives a quite inadequate account of its importance to the editorialists. About John Major, the word signalled weakness and lack of control, especially in handling the sexual and financial misdemean-ours which the oozy word sleaze connoted and in his treatment of the

2. Topics in editorials 17 March–1 May 1997

Editorial Principally about:	D. Mail	D. Mirror	D. Star	D. Telegraph	Express	Financial Times	Guardian	Independent	Sun	The Times	Total	% Voters ranking
Manifestos, campaign, party records	14	13	12	17	11	4	16	18	8	15	128	–
Sleaze	7	10	4	7	5	1	10	3	11	5	63	–
Europe	11	1	2	12	4	3	4	4	12	10	63	24
Trades Unions/Ind. Rel	3	1	4	6	1	1	2	1	2	1	22	–
TV debates	2	1	4	3	2	–	2	1	1	3	19	10
Leadership	1	4	–	2	3	2	2	2	1	2	19	–
Ulster/IRA	1	1	–	3	2	2	3	1	2	2	17	11
Economy	2	1	–	1	1	2	3	1	1	2	14	32
Education	–	1	–	1	–	2	2	3	1	–	10	62
Tax	1	1	–	1	–	4	1	–	2	–	10	35
Health	–	5	–	1	1	1	–	–	–	1	9	70
Pensions	2	–	–	1	2	1	–	–	1	1	8	42
Crime	–	2	2	–	–	–	1	–	–	–	5	50
Devolution	–	–	–	2	–	1	1	–	–	–	4	10
Privatisation	–	–	–	1	1	–	1	–	1	–	4	–
Lottery	–	–	–	1	–	–	1	–	1	1	4	–
Social Policy	–	–	–	–	–	1	2	1	–	–	4	–
Employment	–	1	–	–	–	2	–	–	–	–	3	45
Local Government	–	–	–	1	–	–	1	–	–	–	2	–
Foreign Policy	1	–	–	–	–	–	–	–	–	1	2	–
Immigration	1	–	–	1	–	–	–	–	–	–	2	–
Water	1	–	–	–	–	–	–	–	–	–	1	–
Transport	–	–	–	–	–	–	–	–	–	1	1	21
Religion	–	–	–	–	–	1	–	–	–	–	1	–
Civil Service	–	–	–	–	–	–	–	1	–	–	1	–
Housing/Homelessness	–	1	–	–	–	–	–	–	–	–	1	28
Sport	–	–	–	1	–	–	–	–	–	–	1	–
Total Topics	12	14	5	18	10	11	16	11	14	14		
Total election editorials	57	47	20	65	34	24	54	41	56	49	398	
Total sq.ins.	1084	937	274	1942	539	679	1841	1251	1045	1527		

Note: '% voters ranking' refers to a MORI poll published in the *Independent on Sunday*, 6 April 1997. All voters polled were asked 'which of these issues will be very important to you in helping to decide which party to vote for?'.

Conservatives' divisions over Europe. For Tony Blair, leadership was mainly a question about trust. Time and again Labour's new editorial friends confided their hesitations. Partly these were about the risk that the smells of old Labour (trade union power, typically) might swamp the scents of today. Partly, they were a worry about Blair's inexperience—for example, in European negotiation. Partly, too, they were an irritation with campaign managers such as Peter Mandelson, for keeping Blair resolutely unspecific about so many policies. 'Face the tough questions and earn the people's trust, Mr Blair', urged the *Daily Express* in its comment on the Labour manifesto (4.4.97).

The last column in the table ranks the issues which voters said, in mid-campaign, would be very important in helping them decide which party to vote for. Health is easily top. Yet in half the papers it was not given a leading article to itself at all, and in most of the others it had just one. Only in the *Daily Mirror* did it get top treatment among the traditional policy areas. Trade unions, conversely, came nearly bottom of the voters' list but were second after Europe in the papers' list. Europe itself was a greater concern for the papers than for the voters. Tony Blair's favourite subject—education—reflected voters' priorities but was fairly low down the papers' list.

The table implicitly illustrates papers' partisan preferences. The *Daily Telegraph* and *Daily Mail* banged on about trade unions because they were against them. The *Daily Mirror* emphasised health because it believed Labour would look after the NHS. The *Guardian* gave so much attention to sleaze because it had been leading the campaign to expose the issue of MPs abusing their positions when acting as paid lobbyists, for example by receiving payment in return for asking parliamentary questions. The *Daily Mirror* and *Sun*, as Labour supporters, hammered away too. Indeed the *Sun* actually set up Tory backbencher Piers Merchant, introducing the word if not the idea of 'entrapment' to the tabloid thesaurus, when it arranged for him to be photographed cuddling in the park with a teenage nightclub hostess (although, in the event, he retained his seat). Europe, too, absorbed the eurosceptic papers much more than the others.

The table is no help, however, in illustrating the phasing of editorial discussion. This broadly coincided with the course of the campaign. Right at the start, after months of anticipation, it was predictable that editorial comment should focus on the nature of the coming campaign and the role of media in it. In addition to the drama of the *Sun*'s conversion to Labour, the possibility of televised debates between the party leaders naturally attracted comment—more than once, since the idea became snarled in negotiations. Papers disagreed about where the fault lay, and most were disappointed that the debates never happened. Then sleaze itself was very much an issue about the role of the press as participants in the election, rather than as reactive observers. The *Guardian*'s row with Neil Hamilton long preceded the campaign and strictly had nothing to do with it. But the timing was fortunate for an anti-Conservative paper. The fortunes of other sleazy candidates, such as Piers Merchant, kept the issue alive from the announcement of the election till the end of March. The arrival of Martin Bell as the independent challenger to Hamilton in Tatton started the story up again. Bell could keep electoral semioticians happy for years. A Bosnia war hero (of a kind, since he received wounds as a journalist, which may be more heroic still); Mr Clean, in his trademark white suit; bearer of a surname that rang with integrity and tolled for his opponent; managed by a photogenic daughter; and with a campaign team which, initially at least, worked out of an honest-to-God, traditional British institution, a pub. The layers of meaning are endless.

Not all papers approved of Bell's intervention. The *Daily Telegraph*, for instance, thought it was an arrogant abuse of media power. One or two other papers (including the *Independent*) also thought Hamilton should not stand down, since the parliamentary report which would pronounce on his conduct had not been published and the issue needed debating. Merchant received little sympathy. Sleaze, in the leader columns, was a very bad start for the Conservatives indeed. It knocked their agenda aside for the first two weeks of the campaign and barged in again at the end of the third.

The other major issue, Europe, featured largely in the second half of the campaign. Papers' editorial attitudes are indicated in Table 3. For Eurosceptic papers it was a cause of frustration that, as the *Daily Mail* put it (18.3.97), there was a 'bipartisan pact of non-divulgence' about a European currency and European sovereignty. On 16 April, the *Daily Express* called Major's 'wait and see' policy on the currency 'a feeble battle cry': 'Who goes over the top shouting "wait and see"?'. 'IT'S TIME TO COME CLEAN ON EUROPE' was the front page headline. The next day the *Sun* agreed that Europe was 'in danger of becoming the forgotten issue'. On 21 April, the *Daily Telegraph* described Europe as having 'forced itself' onto the agenda; 'At last this election is getting

3. **Editorial attitudes to the European Union**

Daily Mail	Eurosceptic: 'No more power should be transferred from Britain' (29 April)
Daily Mirror	Sympathetic: '. . . where our future must lie' (12 April)
Daily Star	Eurosceptic: suspicious of 'a European superstate'' (30 April)
Daily Telegraph	Eurosceptic: single currency would mean not 'One nation: we would be no nation' (16 April)
Express	Eurosceptic: sovereignty 'too high a price to pay' for single currency (16 April)
Financial Times	Sympathetic: favours 'an outward looking Europe' (29 April)
Guardian	Sympathetic: '. . . instinctively pro-European' (30 April)
Independent	Sympathetic: 'proud but not slavish pro-European' (30 April)
Sun	Eurosceptic: Britons want to 'trade our goods but not sell our birthright (17 March)
The Times	Eurosceptic: 'no more power' should be transferred from Britain (29 April)

Total circulation ('000s): eurosceptic 9,714 (71%); sympathetic 4,043 (29%)

exciting ... the first in modern times which refuses to stick to the agenda laid down by the party leaders'. The *Daily Telegraph*, *Daily Mail*, the *Sun* and *The Times* each urged Conservative candidates to make plain their personal positions on Europe. The *Daily Mail* canvassed candidates directly and the *Daily Telegraph* analysed their election addresses. All those papers except the *Sun* published various running tallies of them. By 30 April, the *Daily Mail* reported 308 out of 648 Conservative candidates declaring themselves eurosceptic.

The attraction of Europe was complex. The eurosceptic papers, but not only they, recognised it as a fundamental issue, which justified attention on that ground alone. Hence the *Daily Mail* made its first big editorial on the subject its frontpage lead, under the banner headline, 'THE BATTLE FOR BRITAIN'. It was attractive too because it was contentious and newsy, and journalistic values are slighted by election campaigns in which the parties will not engage one another ('The Election Springs to Life' was the heading to the *Guardian*'s editorial on 19 April about the row over a Conservative anti-Labour advertisement about Europe). Most importantly, the Tory eurosceptics (excluding on this occasion *The Times*), saw Europe as the one issue which might even now help to stem the Labour tide. They returned to the topic repeatedly, approving, in the *Daily Telegraph*'s words, the 'steady disintegration' of John Major's wait-and-see policy. Towards the end of the campaign, both the *Daily Telegraph* and the *Daily Mail* seemed to get some satisfaction from the belief that in practice the Conservative party was now overwhelmingly against a single currency. The exception to this approach was the *Express*, which, though firmly Eurosceptic, tucked its two most hostile comments on the subject among the news pages and barely mentioned the subject in its keynote editorials.

Overall, Europe was editorially the prime issue of the election. In addition to its intrinsic and historic importance, it touched on the question of John Major's leadership and, by extension, the apparently superior leadership skills of his opponent. Only one voter in four gave it much weight, according to the MORI poll reported in Table 2. But it was a key factor in the confounding of traditional newspaper partisanship. The *Mail* and *Telegraph* papers found themselves heavily compromised—although the certainty of defeat made it easier than otherwise to criticise their own party. The *Sun*, meanwhile, found itself paradoxically rooting for a Labour leader of marked, if currently muffled, europhile sympathies.

Editorials and party leaders

Table 4 gives a different view of editorials, based on the politicians named in them, not on their subjects (Sunday papers are omitted, since the number of editorials during the campaign was small). Most striking, perhaps, is the almost complete disregard of the Liberal Democrats. In nine of the national dailies Paddy Ashdown was the only Lib-Dem named. In the *Guardian*, Emma Nicholson was named too, once. Ashdown himself was mentioned more than four times only in the *Guardian* (six times) and the *Independent* (seven); this, despite 17% of the vote and 46 seats. The mentions were chiefly about the party's manifesto and tactical voting. Recommendations about the latter featured in the editorial advice of Eurosceptic and anti-conservative papers. Typical of comment on the Lib Dems was the *Independent*'s conclusion that they had 'stretched the envelope of political debate' (29.4.97). It is the fate of minor parties to be noticed only to the extent of their importance in relation to the major parties. The Lib Dems were irrelevant this time, so they became a non-party in the leader columns.

One would expect the broadsheet papers to name more politicians than the tabloids, but the difference was not great, except at the extremes. *The Times* (44) and *Daily Telegraph* (42) mentioned twice as many as the *Express* and (nearly) the *Sun*. But the *Daily Mail* (31) mentioned nearly as many as the *Guardian* (34) and the *Independent* (35). Neither the *Daily Star* nor the *Financial Times* published a large number of editorials at all. Conservative mentions outnumbered Labour everywhere, as might be predicted. In the *Daily Mail* there were fewer references to Conservatives than to Labour—possibly a case of attacking the enemy more than praising one's friends—but more than two-thirds of the references were to Tony Blair. The Conservative numbers were noticeably swelled by the hand-wringing about Neil Hamilton, Tim Smith and others in the jetstream of sleaze. Margaret Thatcher still managed to get more mentions than any other Conservative (apart from Major) in several papers. Apart from Heseltine, Clarke and Howard, few cabinet ministers were mentioned.

The two leaders dominated discussion of their parties. The table measures their mentions as a proportion of the total numbers both of editorials and of party colleagues named. Across the board, Blair was mentioned in proportionately more editorials than Major, and he scored overwhelmingly higher in relation to his colleagues. Neither fact is surprising. Not only does a leader tend to personify his party, especially for a tabloid paper; but with new Labour, the leader is central to its electoral appeal. Even in the majority of the broadsheets, therefore, Blair accounted for well over half the references to Labour. Prescott, Cook, Gordon Brown and Mandelson were the others who featured most.

Table 4 simply lists names. Table 5 sums the amount of space given to each leader in each paper (daily and Sunday) and classifies it as tending towards positive, neutral, or negative.[4] By far the greater part of the coverage was neutral or negative. For John Major less than ten per cent overall was positive in the daily papers and exactly ten per cent (a very small absolute number) in the Sundays. This is an emphatic mark—a crude lifted finger—of his political unpopularity. Disregarding the small *Daily Star* quantity, the *Daily Telegraph* had the most positive

4. Politicians Named in Editorials, 17 March–1 May 1997
No (%) of editorials; [% of own party politicians named]

Politicians Named	D. Mail	D. Mirror	D. Star	D. Telegraph	Express	Fin. Times	The Guardian	The Independ.	Sun	The Times
Conservative										
Major	21 (37) [41]	22 (47) [44]	9 (45) [56]	29 (45) [43]	16 (47) [44]	9 (38) [64]	28 (52) [40]	24 (59) [38]	28 (50) [47]	27 (55) [34]
Heseltine	2	2	1	2	1		4	5	2	6
Clarke	2			4	2	1	5	7	3	3
Howard	2	2	2	3	2	2	6	3	1	1
Portillo	1	2			1		1	1	1	2
Waldegrave				1				1		
Lilley										2
Hague										5
Forsyth										2
Dorrell		2							1	
Redwood	1				2		1			1
Rifkind				1				2	1	1
Thatcher	4	3	1	4	3	2	4	7	8	12
Heath				3	1			1	1	1
Hamilton	5	7	2	6	2		8	3	5	5
T. Smith	2	3		3	1		4	2	1	4
Merchant	3	2	1	3	2		2	1	4	1
Currie	1			2				2		1
Others	6	5		7	3		6	2	4	3
TOTAL	50	53	16	68	36	14	69	62	60	77
Labour										
Blair	40 (70) [70]	20 (43) [6]	8 (40) [89]	36 (55) [54]	17 (50) [89]	12 (50) [86]	24 (44) [62]	26 (63) [55]	28 (50) [76]	30 (61) [50]
Prescott	2	1	1	2	1		1	1	1	1
Brown	4	2		7		1		7	4	5
Cook	1	1		2			3	1	1	5
Beckett		2		1			1			
Blunkett	3	1		1			2	3	1	5
Straw				1				1		2
Mowlam	1			1					2	1
Field	1						1			1
Mandelson		1		5				1		1

J. Smith				1				1		2
Callaghan		2		1			2			
Kinnock		1		4	1	1	1	2		
Foot	1			1			2	1		
Others	2	1		4				3		7
TOTAL	55	33	9	67	19	14	39	47	37	60
Lib-Dem										
Ashdown	2 (4) [100]	3 (6) [100]	3 (15) [100]	2 (3) [100]	4 (12) [100]	2 (8) [100]	6 (11) [86]	7 (17) [100]	1 [100]	4 (8) [50]
Nicholson							1			
Hughes										2
Lynne										2
TOTAL	2	3	3	2	4	2	7	7	1	8
Others	1	2		5	3	3	4	4	1	4
Total Politicians Named	29	28	9	42	21	11	33	34	24	44
Total Mentions	108	88	28	142	62	33	119	120	99	153
Total Election Editorials	57	47	20	65	34	24	54	41	56	49

5. Coverage of Party Leaders in Editorials, 17 March–1 May 1997: Positive, Neutral, Negative Square ins. (% of each Leader's total)

Daily Papers:	Major				Blair				Ashdown				Total Leader Cov.	Total Cov.
	Pos.	Neu.	Neg.	Total	Pos.	Neu.	Neg.	Total	Pos.	Neu.	Neg.	Total		
Daily Mail	9 (20)	16 (36)	19 (43)	44	16 (14)	46 (40)	52 (46)	114	–	1 (17)	5 (83)	6	164 (15)	1084
Daily Mirror	2 (1)	10 (7)	142 (92)	154	96 (90)	9 (8)	2 (2)	107	–	2 (67)	1 (33)	3	264 (28)	937
Daily Star	4 (36)	5 (46)	2 (18)	11	12 (63)	7 (37)	–	19	2 (40)	2 (40)	1 (20)	5	35 (13)	274
Daily Telegraph	16 (29)	34 (61)	6 (11)	56	10 (4)	96 (43)	119 (53)	225	–	6 (75)	2 (25)	8	289 (15)	1942
Express	4 (13)	25 (78)	3 (9)	32	10 (16)	39 (62)	14 (22)	63	–	8 (100)	–	8	103 (38)	539
Financial Times	2 (9)	13 (62)	6 (29)	21	6 (18)	21 (64)	6 (18)	33	–	2 (100)	–	2	56 (8)	679
Guardian	6 (7)	20 (22)	65 (71)	91	47 (49)	31 (32)	18 (19)	96	5 (26)	9 (47)	5 (26)	19	206 (11)	1841
Independent	4 (6)	40 (60)	23 (34)	67	15 (15)	58 (57)	28 (28)	101	8 (40)	12 (60)	–	20	188 (9)	1251
Sun	2 (2)	16 (16)	84 (82)	102	158 (87)	12 (13)	–	181	–	–	3 (100)	3	286 (27)	1045
The Times	8 (7)	74 (64)	33 (29)	115	21 (14)	101 (67)	28 (19)	150	1 (10)	9 (90)	–	10	275 (18)	1527
Total Dailies	57 (8)	253 (37)	383 (55)	693	391 (36)	432 (40)	267 (24)	1089	16 (19)	51 (61)	17 (20)	84	1866 (17)	11119
%				(100)				(100)						(100)

Sunday Papers:

Express on Sunday	3 (27)	7 (64)	1 (9)	11	3 (17)	9 (50)	6 (33)	18	–	–	–	–	29 (18)	161
Independent on Sunday	–	5 (28)	13 (72)	18	2 (9)	20 (91)	–	22	–	1 (100)	–	1	41 (11)	379
Mail on Sunday	3 (25)	8 (67)	1 (8)	12	3 (13)	17 (74)	3 (13)	23	–	1 (100)	–	1	36 (13)	277
News of the World	–	4 (50)	4 (50)	8	14 (48)	9 (31)	6 (21)	29	–	–	–	–	37 (19)	192
Observer	–	1 (17)	5 (83)	6	3 (60)	2 (40)	–	5	–	–	–	–	11 (4)	248
People	2 (40)	2 (40)	1 (20)	5	3 (60)	2 (40)	–	5	–	1 (100)	–	1	11 (9)	118
Sunday Mirror	–	1 (17)	5 (83)	6	1 (50)	1 (50)	–	2	–	–	–	–	8 (3)	243
Sunday Telegraph	2 (8)	18 (75)	4 (17)	24	–	33 (47)	35 (53)	68	–	1 (50)	1 (50)	2	94 (21)	441
Sunday Times	3 (9)	29 (83)	3 (9)	35	1 (2)	32 (76)	9 (21)	42	–	–	1 (100)	1	78 (19)	
Total Sundays	**13**	**75**	**37**	**125**	**30**	**125**	**59**	**214**	**–**	**4**	**2**	**6**	**345**	**2468**
%	(10)	(60)	(30)	(100)	(14)	(58)	(28)	(100)	–	(2)	(1)	(100)	(14)	(100)

to say about the Prime Minister. Even the *Daily Mail* had twice as much bad as good. In those Sunday papers that had much in them at all, the *Sunday Times* was equivocal and only the *Mail* and *Express* titles had more positive than negative. Most of this positive coverage was about Major's personal qualities.

Tony Blair, by contrast, had plenty of negative comment but also, in the *Daily Mirror*, the *Guardian*, the *Sun* and (on a small scale) the *Daily Star*, cheerleaders. The *Sun* could not seem to find a word to say against him. In a succession of editorials during the last week of the campaign, the paper frolicked in a bouncy castle of happy talk: vision, principle, determination, enthusiasm, energy, good humour; fresh, impassioned, trustworthy, dynamic, purposeful, strong; new dawn. On it went. In the same spirit of whoopee optimism, the paper imitated the National Lottery's advertising image for its polling day front page. A pointing finger, spangled with stars, touched the head of Blair, with the headline, 'IT MUST BE YOU'. In the Sunday press, Blair had no such zealots. Only the *News of the World*, among editorialists who wrote about the leaders at length, was substantially positive.

A similar analysis is reported, finally, in Table 6. This shows papers' partisan leanings not just in relation to the leaders but to parties as a whole. Moreover, the attitudes in editorials (where a party leaning was apparent) are broken down by subject, so that the numbers refer to aggregates of topics not of articles. They are listed both by specific parties and by each paper's preferred party. The figures illustrate two tendencies. First, they show how far papers' partisanship was expressed by writing positively about their own party or negatively about their opponents. Secondly, those two figures combined can be compared with the corresponding figures about their opponents, to give an indication of papers' evenhandedness. The *Daily Mail* provides the extreme case of knocking Labour more than writing positively about the Conservatives. The *Daily Telegraph* did much the same, but the *Daily Express* both had fewer partisan comments and divided them more evenly. The Labour supporters were proportionately rather more positive about Labour than were those other papers about the Conservatives. But the greater part of their efforts, nonetheless, were spent knocking their opponents. The combined totals in the bottom part of the table confirm again that the *Daily Express* and the *Independent* were the most evenhanded papers editorially, in the sense that the weight of their commentary included a substantial amount sympathetic to their opponents.

Conclusions

'IT'S THE *SUN* WOT SWUNG IT'. In an echo of its 1992 headline, the *Sun* published on 2 May (on page 2 this time, not on the front page) a claim that for the second time in five years a political leader had said 'Thanks my *Sun*' for helping him to electoral victory. The size of the 1997

6. Editorial References Favouring Political Parties, 17 March–1 May 1977

Tendency in Editorial comment:	Daily Mail	Daily Mirror	Daily Telegraph	Daily Star	Express	Financial Times	Guardian	Independent	Sun	The Times
Pro-Conservative	4	–	7	2	9	4	4	1	–	4
Anti-Conservative	9	29	7	7	8	12	27	10	26	19
Pro-Labour	2	18	1	4	4	9	10	5	21	11
Anti-Labour	26	–	37	3	8	15	8	8	8	18
Total favouring preferred party (%)	30 (73) Con	47 (100) Lab	44 (85) Con	11 (69) Lab	17 (59) Con	21 (53) Lab	37 (76) Lab	15 (63) Lab	47 (85) Lab	n.a
Total favouring opposing party (%)	11 (27)	–	8 (15)	5 (31)	12 (41)	19 (47)	12 (24)	9 (37)	8 (15)	

Note: Some editorials are counted in more than one category.

victory makes the influence of the press over the result a question of minor importance. Did the press set the agenda? On the evidence of editorials, it certainly helped. Did it sway votes? Some, no doubt, as it always does. But no one would try to credit the press with Labour's landslide. The shift of papers into the Labour camp was as much a part of the slide as a cause. If the press helped to change voters' opinions, it was during the five years since the 1992 election; and all the campaigning of a Tory press that had stayed loyal would not have brought them back into the Tory fold during the course even of a six-week campaign (barring a total Labour calamity).

The intriguing question, therefore, is for the future. Is new Labour's press support for the short term or for the long? Have we seen a fracture of the system that has lasted since at least 1945, in which Conservative papers wavered from time to time and were often hostile to Conservative governments, but in which they almost never actually went over in elections to the other side? There have been postwar periods of relatively low-key press partisanship, but the basic orientation of the press system as a whole and of the papers within it has not changed.

The arguments for seeing the change as short term are clear. In most constituencies, the *Independent* concluded, it would cast its vote for Blair with 'a degree of optimism that is not entirely justified by the evidence' (30.4.97). Newspapers were attracted by 'time for a change'. Only the *Express* had supported John Major in the Conservative leadership election in 1995, and that was under an old editor and a Conservative publisher. The new editor supported him on the shaky ground of 'better the devil you know'. But what if the *Express* was right and the change proved a failure: new Labour, new devil? 'Change for change's sake' is hardly a sufficient basis on which to construct a long term future. Unless a Blair government satisfied the Conservative instincts of the mid-market tabloids and the business interests of the Murdoch empire, support could quickly evaporate.

In the same way, Tony Blair had strong personal appeal, and he had carried through the modernising reforms of the Labour party which made Labour electable. But appeal resting on personality causes greater problems of transition to the next generation than that which is rooted in principle. 'Thatcherism' was always a matter of style as well as substance; and part of John Major's difficulty after his honeymoon period, as newspapers' harping on the leadership issue confirms, was that he was not Margaret Thatcher. Editorialists' worries (including the *Sun*'s) about Blair's trustworthiness showed that, however charming, he might find his popularity slump after some not especially Black Wednesday of his own (see Rose in this volume). It is worth emphasising again at this point, too, the new generation of national editors. Piers Morgan at the *Daily Mirror* and Andrew Marr at the *Independent* were both teenagers when Mrs Thatcher came to power; and the average age at that time of the 1997 editors was only 26. Most were not long out of public school and/or Oxbridge. The 1997 election marks a generational shift in the political experience of the national editors.

The third reason for seeing the change as short term is the special significance of Europe. The Conservative waverers and the Murdoch papers were all eurosceptic. If John Major had been strong enough to impose his authority about his party's policy on the single currency and the political development of Europe, the editorialists would have been much less cross-pressured. How quickly they might return home would therefore depend partly on how soon the Conservative party sorted out its European policy.

The alternative arguments are more fairly described as making the case not for an indefinite pro-Labour majority in the press but for long term volatility, in line with that of voters themselves. There is first the simple truth that papers cannot for too long preach, without risk to their sales, opinions at odds with large numbers of their readers. This is notwithstanding the reservations about the proportionately large number of floating voters among *Sun* readers, for instance, and their comparatively low interest in party politics. Nor, arguably, is this truth affected by the continuing drift of the mass market tabloids away from 'public affairs' content and towards being daily magazines dominated by sport, showbiz and celebs. Since its foundation in 1978 the working class *Daily Star*, the extreme case, has always chosen cautiously its words of (until now) Tory comfort.

The second argument is the claimed 'presidential' tendency in British politics. This can be linked to a possible long term decline in the political role of parties in general and the rise of limited-issue pressure groups. The reaction of newspapers may be a tendency not only to align themselves with seemingly non-ideological party leaders, but to avoid committing themselves unreservedly to political parties at all. The ritual quality of some editorial argument in 1997 supports this view. By the end of the campaign there was something vacuous in the *Sun*'s happy talk about Blair and the thumping rhetoric of the *Daily Mirror*. How many different ways can you find to extol a fresh face or an old ally, in a world where the limitations on what governments can achieve are well known? Such a tendency is consistent with the historical connection between newspapers and parties. The two used often to flourish together. A paper was a focus of organisation and an instrument of leadership and propaganda. The relationship was epitomised in the link between Labour and the *Daily Herald*, in which the TUC owned nearly half the shares and controlled the editorial policy (the editor had to account for himself annually at the Labour Party Conference).

A decline in wholehearted commitment would also reflect what may be a long term change in the nature of editorial opinion. The editorial is no longer the largely exclusive fount of a paper's political wisdom. Thick newspapers, divided into sections, mean more space for comment and more specialised comment in individual sections (e.g. on finance, health, education). Columnists have proliferated. No longer do broadsheets have 'the leader (i.e. editorial) page': they have 'op-ed pages' in the American style. The corollary of the accompanying abandonment of anonymity ('our political correspondent'), largely in the Wilson era, has been the rise of the high-profile named columnist. The very identifiability of Simon Heffer (*Daily Mail*), Hugo Young (*Guardian*) or Anne McElvoy (*Daily Telegraph*) virtually requires that they argue a personal case in a distinctive style, rather than stick closely to an official line. In a further twist, the *Independent*'s editor, Andrew Marr, wrote a regular signed column during the 1997 campaign, including a very strong attack on Blair for contributing contradictory messages about Europe to different europhile and europhobe papers. Former editors of *The Times* (William Rees-Mogg, Simon Jenkins), the *Guardian* (Peter Preston) and the *Daily Telegraph* (William Deedes) wrote regular columns in those papers. In such ways is the single editorial voice blurred and its authority, perhaps, diminished. On the basis of change both in the party system and in the press, therefore, we might expect to see less consistent and less categorical partisanship by newspapers in future elections. Already in 1997 their attitudes looked less like firm endorsements than starting positions in a debate with a new government and a riven Conservative party. But whatever the future, the balance of editorial opinion in the national press was an integral part of Labour's triumph and was a unique phenomenon.

1 The author acknowledges with thanks assistance in the preparation of this article from the Goldsmith Awards Program of the Joan Shorenstein Center, Harvard University; and from the Social Sciences Faculty Research Fund, University of Kent at Canterbury. He is grateful to Paul Bacon and Stephan Reynolds for their help with content analysis.
2 The different viewpoints are discussed in M. Linton, 'Maybe the *Sun* Won it After All', *British Journalism Review* 7 1996; and J. Curtice, 'Is the *Sun* Shining on Tony Blair?', *Harvard International Journal of Press/Politics* Spring 1997.
3 Interview in the *Guardian*, 19.5.97.
4 The space figure is fairly arbitrary, since the decision how much of an article refers to the persons named in it can be very subjective. But the coding has been done consistently.

Television

BY HOLLI A. SEMETKO*, MARGARET SCAMMELL† AND
PETER GODDARD‡

NO ONE could say that television did not try. Politics was available for breakfast, lunch and tea with all major party manifestos, policies and campaigns reported in exhaustive detail. Yet, despite following the traditions of public service broadcasting, and making extensive efforts to inform the public, television's election coverage has been severely criticised. Tony Blair, inverting John Birt's famous 'mission to explain' dictum, accused television of a 'conspiracy against understanding'. Newspapers complained of overkill, saturation and boredom. 'Oh no, not the Nine O'Clock News again', moaned the *Telegraph*'s Allison Pearson's April Mediawatch column. Once over, the post-mortem began. Did television contribute to a dispiriting campaign, a turned-off electorate, and the lowest turnout since 1935? Why did an extraordinary election, with historic consequences, feel so dull, flat and repetitive to so many commentators? In the context of these concerns, this article examines some of the key influences on the content of election news. We summarise how the election was covered on the major channels, focusing in particular on whether the news values which shaped broadcasters' coverage, particularly the conceptions of 'balance', served the broader public interest.

Coverage of the election in the news and current affairs

British television devoted far more time to its national election than is common in many other countries.[1] A typical evening during the British campaign presented viewers with the following: the early evening news on BBC1 and ITV (Channel 3), then Channel 4 News (7–8), Channel 5 News (8.30–9), followed by BBC1's extended Nine O'Clock News (9–9.50), the flagship ITN News at Ten (10–10.30), BBC2's Newsnight (10.30–11.30) and, if one was still in the mood, Channel 4's After Midnight. The next morning viewers awoke to the campaign for breakfast on all channels followed by Election Call on BBC1, featuring electors' questions to a different politician each day. There were numerous other special election programmes in which the public interviewed the politicians—BBC's Question Time and the panel of

* Professor of Communications at the University of Amsterdam.
† Senior Lecturer in Communication Studies at Liverpool University.
‡ Research Assistant in Communication Studies at Liverpool University.

electors in ITV's Election 500, for example—and unprecedented 'inter-active' opportunities via ITV's Online and the BBC's Election '97 website. Sky News, available via satellite, mounted a full election operation for six weeks, live throughout the day—from the morning press conferences through to the evening news beginning with 'Live at Five' and political editor Adam Boulton's regular interviews with key politicians. And on election night from 10pm onwards, exit polls conducted by NOP for the BBC and by MORI for ITV provided the first glimpse of the extent of Labour's victory, followed by non-stop live coverage throughout the following morning and afternoon. Those with satellites could also zap to Sky's live election special, while viewers around the world could turn to BBC World's in-studio team of experts who commented throughout the night, and to CNN's election special.

How did each programme approach coverage? BBC1's Nine O'Clock News looked much as it did in 1992, with the campaign leading the news almost without exception throughout the election. In its extended format from 1 April, the opening fifteen minutes reviewed the day's events in an overview from political editor Robin Oakley and reports from those travelling with each of the leaders. The programme then turned to the rest of the days' news with a promise to return to the election later. On the half-hour, Ann Perkins gave a ten minute round-up from the Westminster Studio followed by a field report (often focusing on a region or a set of voters) and studio interviews from Robin Oakley, economics editor Peter Jay, social affairs correspondent Niall Dickson, or opinion poll analyst Peter Snow.

In the first two weeks of the campaign ITV's News At Ten often opened with two or three party leader field reports, with political editor Michael Brunson bringing together the themes of the day in a single report at some point during the programme. But in the final weeks of the campaign, election news largely dominated the first half of the programme. Brunson reported on the campaign each day and there were daily reports from the campaign trail and various constituencies. At the end of each week there were graphics charting the polls accompanied by a 'health warning'. Throughout the campaign, News at Ten never led with a poll story.

Channel 4 News has a loyal, upmarket and politically interested audience of approximately 850,000 most of whom stayed tuned in throughout the campaign. Election news occupied substantial parts of the programme, with political editor Elinor Goodman's daily packages on campaign issues and events, and anchor Jon Snow's studio interviews with politicians and party leaders. There were also regular panel debates—on issues such as education and health, held in different regional locations around the country, with representatives from each of the three main parties—as well as various regional reports. The election was also linked to other stories. Economics correspondent Steve Levinson, for example, drew connections between business news and the campaign. News values largely determined story selection and placement, and exclusive stories that reflected the investigative talents of the programme were put up front.

Channel 5 News, with its unique open-plan studio and computer-like graphics formats, hosted by Kirsty Young, an authoritative 'Generation X' Scot, attracted new audiences of up to 300,000 during the campaign. For computer game lovers, the highlight most evenings was the 'Minute Manifesto', with screen graphics displaying one by one the five main points of each of the three parties' key policies, as the seconds ticked away, until the virtual steel doors on the screen slammed shut 'TIME UP!' It too offered a review of election news during its half-hour bulletin each evening. Campaign trail reports from political editor Mark Easton were often laced with amusing analogies, both visual and verbal. According to Easton: 'My political coverage is to give people basic factual information and steer clear of the rhetoric . . . There are some very big issues right now—about the single currency, the safety of food, welfare states, very big questions about the future. Most people don't know very much about them, if anything. In fact they tend to switch off because they require a lot of background knowledge before you can take on the latest event. TV unnecessarily clutters itself up by using a conventionally formulaic approach and I believe we can deconstruct the way we tell stories using far more tricks of TV than the tricks of just newspapers to tell stories. Newspapers use quotes. TV news gets most of its ideas from newspapers. I'm arguing that we should use the tricks of TV to do what we want to do which is to tell stories.'

BBC2's Newsnight, with its late evening slot (beginning at 10.30pm), also retained most of its audience despite the considerable amount of election-related news. Jeremy Paxman and Kirsty Wark anchored two debates—one on constitutional reform and devolution, and the other on Europe, as well as five 'Millennium Challenge' programmes in which education, health, crime, job insecurity, and inequality, were each the subject of discussion between a panel of politicians and pre-selected voters with first-hand experience of the issues, and three 'Big Ideas' programmes in which a single politician from each of the three main parties faced questions from a pre-selected studio audience. Newsnight also gained viewers with its new 'relaxed' Saturday programme, aired in the early evening (7pm), in which different perspectives on the election were featured, for example, entertainers such as Simply Red's lead singer, writers, and political luminaries such as Sir David Steel. Each of the major news programmes therefore devoted considerable resources to the campaign, although the format and approach reflected the distinctive philosophies and audiences of each channel.

Criteria guiding news coverage

Why did television give so much attention to the election and how did broadcasters decide what stories should be prioritised? Journalists, editors and producers regarded the election as a critical event in British political history which therefore deserved full and sustained coverage. In terms of sheer news value the 1997 election was widely seen to represent a watershed. A Tory win would produce an historic fifth consecutive triumph whilst a Labour victory would mean the biggest swing in decades and a new generation of political leaders. Other scenarios—a minority government, a hung parliament, a coalition— also made fascinating news. This reading of the news opportunities underpinned broadcasting decisions to devote so much attention to the campaign. And the broadcasters took all the various scenarios seriously, despite Labour's long and strong poll lead. Throughout the course of the six-week campaign, and indeed over the twelve months which preceded it, an average of the published polls showed Labour's lead over the Conservatives consistently between 15–20 percentage points. But the ghosts of 1992 loomed large. The possibility of the polls being wrong again was considered a real one (see Crewe this volume). Broadcasters took this into account in planning their approach to the 1997 campaign.

Many factors may have influenced decisions concerning how to cover the election. As in previous elections, the primary one which has long dominated television coverage of British elections is the concept of 'stop-watch' balance.[2] News programmes claim that the stopwatch does not dictate the news, but all pay attention to the times and nevertheless keep tallies for the purposes of remaining balanced, not only within the terms of the Representation of the People Act but also within the broadcasters' agreed ratio for maintaining balance between the parties. The problem with the tallies is, as one senior editor describes it 'the Michael Foot syndrome', in other words, more time in the news may hurt rather than help the party. But what are the consequences for the viewer of a stopwatch approach versus a news values approach? The balance requirement gave the parties greater opportunities to promote their favourite topics. But the effect on the viewer may sometimes be to diminish, rather than enhance, understanding of the issues.

An illustration of the contrasts between conceptions of balance, which predominated at the BBC, and conceptions of news values driving the agenda at ITN, can be shown by coverage on Tuesday, 25 March. BBC1's Nine O'Clock News (before the programme was extended to 50 minutes) took a very different approach to ITN's News at Ten. The BBC news was more varied and inclusive of various statements, but it also appeared more fragmented. Unions were mentioned briefly by the reporter, followed by three soundbites, one from each main party. While these faithfully reflected the parties' agendas, they did not connect substantively but rather as evidence of the parties attacking one another: a soundbite from Michael Heseltine attacking Labour on unions, followed by one from Robin Cook attacking the Tories as divided, and disloyal on Europe, followed by a soundbite from Paddy Ashdown about the environment during his visit to a recycling plant. By contrast, ITN's Michael Brunson focused his report on unions as the story of the day, and sought out soundbites from each of the main parties on this theme. Balancing the news by faithfully reflecting the parties' agendas may have had the unintended consequence of a 'bias against understanding,' and this may have been exacerbated in the extended Nine O'Clock News.

Interestingly, that same day, 25 March, Channel 4 News and Channel 5 News ignored the union story and the press conference soundbites, and instead focused on the environment as the most important story of the day. Why? According to Channel 4's Jon Snow: 'It was the first head-to-head debate of the whole campaign . . . on one issue . . . and so we went with it.' Friends of the Earth organized a three-way debate between leading politicians, which Channels 4 and 5 reported, because in the words of Channel 5 news editor Chris Smith it provided 'a genuine spontaneous difference of opinion between the Labour and Tory front bench spokespeople, and the Liberal Democrats have a very distinctive environmental policy.' There was no mention of the Friends of the Earth debate on BBC's extended Nine O'Clock News or ITN's News at Ten that same day. This is an illustration of the difference between conceptions of balance or news values setting the media agenda. Whether one approach is better than another is an open question. Research on viewers' information processing could assess which of the different formats was actually more effective for learning.

In practice, the concept of balance meant extensive coverage of politicians on the campaign trail, and this often highlighted negative news, in particular the personal attacks made in soundbites (see Gavin and Sanders in this volume). Take the attack on Mr Blair by Heseltine, for example, in an evening speech, on 25 April 1997: 'You stand for new Labour. You can keep it. You can stuff it back in all those smiling glitzy soundbites that you've imported from the worst of transatlantic political campaigning. You are not fit to be leader of the Labour Party and you are certainly not fit to be Prime Minister of this country' (applause). This was on the BBC Nine O'Clock news Westminster Report from Ann Perkins. Earlier in the campaign, John Major was on the attack. Here is an example from the top of Michael Brunson's report on News at Ten, 18 April 1997:

Brunson: Mr Major began his week by attacking Tony Blair on Europe and he ended it . . . by attacking Tony Blair on Europe. Mr Blair's inexperience, his unwillingness to be isolated, would put him at the mercy of the other heads of government, he said.

Soundbite of John Major: I know those Europeans, they'd eat him alive. It would be like sending a fly to a spiders' convention.

Brunson: Same message, different delivery in Tory newspaper ads this morning. The boy Blair sitting on Chancellor Kohl's knee. Several German politicians said it was well out of order. But from Mr Major, no apology.

Tony Blair responded by criticising Major's record as Prime Minister and inability to keep his party together on Europe. But Blair also criticised the news media for making conflict and attacks too prominent in the coverage. As he said,

One of the great problems of this election campaign, for you in the media, and for us the politicians, is what I call the battle for the stories, as opposed to the issues. The most frustrating experience is that we go around and give these speeches, I gave three myself last week, one on education, one on the welfare state, one on the nature of society and how we develop it, on business, and its actually quite difficult to get coverage for those things during the course of the campaign. It is perhaps natural that it means that some of the passion and the conviction and the articulation of the different positions, which is what people want from the campaign, get pushed to the side if someone made a gaffe today, if I attack John Major, or if John Major attacks me. It's quite difficult for the public, I think, a lot of the time, sitting there and listening to this, to understand that there are issues of considerable importance that are going to be decided, and working out exactly what their positions are (*London Press Club*, 22.4.96).

The problem is that conceptions of balance may drive coverage, and if politicians spend their time attacking each other, television journalists may feel this has to be faithfully reported, even if this fails to illuminate the serious policy issues facing the electorate.

Conclusions

In 1997, British election television news was voluminous, substantive, and more detailed than in many other countries. Nevertheless our brief look at election television suggests that the news was more negative in 1997 than in previous campaigns, and this process may turn voters off.[3] It is too simple to blame the journalists for this emphasis in the news. Politicians are almost always the initiators of these statements, and they are well aware of reporters' predilection for conflict. Politicians were largely responsible for launching these attacks on a daily basis, and although broadcasters had the freedom to reject this emphasis in the news they chose not to, given their conception of 'balance'. Section 93 of the Representation of the People Act prohibits broadcasters from airing an interview or broadcast about a constituency unless all candidates for the seat agree, or actually take part in the broadcast themselves. Party leaders were interviewed repeatedly in 1997, as in past elections, in special current affairs and main evening news programmes. The leaders also received the overwhelming bulk of the attention in the news from the campaign trail each day, not only because each literally carried his party's campaign, but because of Section 93 which, according to Richard Tait, editor-in-chief of ITN, makes 'politics on television during elections seem an almost exclusively male, white and middle-aged activity'. As a result, in Tait's view, the press had more freedom than television news to cover the interesting stories at local level: 'Just think of all the interesting stories and issues which you could read about in the press but appeared on television only in a very constricted form. Where was the blow-by-blow coverage of Tatton, one of the most remarkable constituency battles since the second world war? What about the unprecedented numbers of women candidates in winnable seats, or the growing number of black and Asian candidates, or the impressive group of very young candidates?' (*Guardian*, 20.5.97).

Television is widely regarded as the most trusted source for information about the general election campaign. Would television lose its credibility if released from the restrictive Section 93 of the Representation of the People Act, which many believe, in Tait's words, 'in its present form, is an obstacle, not an aid, to fair and full election coverage?' It is a question that deserves serious consideration by politicians and policy-makers in the coming years. It was ironic that the special efforts extended by the broadcasters, especially the BBC's Nine O'Clock News, may have led to millions of turned-off viewers. The challenge for all broadcasters in the next election will be to improve upon the quality of election news, with innovative formats that enhance public understanding of the important issues of the campaign. This task is hampered from the outset, given the restrictions imposed by Section 93 of the Representation of the Peoples Act. The radical challenge for the new Labour government, and for broadcasters, in the coming years is to reform the restrictions on election broadcasting, giving television more room to use creative talent and to provide thoughtful and newsworthy reporting for voters. The 'balance requirement', despite all its good intentions, often resulted in regimented soundbites and negative conflict that may in fact have conspired against understanding. Michael Jermey, deputy editor of ITN, emphasised that trust, credibility, and respect for different political viewpoints was central to the mission of ITV's news programmes: ' . . . the end result of our coverage should be that ITV viewers feel well informed and able to cast a considered vote.' Whether television achieved these aims is open to debate.

This study is part of an ESRC supported research project on political communications in the 1997 election directed by Margaret Scammell and Holli Semetko. Special thanks to those who took time to be interviewed and provided valuable documentation and materials for this research.

1 H.A. Semetko, 'The Media', L. LeDuc, R. Neimi and P. Norris (eds), *Comparing Democracies* (Sage, 1996).

2 H.A. Semetko, 'Journalistic Culture in Comparative Perspective: The Concept of "Balance" in US, British and Germany TV News', *The Harvard International Journal of Press/Politics* 1/1996; H.A. Semetko, M. Scammell and T.J. Nossiter, 'Media Coverage of the 1992 British General Election Campaign' in A. Heath, R. Jowell and J. Curtice (eds), *Labour's Last Chance? The 1992 Election and Beyond* (Dartmouth, 1994); M. Scammell, 'Political Advertising and the Broadcasting Revolution', *Political Quarterly*, 61/1990.

3 See, for example, S. Ansolebehere and S. Iyengar, *Going Negative* (MIT Press, 1996); T.E. Patterson, *Out of Order* (Vintage, 1994).

Why the Tories were Trounced

BY PETER KELLNER*

HOW DID Britain vote, what was the impact of major issues like the economy and Europe, and how much did leadership and party image count? To examine these issues the BBC commissioned two NOP polls of voters as they exited polling stations on election day: a 'prediction poll' (17,073 voters completed short questionnaires, which asked how they had just voted, and how they had voted in 1992); and an 'analysis poll' (2,356 voters completed longer questionnaires, which sought their responses to a wider range of issues). This chapter reports and explores the findings of these surveys.[1] What emerges is that the perceived poor economic record, divisions and weak leadership of the Conservative government did help to produce a change of government; but the scale of Labour's landslide victory was also a product of the positive popularity of the Labour Party and, in particular, the appeal of Tony Blair. It also emerges that—contrary to some commentaries immediately following the election—the recovery in Britain's economy in the years prior to the election did help the Conservatives avoid complete annihilation: their losses, heavy though they were, would have been even greater had the economy not shown clear signs of growth.

How Britain voted

The first table shows how each of the main demographic groups voted in 1997, and compares the figures for each party with the BBC/NOP exit poll from the 1992 election. There is little evidence of any gender gap in 1997 (more accurately, if there was a gender gap this time, it was too small to escape the clutches of sampling error). For the first time since 1945, the votes of women alone would have given Labour a clear victory. Labour's other postwar victories—1964, 1966 and 1974—depended on the male vote: either the Tories retained a lead among women (1964 and both 1974 elections), or Labour's lead was so small among women that the result would have been a hung Parliament (1966). Furthermore, according to the BBC/NOP exit poll in 1997 there was a marked difference in the swing to Labour among different age groups. This had the effect of increasing the generation gap between young and old voters. The under thirties, already the most pro-Labour age group, swung the most; the over-65s, already more pro-Conservative than the average, swung the least. Indeed, Labour's share of the

---

* Political correspondent for BBC Television and the *Independent*.

1. Vote by group (%)

	Con		Lab		Lib Dem	
	1997	Change since 1992	1997	Change since 1992	1997	Change since 1992
All	31	−11	44	+9	17	−1
Men	31	−11	45	+8	17	0
Women	32	−12	45	+11	17	−2
18–29	22	−19	56	+18	18	+1
30–44	26	−15	49	+15	17	−5
45–64	33	−14	43	+9	18	+1
65+	44	−3	34	−1	17	+1
AB voters (managerial/ professional)	42	−14	31	+11	21	0
C1 (white collar)	26	−15	47	+15	19	−4
C2 (skilled workers)	25	−13	54	+13	14	−4
DE (semi-skilled, unskilled, state pensioners)	21	−16	61	+15	13	−2
Own home outright	41	−14	35	+10	16	−2
Mortgage-payers	31	−16	44	+15	18	−2
Council tenants	13	−8	66	+1	15	+4

Source: BBC/NOP Exit poll: sample of 2,356 voters polled on 1 May, having just voted.

vote fell fractionally among the elderly. In 1992, the Conservatives led by three points among 18–29 year-olds, seven among 30–44 year-olds, 13 among 45–64 year-olds and 12 among over 65s. The figures for the same age groups this time were: −34, −23, −10, +10.

This has had a marked effect on the age profile of each party's vote. Half of Labour's voters were under 45, while half were over 45; however only a third of Conservative voters were under 45, while fully two-thirds were over 45. These figures suggest that the Tories' core support resembles the readership of the *Sunday Express* in the seventies and eighties: tilted heavily towards older people, and destined to decline remorselessly unless some means can be found to attract young recruits. Can the Tories succeed over the next five years where the *Sunday Express* has failed over the past quarter century? Moreover, this may have important implications for future support. If past demographic trends continue, and the present Parliament lasts a full five years, 1.1 million people who voted Conservative at this year's election are likely to die before the next general election, compared with 800,000 Labour voters and 400,000 Liberal Democrats. This means that the baseline at the next general election—that is survivors from the 1997 general election—will be: Labour 12.7m, Conservatives 8.5m, Lib Dems 4.8m, others 2.1m. This translates into the following percentages: Labour 45.2, Conservatives 30.2, Lib Dems 17.1, others 7.5. Labour will start with a 15% lead among the survivors from 1997, rather than the 13% lead it actually achieved on polling day.

Table 1 also shows how each social class voted. These figures are not strictly comparable with those from other surveys, as voters were asked to classify their own social class from a simplified list of examples of occupations. The effect, as in 1992, was to inflate the number of ABs, compared with conventional surveys, and depress the number of C1s and DEs. The figures for self-classification in the BBC/NOP exit poll were: AB: 38%, C1: 21%, C2: 24%, DE: 16%. The differences in the swing among the different social groups were not statistically significant. All were above the national average: a phenomenon which reflects class-drift since 1992 (more voters classifying themselves as AB and fewer as DE). There does, however, seem to have been a significant pattern according to housing tenure, with mortgage payers swinging more heavily to Labour (15.5%) than either people who own their homes outright (12%) or council tenants (4.5%). This is one example of evidence from the analysis exit poll that economic factors did matter in the election; for it is among a significant minority of mortgage payers that the problem of falling house prices in general, and negative equity in particular, was acute in the early nineties.

The larger prediction poll enables us to compare how people leaving polling stations said they had just voted in 1997 with how they recalled voting in 1992. The detailed figures are given in Table 2. As many as 29% of those who recalled voting Conservative in 1992 said they had switched parties, compared with just 10% of people who recalled voting Labour. While 13% of 1992—Tories switched to Labour, just 2% of 1992—Labour voters made the opposite journey. Labour also picked up the votes of 19% of those who recalled voting Liberal Democrat in 1992—more than twice as many switchers as the Conservatives attracted. As with all exercises involving vote recall, care must be taken with the interpretation of these figures. Previous work done by MORI, ICM, the British Election Study and the British Household Panel Study, has shown that a significant minority of people are liable to suffer from 'false memory syndrome' and to give different recall answers when asked the same question on different occasions. The biggest systematic effect after 1992 was that too many people 'remembered' voting Labour, while too few 'remembered' voting Liberal Democrat. It seems likely that many of the 1992—Lib Dem voters who subsequently 'remembered' voting Labour are people who normally support Labour but decided in 1992 to vote Liberal Democrat instead. If this is so, then the number of people who switched from Lib Dem to Labour in 1997

2. Flow of the vote 1992–97—recall vote % (1992)

	Con	Lab	Lib Dem	Nat	Other	Too young	Did not vote	Cannot remember	Refused
1992 total	35	34	12	2	1	4	7	2	3
1997 vote:									
Conservative	71	2	7	2	7	30	27	22	35
Labour	13	90	19	12	30	40	47	41	36
Lib-Dem	11	5	69	6	14	21	19	28	20
Scot Nat/PC	1	1	1	78	2	5	1	3	2
Referendum	3	1	2	1	14	3	3	4	5
Other	1	1	2	1	33	1	3	2	2
	100	100	100	100	100	100	100	100	100

Source: BBC/NOP prediction poll, n = 17,073

is rather greater than the 19% shown in the table. Moreover, one myth that the poll does demolish is that the Referendum Party attracted almost all its support from the Conservatives. In fact, only around half its voters recalled supporting the Tories in 1992.

The analysis poll asked voters when they had decided which party to support (Table 3). One in ten said 'today', with the Liberal Democrats gaining most from late deciders: 16% of their voters made up their minds on the day. In contrast, 65% of Labour's supporters had made up their minds before the campaign started—higher than the Tories' 58% and much higher than the Lib Dems' 34%. These figures are broadly consistent with the story told by the opinion polls during the campaign, with Labour's vote slipping and the Lib Dems gaining ground. The prediction poll also allows us to test with some precision various beliefs about when the supporters of different parties turnout to vote. Two main points emerge: first, almost half the votes cast on 1 May were cast after 5pm; second, the time-profile of each party's support is broadly similar. A higher proportion of Labour voters than Tories went to the polling stations in the morning; and a higher proportion of Tories voted in the afternoon and evening; however the differences were not great. This data provides no support for the notion that Labour voters mainly tend to visit the polling station on the way to or from work, while mid-morning to mid-afternoon voters are mainly Tory. Whether or not this was true in the past, it was certainly not true in 1997.

3. Timing of voting decision

%	All	Con	Lab	Lib Dem
Today	11	11	9	16
Within the last week	14	12	10	25
Since election was called	18	18	15	25
Before election was called	57	58	65	34
Time of vote				
7–9am	9.0	9.1	9 .1	10.1
9–11am	13.4	12.5	14.7	12.5
11am–1pm	9.8	8.9	10.5	9.4
1–3pm	10.2	10.4	9.5	10.7
3–5pm	12.0	12.5	11.5	11.9
5–7pm	21.1	21.0	20.4	21.2
7–9pm	21.3	21.8	20.6	22.1
9–10pm	3.3	3.7	3.6	2.1

Note: The Table represents responses to the question, 'When did you make up your mind how you would vote today?'

Source: BBC/NOP prediction poll

The Conservative record

All elections are, to a lesser or greater extent, verdicts on the party seeking re-election. In 1997, the Conservatives could point to a record of steady growth, low inflation, falling unemployment and a buoyant housing market. So how was it that they won the lowest share of the

4. The Conservative record

%	All	Con	Lab	Lib Dem	Ex-Con	New Lab
(a) Standard of living						
Better	25	52	11	15	18	16
About the same	37	41	32	43	42	33
Worse	38	6	57	42	40	52
(b) Economy						
Stronger	35	74	13	27	32	17
About the same	34	21	39	40	39	40
Weaker	31	4	47	31	28	41

Note: The Table represents responses to the questions, 'Compared with five years ago, at the time of the election (a) have the living standards of you and your family got worse, stayed the same or got better? (b) is the economy weaker now, stronger now or about the same?'. 'Ex-Con' are voters who recall voting Conservative in 1992, but voted for another party in 1997; 'New Lab' are voters who did not vote Labour in 1992, but did in 1997

	All	Con	Lab	Lib Dem	Ex-Con	New Lab
'It's time for a change; the Conservatives have done a bad job'	44	3	71	48	40	60
'This is no time for a change; Labour wouldn't do any better'	32	92	3	9	8	3
'No matter how well or badly the Conservatives have done, it's simply time for a change'	23	5	26	42	51	37

Note: The Table represents responses to the question, 'Which of the following comes closest to your view . . .'

Source: BBC/NOP exit poll

vote of any governing party in the twentieth century? The analysis poll's questions on the Conservative record throw some light on this (Table 4). Only a quarter of voters said their own standard of living was higher now, compared with 1992. Many more (38%) said their standard of living had got worse. However, when voters made a similar five-year comparison, but about the state of the British economy, the figures were rather different: more voters thought the economy was now stronger (35%) rather than weaker (31%).

Two reasons may be adduced for the difference between these two questions. First, some people feel that they have been left behind during the recovery. Indeed, for them, the Conservative slogan, 'Britain is booming', may have been counterproductive, for it induced some voters to react: 'Maybe it is, but I am not'. Of those voters who said the economy was stronger, but their families standard of living had deteriorated, more than eight out of ten voted Labour or Liberal Democrat. Second, it may be that 'the economy' is mainly about money, whereas 'standard of living' embraces not just the purse or wallet, but a wider sense of the quality of life, including the quality of the health and education services, public transport and so on. Although these were not tested directly in the exit poll, other surveys have shown that large majorities of people feel that the public services have deteriorated since 1992.

It also seems clear that the Conservatives suffered from having been in power so long, and that 'time for a change' struck a chord with many voters. The analysis poll asked voters which of three statements came closest to their own view. Among people who recalled voting Tory in 1992, but had just voted for another party, fully 51% chose: 'No matter how well or badly the Conservatives have done, it's simply time for a change'; rather fewer, 40%, said: 'It's time for a change; the Conservatives have done a bad job'. Seven out of ten Labour voters agreed that the Conservatives had done a 'bad job'; but one in four opted instead for the view that it was time for a change, irrespective of the Tories' performance in office.

Party ratings on the main issues

As Table 5 shows, Labour matched the Tories in 1997 when voters were asked which party they trusted most to take the right decisions about the economy—a far cry from 1992, when the Tories led Labour on this issue by 53 to 33%. On income tax, the shift has been even greater. In 1992 the Tories led Labour by 22 points as the party most trusted to take the right decisions; in 1997 Labour led the Tories by 8 points. The poll suggests that the Conservative record on income tax was particularly important in persuading many people who had voted Conservative in 1992 to switch parties. Ex-Conservative put the two main parties level-pegging on the economy in general—as did voters as a whole. But on income tax, Labour led by 18 points among ex-Conservatives, compared with just 8 points among voters generally. The

	Conservative		Labour		Lib Dem	
	1997	Change since 1992	1997	Change since 1992	1997	Change since 1992
The economy	42	−11	44	+11	13	0
Income tax	36	−19	44	+13	20	+6
Schools/education	26	−14	48	+9	26	+5
Dealing with sleaze	23	n/a	49	n/a	29	n/a

5. Party ratings on the main issues (%)

	All	Con	Lab	Lib Dem	Ex-Con	New Lab
(a) Economy						
Conservative	42	97	11	22	39	18
Labour	44	3	87	14	38	79
Liberal Democrat	13	0	3	64	23	4
(b) Income tax						
Conservative	36	92	7	11	26	12
Labour	44	5	85	11	44	80
Liberal Democrat	20	4	8	78	30	9
(c) Schools/education						
Conservative	26	77	2	3	10	4
Labour	48	9	89	14	50	83
Liberal Democrat	26	14	9	83	40	13
(d) Dealing with 'sleaze'						
Conservative	23	66	3	3	6	4
Labour	49	11	87	16	46	79
Liberal Democrat	29	22	10	82	48	17

Note: The Tables represent responses to the question, 'Which party do you trust most to take the right decisions about . . .'

Source: BBC/NOP exit poll

difference is explained not by the number saying Labour had the best policies (44% among voters as a whole, the same as among ex-Tories), but by the numbers naming the Tories (36% among all voters, but just 26% among ex-Tories). Even more ex-Tories were dubious about Conservative policies on education and 'sleaze'; but this is less surprising, for neither is a home-ground issue for the party. Income tax, on the other hand, has traditionally been one of the party's strongest issues — but not in 1997.

It should also be noted that the Liberal Democrats scored well on both tax (20% among voters generally) and education (26%), relative to their national vote (17%). The key policy that the party stressed during the campaign was that it would increase the standard rate of income tax by 1p in the £, and spend the money on education. These figures confirm the findings of campaign polls: this was a popular policy (see 'voters' values', below) which may have contributed to the fact that the Liberal Democrats were the only party to gain support significantly during the course of the election campaign. The Liberal Democrats were also widely trusted as the best party to deal with 'sleaze', scoring more (29%) than the Tories (23%). These figures suggest that sleaze did help drag the Conservative vote down, and that the Liberal Democrats' attempt to portray themselves as a fresher, cleaner, more positive party did them some good.

Expectations

If the Conservatives were hampered by their record, and as a result by their perceived weakness on the economy, Labour benefited from having banished the 'fear factor' which the Conservatives exploited so skilfully in 1992. As Table 6 shows, 57% expected Labour policies generally 'to

6. Expectations (%)

	Labour policies . . .			Conservative policies		
	All	Ex-Con	Lab	All	Ex-Con	New Lab
A lot better	24	17	40	8	1	2
A little better	33	42	54	23	15	5
Would make no difference	11	18	3	19	34	22
A little worse	16	18	1	18	30	33
A lot worse	17	6	1	31	19	38

Note: The Table represent responses to the questions, 'If Labour wins the election, do you think that, overall, Labour policies will make things in Britain . . .' and 'If the Conservatives win the election, do you think that, overall, Conservative policies will make things in Britain . . .'

	If Conservatives won			If Labour won . . .		
	All	Ex-Con	Lab	All	Ex-Con	New Lab
Taxes would go up	59	65	76	61	65	39
Taxes would go down	5	4	5	9	6	15
Taxes would stay about the same	35	31	19	30	29	46

Note: The Table represent responses to the questions, 'If the Conservatives won the election do you think that taxes overall would go up, go down or stay about the same?' and 'If Labour won the election do you think that taxes overall would go up, go down or stay about the same?'

Source: BBC/NOP exit poll

make things better', while just 33% expected them to make things worse. For the Tories the figures were almost the reverse: just 31% expected them to make things better, while 49% expected them to make things worse. Within those broad categories, we should note that Labour successfully managed to minimise expectations: of those who thought things would get better under Labour, most thought they would get only 'a little better'. Yet, for many people fear of a fifth Conservative term was intense: most of those who expected things to get worse with Conservative policies thought they would get 'a lot worse'. However, when a specific feature of government policy was tested—what would happen to taxes—there was little difference between perceptions of the two main parties. Six out of ten voters expected taxes to rise, whoever was in charge. Among ex-Conservatives, 65% expected taxes to rise under either Labour or Tory. Very few expected taxes to fall.

So why did Labour lead the Tories when voters judged which party they trusted most on income tax; and why did Labour score so much better than the Tories as the party that would generally 'make things better'? Perhaps Labour's specific commitments not to raise the basic or higher rate of income tax played a part. It may also be that Labour managed to reverse the pattern found in 1992. Then most people expected Labour to raise taxes simply to pay for their economic incompetence, rather than to improve public services; the Tories, in contrast were perceived as economically competent, and managing to keep taxes down as a result. In 1997, the Conservatives seem to have acquired the reputation for tax-raising incompetence; whereas Labour was seen as a party that would use its tax-income wisely, and to raise taxes either to improve public services or to pick up the bill left by the Conservatives. In other words, expectations of future tax increases under Labour may reflect a judgement of past Conservative failure rather than future Labour incompetence.

Voters' values

Table 7 sets voters' views about the parties and taxation in the wider context of their own values. By a large majority, they felt that income tax should be increased by 1p in the pound, and the money spent on Britain's schools. Large majorities of supporters of all parties expressed this view: a two-to-one majority of Tories, as well as a four-to-one majority of Labour voters and a six-to-one majority of Liberal Democrats. These findings are consistent with those from other surveys in recent years. However the question is worded, and whatever allowance one makes for the undoubted desire among more respondents to give the 'socially correct' answer rather than the selfish one, it seems clear that many millions of voters would prefer money to be spent on better front-line public services rather than lower taxes. The policy being tested here was a Liberal Democrat rather than a Labour policy; nevertheless, it may help to explain why Labour policies were seen as

7. Voters' values (%)

Whoever wins today's election, do you think the new government should or should not carry out any further privatisation?

	All	Con	Lab	Lib Dem	Ex-Con	New Lab
Should	20	41	10	11	22	15
Should not	73	52	84	82	75	73
No answer	7	7	6	7	3	12

Whoever wins today, do you think the new government should or should not increase income tax by 1p in the pound and spend it on Britain's schools?

Should	72	61	75	83	79	71
Should not	23	32	19	14	19	18
No answer	5	7	6	3	2	11

Q: How much do you or disagree with the following statements: 'Private enterprise is the best way to solve Britain's problems'

	1992 All	1997 All	Change	1997 Old Lab	1997 New Lab
Agree strongly	18	13	−5	7	7
Agree	29	28	−1	12	26
Neither	27	32	+5	32	34
Disagree	20	20	0	36	24
Disagree strongly	6	7	+1	13	9

'The government should redistribute income from the better-off to those who are less well-off'

Agree strongly	27	30	+3	50	32
Agree	33	31	−2	30	33
Neither	21	23	+2	15	22
Disagree	13	12	−1	3	10
Disagree strongly	6	5	−1	2	3

Note: 'Old Lab' are people who voted Labour in 1992 and 1997

Source: BBC/NOP exit poll

doing more than Conservative policies to 'make things better', despite the belief that Labour would be as likely to raise taxes as the Tories. Despite Labour's insistence that it would stick to the Conservative spending targets it would inherit in government, it seems likely that many voters expected and wanted Labour to raise taxes to spend more on public services. What is certain is that the mood of most voters was more radical on tax-and-spend than Labour's manifesto.

The same is true in other areas. Early in the campaign, Labour had some difficulty explaining its attitude towards Britain's air traffic control: would a Labour government implement plans to privatise it, despite having said publicly in October 1996 that it would not? The issue arose in the election campaign because the revenue from privatisation was built into the Conservatives' projections for the late nineties. However, Labour appeared generally nervous about being seen to be anti-privatisation. It should not have been. Three our of four voters thought the new government, after the election, 'should not carry out any further privatisation'. Were 'new Labour' voters—those who voted Labour in 1997 but not 1992—keener on privatisation than 'old Labour' voters? A little: new Labour voters divided 73 to 15% against privatisation, while old Labour voters divided 91 to 7% against.

The exit poll also re-tested two propositions that it had included in the equivalent survey in 1992, on private enterprise and on redistribution. It found no evidence that voters had grown any more inclined over the five years to believe in private enterprise, or any less inclined to favour redistribution. Indeed, the proportion agreeing that 'private enterprise is the best way to solve Britain's problems' fell from 47 to 41%, while the proportion agreeing that 'the government should redistribute income from the better-off to those who are less well-off' was virtually unchanged at 61%. These questions did, however, reveal some difference in attitudes in 1997 between 'old Labour' and 'new Labour' voters. 'Old Labour' divided two-to-one against the proposition that 'private enterprise is the best way to solve Britain's problems' (19% agreed, 39% disagreed), while 'new Labour' voters were evenly divided: 33% agreed, 33% disagreed. When asked whether 'the government should redistribute income from the better-off to those who are less well-off', 'old Labour' voters divided: 80% agree, 5% disagree, while 'new Labour' voters were less enthusiastic redistributionists: 65% agreed, 13% disagreed. By far the biggest single difference concerned those who 'strongly' agreed: 50% of 'old Labour' voters, but only 32% of 'new Labour' voters.

Best Prime Minister

Many of the findings concerning the perceived competence, record and likely future performance of the main parties reflect the way the Labour and Conservative parties had evolved under Tony Blair and John Major. But what about the reputations of the leaders themselves? The analysis poll asked voters who they thought would make the best Prime Minister, irrespective of how they had just voted. The division of opinion almost exactly reflected the three-party division of the national vote, with 47% saying Blair, 33% Major and 20% Paddy Ashdown.

Yet within these overall figures lies some intriguing political cross-dressing. Tory voters were actually more loyal to Major (89% naming him as best Prime Minister) than Labour voters were to Blair (84%). The difference is accounted for mainly by the 12% of Labour supporters who thought that Ashdown would make the best premier (compared with only 5% of Tories who held that view). A large minority of Liberal Democrats returned the compliment: 30% of them named Blair as the best Prime Minister (a figure that helps to explains why Ashdown's overall rating was down from 26% to 20% since 1992: five years earlier only 13% of Liberal Democrats had named Neil Kinnock as the best Prime Minister). As percentages of the overall voting population, 12% of Labour supporters and 30% of Liberal Democrats amount to almost exactly the same number: 5% of all voters. If we count them as a rough proxy for the number of tactical voters, then it would seem that fully 10% of all voters plumped tactically for Labour or the Liberal Democrats in order to defeat the Conservatives. That figure must obviously be treated with great caution. Some Labour voters undoubtedly held

8. Best Prime Minister (%)

Q: Regardless of how you voted today, who do you think would make the best Prime Minister?

	1992 %	1997 %	Change
Neil Kinnock/Tony Blair	30	47	+17
John Major	45	33	−12
Paddy Ashdown	26	20	−6

%	All	Con	Lab	Lib Dem	Ex-Con	New Lab
Tony Blair	47	6	84	30	42	79
John Major	33	89	4	13	27	7
Paddy Ashdown	20	5	12	57	31	14

Q: Regardless of how you voted do you think that (a) John Major is a strong leader of a weak leader, or (b) Tony Blair is a strong leader or a weak leader?

	All ...		Ex-Conservative		New Labour	
		%				
	Major	Blair	Major	Blair	Major	Blair
Strong	35	77	28	80	10	96
Weak	65	23	72	20	90	4

Q: Regardless of how you voted do you think that (a) John Major can be trusted or cannot be trusted, or (b) Tony Blair can be trusted or cannot be trusted?

Can be trusted	57	56	58	61	33	90
Cannot be trusted	43	44	42	39	67	10

Source: BBC/NOP exit poll

Ashdown in high regard without any thought of tactical voting; likewise some Lib Dem voters think highly of Tony Blair. However, the scale of the cross-dressing does seem broadly consistent with the scale of tactical voting evident in the pattern of constituency results.

The analysis poll also asked about two key attributes of the two main parties leaders: their strength and their trustworthiness. Blair was seen as far stronger than Major—but no more trustworthy. The pattern was particularly marked among ex-Conservatives. Almost as many of them were willing to put their trust in Major (58%) as into Blair (61%). However, when they were asked whether each leader was strong or weak, the figures for the two leaders could scarcely have been more different: Major—strong 28%, weak 72%; Blair—strong 80%, weak 20%.

Party images

If the figures for the images of the rival party leaders contained a mixed message, the figures for the images of the parties did not. The exit poll looked at them in two distinct ways; Labour easily outscored the Conservatives on both (Table 9). Voters divided two-to-one in favour of the view that Labour was good for all classes, not just one. The figures for the Tories was almost exactly the reverse. Among Conservative defectors, 71% said the Tories were good for only one class; while among converts to Labour, as many as 87% said Labour was good for all classes. This question has proved in the past to be strongly associated with the ups and downs of party fortunes and 1997 proved to be no exception: Labour clearly won the battle to be perceived as the 'one

9. Party images %

Q: Regardless of how you voted today, do you think that the Conservative Party is good for one class or good for all classes? Regardless of how you voted today, do you think that the Labour Party is good for one class or good for all classes?

	All ...		Ex-Conservative voters ...		New Labour voters ...	
	Con	Lab	Con	Lab	Con	Lab
Good for one class	68	31	71	38	84	13
Good for all classes	32	69	29	62	16	87

Q: Regardless of how you voted today, do you think that the Conservative Party is united or divided?
Q: Regardless of how you voted today, do you think that the Labour Party is united or divided?

United	16	66	11	57	7	83
Divided	84	34	89	43	93	17

Source: BBC/NOP exit poll

nation' party. It is worth recalling the origin of the phrase. In *Sybil* Disraeli depicted 'two nations; between whom there is no intercourse and no sympathy ... the rich and the poor'. That seems to be a fair description of how many voters in 1997 viewed Britain after eighteen years of Conservative rule, with the Tory party associated firmly with the rich.

An even greater contrast between Labour and Conservative emerged when voters were asked whether they thought the two main parties were united or divided. A two-to-one majority thought Labour was united; but only 16% thought the Conservatives were united. Among Conservative defectors, 93% thought the party divided, while only 7% said it was united. Even loyal Tory voters were largely unconvinced by the protestations of their party's leaders that the Conservatives were in one mind. Tory voters who regarded the party as divided outnumbered those who thought it united by three-to-two.

Europe

Finally, one of the core issues in the campaign was Europe. The exit poll asked a specific question about the single currency. As Table 10 shows, only 17% thought Britain should say now that it will join a single currency; twice as many (36%) thought Britain should say now it will never join a single currency. However, the largest group (47%) approved of the 'wait and see' approach. The 'wait and see' plurality was highest among Conservative voters. Liberal Democrat supporters

10. Attitudes to EMU %

Q: There are proposals for the pound to be replaced by a new single European Currency throughout Europe—the Euro. What do you think the government's policy should be?

	All	Con	Lab	Lib Dem	Ex-Con	New Lab
To say now that Britain will *never* join the single currency	36	41	30	36	44	34
To say now that Britain *will* join the single currency	17	8	23	20	16	22
To wait and see what happens	47	51	48	44	40	44

Source: BBC/NOP exit poll

divided in similar numbers to the electorate as a whole: the exit poll provided no evidence that Lib Dem voters were as enthusiastic as the party leadership about joining the single currency. This is in line with almost every survey of the past twenty years: the Lib Dems, like the SDP and the Liberals in the past, have regularly attracted votes despite of, as much as because of, their pro-European stance. Overall, the responses to the exit poll question on Europe confirm what pre-election polls found: that there is little positive public appetite for abandoning the pound. However, it is surely significant that almost two voters out of three did not oppose the single currency on principle. This suggests that it would be premature to assume that a referendum would kill British participation. The fact that almost half of all voters opt for 'wait and see' indicates that large shifts in opinion may occur—especially in circumstances in which the single currency was in existence and working, and an enthusiastic government campaigned for British participation with the backing of much of industry, the City and the trade union movement.

Conclusions

What conclusions should we draw from this data? Table 11 shows the results of a four-stage multivariate analysis. This shows that social class still counts; as does age. The figures also counter the view that 'the economy, stupid' does not apply to Britain: fairly or unfairly, judgements of the Tories' economic record counted against them. Controlling for social class and economic factors, the reputations of Tony Blair and the image of new Labour contributed significantly to the size of the government's majority. These findings underline what the opinion polls found during the 1992–97 Parliament. The 'feelgood factor' declined sharply after sterling left Europe's exchange rate mechanism in September 1992; and this precipitated a marked fall in Conservative support. In 1994, the feelgood factor started to improve—but the Tories fell back further (as did the Liberal Democrats) following Tony Blair's election as Labour leader. His election undoubtedly created a 'Blair premium' in Labour's support. From the beginning of 1995, Conservative support gradually started to recover, in line with the feelgood factor; however the Tories failed to erode the 'Blair premium', which persisted until the general election.

There are two ways to view the 'Blair premium'; either or both may be valid: time will tell. The first is that it indicates a move towards 'presidential' general elections. In the past, British general elections have appeared to be largely immune to the impact of personalities. In 1979, James Callaghan was far more popular than Margaret Thatcher: yet the Conservatives won the election. Each election has produced speculation, predicting (and usually deploring) the arrival of a campaign decided by leadership-appeal rather than party-choice. Perhaps the 1997 election saw reality begin to converge with the prediction. The second way to view the data is to apply a different label—not (or not only) the 'Blair premium' but the end of the 'old Labour discount'. The annual British Social Attitudes series has shown, each year since 1983, that 'Thatcherite' values never took hold of the British electorate, which consistently showed a preference for more socialised values. It is possible that the main obstacle to Labour returning to power was—the Labour Party. It was seen as old-fashioned, incompetent and over-dependent on the trade unions. Blair's election as Labour Party leader removed the factors that caused Labour's support to remain suppressed, and allowed it to recover to more normal levels. Either way, Labour's huge victory was not simply a product of a negative anti-Conservative vote. The size of the majority owes much to the positive reputation of new Labour and Tony Blair. As Table 11 shows, among Labour voters, the positive attraction of Labour's leader and the party's image was far stronger than the negative rejection of the Tories.

11. Models of voting choice

	Model 1	Model 2	Model 3	Model 4
Social cleavages				
Social class	0.17**	0.08**	0.06**	0.06**
Age	−0.14**	−0.11**	−0.08**	−0.06**
Housing tenure	0.03	0.03	0.01	0.01
Gender	0.00	0.04*	0.02	0.00
Retrospective economy				
Britain's economy last 5 years		−0.29**	−0.17**	−0.11**
Own living standards last 5 years		−0.19**	−0.10**	−0.06*
Leadership image				
Blair best PM			0.30**	0.22**
Blair trustworthy			0.22**	0.14**
Blair strong/weak			0.10**	0.06*
Major trustworthy			−0.09**	−0.04*
Major strong/weak			−0.05*	−0.03
Party image				
Labour policies make things better				0.26**
Labour united/divided				0.14**
Labour good for one class/good for all				0.11**
Con policies make things better				−0.05*
Conservatives united/divided				−0.04
Cons good for once class/good for all				−0.04
R^2	0.06	0.21	0.37	0.46

Note: These models use regression analysis with the Labour/non-Labour vote as the dependent variable and mean substitution for missing data. The figures represent standardized beta coefficients: ** significant at $p > .01$; * significant at $p > .05$

So did the economy count for nothing? Did Britain's voters give Labour its biggest ever victory because they took no account of Britain's record of growth, low inflation, cheap mortgages and tumbling unemployment? No: public perceptions of the economy did matter (see the discussion by Gavin and Sanders in this volume). Bad though the Conservative defeat was, it could have been worse. Had the feelgood factor not risen steadily during the second half of the 1992–97

Parliament, it is likely that the Tory defeat would have been even more catastrophic, and possible that (as happened to the Conservatives in Canada in 1992) they might not even have survived as the main opposition party.

1 The raw data from the 1997 BBC/NOP prediction poll overstated Labour's lead; the raw data from the analysis poll understated the lead. Data from both polls has been adjusted to match the election result, and a similar procedure was followed concerning the 1992 exit poll. That adjusted data forms the basis for this chapter. Both BBC/NOP exit polls, in common with conventional opinion polls, covered Great Britain but not Northern Ireland.

The Economy and Voting

BY NEIL T. GAVIN* AND DAVID SANDERS†

HAROLD WILSON said 'All political history shows that the standing of the government and its ability to hold the confidence of the electorate at the general election depend on the success of its economic policy'. Several decades on, an aide-memoire in Clinton's office at the 1992 election read 'It's the economy, stupid'—a reminder of the centrality of the issue to the public and, therefore, to the campaign. Politicians, pundits and scholars commonly regard the economy as an issue of critical importance at elections. The 1997 campaign was no exception. Compared with our European partners, and the OECD average, the Major government's objective economic record looked remarkably healthy. The Conservative Party certainly thought this was a trump card, and they high-lighted their record of taxation, inflation, economic growth and unemployment prominently in their campaign. Moreover, Gallup polls suggested that the public regarded economic issues in general, and unemployment and inflation in particular, as among the most important issues facing the country. So the paradox for the conventional wisdom of economic voting is why, given their economic record, and the salience of these issues, did the Conservatives suffer their worst result since 1832?

The central argument we shall put forward to explain this conundrum is that the objective economic record of the Major government was remarkably strong, but nevertheless the Conservative reputation for sound economic management was fatally undermined by the ERM crisis in September 1992. Yet sterling crises early in an administration are rarely sufficient by themselves to defeat a government. We suggest that one reason why the Conservatives failed to recover support from their mid-term slump was because of television coverage of their economic record in the six-to-eight month run up to polling day. In particular, a content analysis of economic news on the flagship BBC1 and ITN evening news programmes indicates three important factors which may have contributed towards public perceptions of the Conservative economic record: in coverage of the government's economic record the ratio of good news to bad news stories showed a positive balance, but the margin was relatively modest; moreover the Conservatives could not benefit much from this as the news coverage of Labour's economic

* Lecturer in Politics at Liverpool University.
† Pro-Vice Chancellor and Professor of Government at Essex University.

policy proposals was also relatively positive; and, lastly, coverage of the divisions in Conservative policy towards the proposed single European currency highlighted damaging splits within the party, and obscured other issues during the last part of the campaign. Other contributors to this issue confirm the depths of the government's mid-term slump (see Rose) and also the continuing importance of retrospective evaluations of the government's economic record on voting choice (see Kellner). Together this helps to explain part of the conundrum for theories of economic voting, although we await more detailed surveys of voters to confirm the impact of these factors among the electorate.

The government's economic record 1992–97

The most striking long-term factor influencing Conservative popularity was 'Black Wednesday', on 16 September 1992, which saw sterling suffer its most serious crisis of international confidence since 1967, wildly fluctuating interest rates, and the ignominious exit of Britain from the ERM. In the wake of this catastrophe the Conservatives were excoriated in the normally loyal press (see Seymour-Ure in this volume). The whole episode critically undermined public confidence in the Conservative's ability to handle the economy and, thereby, sowed the seed of electoral disaster in 1997. In terms of Conservative support, the ERM crisis had a profound effect on voters' economic perceptions (see Whiteley in this volume). The feelgood factor, which was already declining, plummeted even further. After September 1992, voters were far more likely to hold the government responsible for the length and depth of the recession than they had been before.[1] Much more seriously, however, the Conservatives' long-standing lead over Labour on economic management competence was dramatically reversed—a position from which the Conservatives never recovered during the 1992 parliament (see Figure 1).

In different circumstances, the loss of this lead might have proved ephemeral. As economic good times returned, the Conservatives might have seen their traditional economic competence lead (and their popularity) restored.[2] In the event, however, this did not happen, for several reasons. The ERM crisis probably crystallised doubts about the Conservatives that were already lurking at the back of voters' minds. First, the Conservatives had promised that their re-election would witness a rapid end to the recession yet by the autumn of 1992 there was little sign that recovery was under way. Second, the Conservatives' 1992 campaign had successfully portrayed Labour as the party of tax increases yet, by the autumn of that year it was already clear that the forthcoming Budget would introduce tax increases in order to rectify the ballooning public finance deficit. This may have undermined public trust in the Conservatives as the tax-cutting party, just like George Bush's betrayal of his 'Read my lips' pledge. Third, the government was obliged to jettison the public explanation that it had previously been

Figure 1. Economic management competence: Conservative lead over Labour

Note: This time-series is constructed from responses to the following survey question, 'With Britain in economic difficulties, which party do you think could handle the problem best — the Conservatives under Mr Major or Labour under Mr Blair?' (% answering 'Conservative' minus % answering 'Labour').

Source: Gallup Political Index

offering in order to justify Britain's membership of the ERM and the economic strictures this entailed, that is, that joining the club was the only viable route to sustained, non-inflationary growth. This was even clearer as Britain's economy began to flourish outside the system, while France, Germany and Spain suffered from long lines at the unemployment office, painful cuts in welfare, and sluggish growth. In the wake of Black Wednesday, the government was obliged to argue that economic growth could best be achieved by Britain's remaining outside the ERM. Such a policy U-turn, without a plausible story to justify it, engendered a loss of public confidence in the government's managerial capabilities. To add insult to Conservative injury, Labour's new moderation and respectability under the stewardship of John Smith and Tony Blair transformed Labour's image in the minds of sufficient electors for new Labour to claim to be the party of both managerial competence and moderate taxation. Combined with the widespread sense of economic insecurity that afflicted large numbers of voters during the 1992–97 parliament, Labour's new-found 'electability' made it difficult for the Conservatives to regain their previous reputation for superior economic management skills.

    In the wake of the ERM crisis, the government sought to rekindle voters' enthusiasm for the Conservative Party by a strategy of low interest rates, export-lead economic recovery, and reductions in taxation which together, it was assumed, would reinforce the recovery and restore the feelgood factor. Indeed, in the run up to the election the economy seemed to show all the signs of steady non-inflationary growth that ought to presage political recovery for the incumbent (see Table 1). At the time of the election the balance of payments deficit had dropped sharply and house prices were showing signs of recovery, even if these were not particularly spectacular. Moreover, inflation had been below 3% for most of the previous three years and was falling. Unemployment too had been falling for a year and had seen some spectacular falls since the autumn of 1996 (only part of which was due to the introduction of the Job Seeker's Allowance).

1. The Conservative economic record

		RPI	GDP	Unemployment	Consumer durable expenditure	Average earnings	Balance of payments
1992	Q1	5.7	−1.4	9.1	7373	7.3	−2681
	Q2	5.3	−0.7	9.5	7589	6.5	−2963
	Q3	4.3	0.0	9.7	7801	5.8	−3321
	Q4	3.7	−0.1	10.1	7914	5.0	−4139
1993	Q1	3.4	1.5	10.5	8058	4.4	−3746
	Q2	2.8	1.7	10.4	8143	3.8	−3257
	Q3	3.1	2.2	10.3	8585	3.3	−3178
	Q4	2.7	2.8	10.1	8667	3.0	−3279
1994	Q1	2.7	3.0	9.9	8760	3.9	−3141
	Q2	2.4	4.0	9.6	8975	3.9	−2539
	Q3	2.2	4.0	9.3	9053	3.8	−2234
	Q4	2.3	4.2	8.9	9320	3.8	−2917
1995	Q1	2.7	3.4	8.5	9254	3.6	−1603
	Q2	2.7	2.7	8.3	9204	3.6	−3193
	Q3	2.9	2.0	8.2	9525	3.3	−3596
	Q4	2.9	1.8	8.1	9372	3.3	−3192
1996	Q1	2.9	2.0	7.9	9615	3.4	−3726
	Q2	2.8	1.9	7.8	9991	3.8	−3008
	Q3	2.9	2.0	7.6	10051	4.0	−2913
	Q4	3.2	2.6	7.2	10204	4.4	−2581
1997	Q1	2.9	*	6.5	*	*	*

Notes: RPI: % change in inflation, excluding mortgages; GDP: gross domestic product, % change over previous year; Unemployment: claimant count as % of the workforce; Consumer durable expenditure: £m; Average earnings: % change over previous year; Balance of payments: trade in goods and services, £m.; * not available.

Source: Economic Trends

Consumer confidence *did* show a modest recovery during 1995–97, but although personal taxation was considerably reduced in April 1996, and again in April 1997, neither this expedient nor the burgeoning 'real' economy produced the political pay-off that Conservative strategists had anticipated. The Conservatives' opinion poll ratings improved during 1995–97, but never sufficiently to make John Major's re-election a realistic possibility. Table 2 shows the party lead on a range of economic topics. The figures are taken from the Gallup Political Index surveys and represent the percentage thinking that Labour could best

2. Perceptions of Labour and Conservative parties on economic issues

	1992	1997	Change
Inflation	−29	+3	+32
Tax	−20	+11	+31
Unemployment	+16	+41	+24

Note: These figures represent the Conservative or Labour party lead as the party best qualified to handle the issue. They are calculated from responses to the survey question. 'I'm going to read a list of problems facing the country. Could you please tell me, for each of them, which party you personally think would handle the problem best?'.

Source: Gallup post-election polls, 2–3.4.92 and 10–11.5.97

handle the issue *minus* the percentage thinking the Conservatives could best handle it. In 1992 Labour were behind the Conservatives on inflation and taxes, and only just ahead on unemployment. By 1997 the party difference had been neutralised on inflation and, most importantly, the lead had tipped in favour of Labour on taxation. Despite government tax cuts and palpable economic recovery, the public were disinclined to give any credit to John Major's party.

Since 1979 successive Conservative chancellors had been able to rely upon a pre-election boom to boost economic expectations and produce a solid recovery in support for the government. The trick had worked splendidly in 1983 (with a little help from the Falklands factor), in 1987, and in 1992. After Black Wednesday, however, the Conservatives found that even quite a large improvement in personal economic expectations elicited only a modest recovery in government support. As Kellner argues elsewhere in this volume, economic calculations still mattered in 1997—both to electors deciding how they should vote and to the government seeking to restore its economic management reputation. Unfortunately for the Conservatives, the Downsian electorate decided that their economic fortunes were more likely to be maximised by a new Labour government under Tony Blair.

Television news coverage of the economy

So improvements in objective economic indicators failed to translate into government support. Why? The failure of the Conservatives to capitalise on the thriving 'real' economy was an important dimension of their defeat in 1997, but it is also an anomaly in terms of the conventional Downsian notion of the 'primacy of the pocketbook'. In this view, people do not require a great deal of information about politics, politicians or policies in order to decide how to vote. People only need a firm sense, as most tend to have, of their own and the country's financial circumstances; an idea of how these have changed since the last election, and are likely to change in the future; and developed views on the retrospective government record and prospective party policies. Yet information about the economy comes to voters directly (through the pocketbook economy) and indirectly (through perceptions of economic conditions provided by the mass media).

Evaluations of the economy by news presenters, journalists and commentators is often thought to be of particular importance.[3] The balance
of good and bad economic news may influence public perceptions of a
government's competence in handling the economy, and, through this,
its popularity.

A good deal of economic news does, however, take the form of
political sniping—with reports of the statements and claims from one
side followed by coverage of counter-statement and counter-claim from
the other. An example of this was the Prime Minister's statement in
September 1996 that the government had produced low taxes—a claim
that brought little more than denial and counter-claim from Labour and
the Liberal Democrats (BBC, 18.8.96). These sorts of conflictual stories
may have a role in shaping the public agenda, but research on the
impact of news both here and in the United States suggests this has a
limited role in determining the public standing of the parties.[4] This
reflects the fact that such stories generally constitute little more than
point-scoring by partisan, and hence untrustworthy, sources. In the
midst of this political dogfight there is, however, a steady stream of
news that may have had a direct bearing on the fortunes of the
government.

To assess the significance of this sort of coverage we used a form of
content analysis to analyse news touching directly on economic matters.
We looked at the period encompassing the all-important 'near-term
campaign' (from autumn 1996 to the election).[5] Television (in contrast
to the press) is commonly found to be the most important and trusted
source of political information for the public and so we centred our
analysis on weekday news from BBC and ITN's flagship, prime-time
news programmes (the Nine O'Clock News and Ten O'Clock News)
from September 1996 up to (and through) the election campaign. The
emphasis here was on the symbolic significance of this news—the
signals it gave about the health or otherwise of the national economy
rather than the statements and claims of politicians. The coding of the
material revolved around the sentences in news text which dealt with
trends in a range of key economic indicators. These included references
to the general state of the economy (features like growth, production
and investment) as well as inflation/prices, tax, jobs, sales, living
standards, wages, the balance of payment, interest rate fluctuations,
PSBR, and the state of the housing market and house prices. In terms of
presentational form these can all be regarded as 'valence' issues, with
upward and downward movement carrying fairly obvious positive and
negative connotations. So, for instance, a sentence carrying a references
to unemployment going down, is counted as 'positive'; alternatively, if
inflation is reported as creeping up, this is counted as 'negative'.[6] All
references of this sort were then added up *within* the story to determine
whether there is, overall, a positive or negative balance (with a positive
balance counting as + 1 for a 'good news' story and a negative balance

counting as –1 for a 'bad news' story). This technique gives a course-grained measure of the balance of 'good' and 'bad' news output, but it has been used successfully in research modelling the influence of news on public opinion. So, did this economic news on television have an impact on the fortunes of the Conservative government? Table 3 below gives an a clear impression of the balance of good and bad news stories over the months leading up to (and through) the election.

3. Balance of economic news on BBC and ITN, September 1996 to May 9

| | BBC | | ITN | | |
	Good news	Bad news	Good news	Bad news	Overall balance
September	7	4	3	1	+5
October	12	7	3	4	+4
November	10	4	5	3	+8
December	4	4	4	3	+1
January	12	8	3	7	0
February	9	4	5	3	+7
March	8	5	6	3	+6
April/Campaign	8	4	2	1	+5

Note: For the definition and methodology see text.

Source: BBC Nine O'Clock and ITN Ten O'Clock News, September 1996 to May 1997.

Although there were fluctuations from month to month, the results suggest that good news outweighed bad news throughout this period. Yet in this overall climate of positive news about the economy, why did the Conservative government fail to make significant headway in the polls? The answer has three parts. Firstly, the balance of news was positive throughout, but it was never overwhelming large: for every story about growth in high street sales (BBC, 18.9.96) or dropping levels of inflation (ITN, 17.4.97) there were frequent corresponding stories with a negative slant – like rising interest rates (ITN, 30.10.96) or job losses at Halewood (BBC, 16.1.97). Here the overall quantity of 'good' news offered a rather limited platform for a pre-election surge in government popularity.

Second, although the health of the economy was reported in a broadly positive light, in 1997 Labour nevertheless achieved relatively positive coverage for its manifesto pledges on the economy. In 1992 commentators on news programmes were often relatively critical about Labour's policies on a range of issues, notably taxation, national insurance and the minimum wage, while they were relatively positive towards the Conservatives.[7] In contrast, the pre-election commentary in 1996–97 was much more finely balanced. In November 1996 the government's policy on 'Workfare' received some positive coverage and the Conservatives could claim some success in the way the debate on the European Court's ruling on the '48 hour week' unfolded. Yet the BBC reported in some detail an IMF warning to the government over the level of public sector borrowing (27.9.96) and there was some critical coverage of the government's Private Finance Initiative (21.10.96). Michael Heseltine's 'astonishing squabble' with leading industrialists (21.1.97) was also prominently reported. Both channels reported the negative impact of the Budget on local government finances and the Council Tax (27.11.96). And in a BBC report on the sustainability of the recovery Peter Jay, in a response to a question about whether 'boom' would turn to 'bust', noted that, '..we could even actually get the bust without ever having had the boom' (24.3.97). On the other hand, Labour had more balanced coverage than in 1992, particularly on tax, where in the pre-election phase a great deal of the coverage was of the 'statement/ counter-statement' variety. Moreover, what appeared like endorsement by the Catholic Church for Labour's policy on a minimum wage was covered on BBC and ITN (21.10.96). The BBC prominently covered a report by Warburgs to the effect that Labour's windfall tax was financially feasible (7.11.96) and flagged a report from leading industrialists that seemed to endorse Labour's economic strategy (21.1.97). Unlike 1992, this balance of economic policy commentary on television gave the Conservative Party no significant advantage that could translate into support in the run up to the election.

During the election campaign both the main channels covered the economy in the full and professional manner we would expect from public service providers of news (see Semetko and Scammell this volume). There was a great deal of coverage of party manifestos, statements about party positions and comments by politicians on their respective promises, liberally peppered with interviews with the party leaders, as well as numerous location reports. Inevitably, however, the 'statement-claim-and-counter-claim' format predominated, a feature slightly more pronounced on ITN than BBC. There were few (if any) gaffes to exploit and, in the event, relatively little *pointed* commentary on the actual weaknesses and strengths of respective positions. Where this did occur, commentators were equally critical of the economic policies of each of the main political parties, whether Liberal Democrat plans to raise and spend £2b; Conservative 'massaging' of growth figures; or, to a limited extent, Labour's minimum wage proposals. As far as television coverage was concerned, however, the Conservatives landed no knock-out punches on Labour's minimum wage proposals, 'windfall tax' policy, or their tax plans generally. There was a tendency on both channels for reporters to suggest that after the election the public might have to pay more tax, irrespective of which party won, which was reflected in public expectations (see Kellner Table 6). This tendency is perhaps exemplified by Peter Jay's comment towards the end of the campaign. In response to a question about whether it would matter, economically speaking, which party a person voted for, he replied, 'Not much, if you assume that both parties will govern precisely according to the scripts in their manifestos' (BBC, 3.4.97).

The final explanation for the government's failure to capitalise on good news about the economy lies in the Conservatives Achilles heel—

news about Tory party policy, and internal splits, concerning Britain's future membership of the European Monetary Union. The seismic rumblings of the Conservative Party's deep divisions on the European single currency, and the acrimonious squabbles between the competing factions that often came in their wake, were regularly and prominently portrayed on television, especially in the last few weeks of the campaign when Europe became the most important issue in coverage (Golding, Deacon and Billig *The Guardian* 2.5.97). Europe came to dominate coverage of the economy. The following examples give a flavour of wording of the opening sentences of economic news stories across the near-term campaign and the election proper: 'John Major steps in to try to limit the damage of a new Tory spat about Europe' (BBC, 24.9.96) and 'Cabinet rift over Rifkind's single currency hostility.' (ITN, 19.2.97). Coverage of this sort appeared on twenty-five separate occasions in the pre-Christmas period alone (a pattern which re-emerged in the campaign). Bearing in mind that there are normally only three to four economic stories on each channel in any particular week — ranging over a very broad spectrum of topics — this represents a considerable quantity of coverage framed in rather uncompromising language. Internal dissent within the Conservative party over the single currency dominated economic news in the third and forth weeks of the campaign, with considerable attention given to Angela Browning, Dame Angela Rumbold and John Horam, and numerous backbenchers, publicly breaking ranks. Divisions culminated in John Major's 'impassioned plea to his election candidates to unite behind the government's line on Europe.' (headline, BBC, 16.4.97) and his attempt '. . . to heal his party's split over Europe by offering backbenchers a free vote on the single currency' (headline, BBC 17.4.97). In contrast, there were few references before or during the campaign to Labour's eurosceptic wing. It is generally considered that the economy is important to a party's electoral prospects. Yet it is also part of established wisdom that it is extremely difficult for a divided party to get elected (or re-elected). In this context it is hardly surprising that the Conservatives were unable to build the momentum necessary to achieve a winning share of the vote in May 1997 when divisions over a major issue of economic policy were so open, and so widely reported (see Kellner on party images in this volume).

Conclusions

We have yet to look at the impact of media coverage on individual voters, and this analysis of television news requires further exploration once data from the 1997 British Election Study is released. Nevertheless this preliminary analysis suggests that, despite the paradox of the Conservative government losing despite a strong economic record, still the economy probably did have a significant impact on the outcome of the 1997 general election. The devastating defeat for the Conservatives had its roots in events of Black Wednesday in September 1992, in particular the British ejection from the ERM and the tax rises required to deal with the ballooning deficit. Ironically, the economic fallout from the ERM crisis produced the climate for the sustainable, low inflationary growth that Britain had sought for decades and which, in normal circumstances, would have given an enormous boost to the standing of the incumbent. But in the event it fatally undermined public confidence in the government's ability to handle the economy. By 1997 the 'green shoots' of a house-price recovery were beginning to show, and in a context of promising balance of payments statistics, falling unemployment and low inflation, the Conservatives could have expected to have made ground on Labour. In the run up to the election, and, indeed, during the campaign, the government did make up some lost ground in terms of public attitudes towards their policies and their general economic management capacities. Without their economic record, as Kellner argues, the Conservatives could have been damaged even more badly. In the event, however, the Conservatives suffered from rather lukewarm coverage of an economy that was, in fact, doing quite well. Unlike 1992 the Conservatives were unable to land any telling punches on Labour, and they were the victims of rancorous, public and all too newsworthy divisions on Europe and the single currency. In the end, it seems likely that good objective economic indicators were insufficient to outweigh these other considerations. Just like George Bush in 1992, in a period of relative peace and prosperity, the public had apparently made up its mind to overturn conventional wisdom and 'throw the rascals out'.

1 See D. Sanders, 'Economic Performance, Management Competence and the Outcome of the Next Election', *Political Studies* 44, 1996.

2 For a useful guide to the respective theoretical strands, see D. Denver and G. Hands, *Issues and Controversies in British Electoral Behaviour* (Harvester and Wheatsheaf, 1992), p. 241. See also M. Lewis-Beck, *Economics and Elections* (University of Michigan Press, 1990).

3 In recent studies, the comment by politicians tend to be excluded from analysis, the assumption being that the public see politicians as self-serving and less than trustworthy source, and so lack persuasive power—see D. Sanders, D. Marsh and D. Ward, 'The Electoral Impact of Press Coverage of the Economy, 1979–87', *British Journal of Political Science* 23, 1993; and N.T. Gavin and D. Sanders, 'Economy, News and Public Opinion: Britain in the Mid-1990s' in N.T. Gavin (ed.), *Economy, Media and Public Knowledge* (Cassell, forthcoming).

4 See the studies cited in note 3, as well as W.J. Severin, *Communication Theories* (Longman, 1988).

5 A term elaborated in D. Butler and D. Kavanagh, *The British General Election of 1992* (Macmillan, 1995).

6 For details of the coding scheme see N.T. Gavin and D. Sanders, 'The Impact of Television News on Public Perceptions of the Economy and Government, 1993–94' in D. Farrell, D. Broughton, D. Denver and J. Fisher (eds), *British Elections and Parties Yearbook, 1996* (Frank Cass, 1996), p. 68.

7 N.T. Gavin, 'Television News and the Economy: The Pre-Campaign Coverage', *Parliamentary Affairs* 45, 1992.

Regional Voting

BY IAN McALLISTER*

ONE of the most significant developments in postwar British politics has been the emergence of a regional divide in voting. Throughout the 1970s and 1980s, the increasing geographical concentration of the vote made the Conservatives the dominant party in the South of England, while Labour was the largest party in the North of England, and in Scotland and Wales. These regional patterns of voting were further exacerbated by the operation of the electoral system, so that the two major parties became either dominant or almost completely absent from large areas of the country. After the 1992 election, for example, Labour held just four of the 109 seats in the South of England, the Conservatives just six of the 36 seats in the North of England. The extent of the regional polarization in voting patterns led some observers to view it as a new political cleavage to rival class in its importance for the parties.[1]

There is little disagreement that there has always been some degree of regionalism in British voting behaviour. Regional factors were integral to the formation of the party system in the 1880s and 1890s, when Labour emerged out of the industrialized North of England, the lowlands of Scotland, and South Wales.[2] In the early part of the century regional divisions weakened in importance, re-emerging in the postwar years.[3] The precise origins of the current patterns of regional voting are disputed. Some have argued that they originate in the mid-1950s[4] or in the 1960s.[5] The major industrial restructuring which took place in the early years of the Thatcher Conservative government has led others to argue that regionalism can be traced to Conservative government policies. In this interpretation, it is these policies which have affected local material conditions in the regions and produced differential economic expectations and local political cultures.[6]

Regional voting, though on a lesser level than previous elections, emerged as a strong element in the Conservative defeat in the 1997 general election. The election left the Conservatives without a single member in Scotland or Wales, although the swing against them in both nations was relatively modest. The most important regional factor which damaged the Conservatives was the swing against them in large parts of the South of England and the Midlands, where they had found strong support during the Thatcher period. Regional voting, then,

* Director of the Research School of Social Sciences at the Australian National University.

coupled with an unprecedented level of tactical voting, helps to explain the devastating result for the Conservatives.

Regional voting in the 1997 election

Under the steady state British party system, near-uniform national swing was the accepted pattern of voting, with each part of the country changing together in the same direction from one general election to the next. As Crewe puts it, 'to know the swing in Cornwall was to know, within a percentage or two, the swing in Caithness'.[7] Uniform national swing had effectively broken down by the 1979 election, and it has been replaced at every general election since by the different regions of Britain moving in different directions and at different levels. The 1997 election was no exception to this pattern of regional diversity. Using the standard regions of England as a measure of regionalism, plus the nations of Scotland and Wales,[8] the mean geographical variation in the vote for the three major parties was nearly 25%, a substantial figure by any standards (Table 1).

Variations in regional voting were generally higher for Labour in 1997 than for either the Conservatives or the Liberal Democrats. The Labour vote ranged from a high of 60.9% in the North of England—a substantial 16.5% higher than the Britain-wide figure—to a low of 26.4% in South West England, representing an overall range of 34.5% of the vote. By contrast, the Conservative vote varied from lows of 17.5% and 19.6% in Scotland and Wales, respectively, and 22.2% in the North of England, to a high of 41.4% in the South East, a range of 23.9% in the vote. The regional variation in the Liberal Democrat vote was, with the exception of the South West where their support is concentrated, considerably less. Excluding the South West, the Liberal Democrat vote varied by 9%.

The Conservatives performed proportionately worse in the regions where they had secured most of their gains during the 1980s. Their

1. Regional voting in the 1997 election

	1997 vote (%)			Mean deviation (%)		
	Con	Lab	Lib Dem	Con	Lab	Lib Dem
England						
North	22.2	60.9	13.3	−9.3	16.5	3.9
North West	26.7	54.2	14.8	−4.8	9.8	−2.4
Yorkshire and Humberside	27.9	51.8	15.9	−3.6	7.4	−1.3
East Midlands	35.5	47.9	12.9	4.0	3.5	−4.3
West Midlands	33.7	47.8	13.8	2.2	3.4	−3.4
London	31.2	49.4	14.6	−0.3	5.0	−2.6
South East	41.4	32.0	21.4	0.3	−12.4	4.2
South West	36.7	26.4	31.3	4.2	−18.0	14.1
East Anglia	38.7	38.3	17.9	7.2	−6.1	0.7
(England total)	32.9	35.7	17.5	1.4	−6.7	0.3
Wales	19.6	54.7	12.4	−11.9	10.3	−4.8
Scotland	17.5	45.6	13.0	−14.0	0.8	−4.2
(Britain total)	31.5	44.4	17.2			

Source: British Parliamentary Constituencies, 1992–97.

greatest losses were in the South: in London the Conservative vote dropped by 14.1%, and in the South East by 13.1% (Table 2). These were the areas where the party had gained most over the previous five general elections. Since 1979, the Conservatives had attracted between 54 and 55% of the vote in the South East, although their share of the vote in London had fluctuated more substantially. Indeed, part of Labour's revival in London can be traced back to the 1992 election, when they attracted 37.1% of the vote, which represented a steady improvement in their vote compared to the disastrous result of 1983, when they gained only 30.4%, little more than six per cent ahead of the Liberal-SDP Alliance. Conversely, the Conservatives suffered their fewest losses in the areas where they were already attracting few votes, notably Wales and Scotland. The party had won just 25.6% of the vote in Scotland in 1992, and there were clearly few additional votes to be lost, even with the intervention of nationalist candidates (see Brown this volume).

2. Changes in the regional vote, 1992–97

	1992–97 vote change (%)		
	Con	Lab	Lib Dem
England			
North	−11.2	+10.2	+2.3
North West	−10.7	+9.7	+1.3
Yorkshire and Humberside	−10.0	+7.5	+0.9
East Midlands	−11.7	+10.7	+1.9
West Midlands	−11.1	+9.0	+1.2
London	−14.1	+12.3	+1.3
South East	−13.1	+11.2	+1.9
South West	−10.9	+7.2	+0.1
East Anglia	−12.3	+10.3	+1.6
(England total)	−11.8	+9.7	+1.4
Wales	−9.0	+5.2	0.0
Scotland	−8.1	+6.6	−0.1
(Britain total)	−11.3	+9.2	+1.2

Source: British Parliamentary Constituencies, 1992–97.

There were also regional variations in electoral participation in the 1997 election. Across Britain as a whole, turnout declined from 77.3% in 1992 to 71.6%, a drop of 5.7% (Table 3). However, there were distinct variations in the level of the decline between the regions. In Scotland, turnout declined by just 3.3%, although it had already been substantially lower than the Britain-wide figure in 1992. Turnout declined much more substantially in the Midlands and in the North of England: the largest decline across the country occurred in the East Midlands, where turnout dropped by 6.8%, albeit from the second highest regional figure in the 1992 election. Clearly, then, there were regional variations not just in the vote in the 1997 election, but in patterns of electoral participation as well (see Denver and Hands this volume).

How does the overall pattern of regional voting in the 1997 election compare with previous elections? Boundary changes make exact com-

3. Regional variations in turnout, 1992–97

England	1992	Turnout (%) 1997	Change
North	75.7	69.7	−6.3
North West	76.5	69.9	−6.6
Yorkshire and Humberside	75.0	68.6	−6.4
East Midlands	80.3	73.5	−6.8
West Midlands	77.3	70.9	−6.4
London	72.9	67.8	−5.1
South East	79.8	73.8	−6.0
South West	80.8	75.1	−5.7
East Anglia	79.8	74.6	−5.2
(England total)	(77.5)	(71.5)	(+1.4)
Wales	78.6	73.5	−5.1
Scotland	74.6	71.3	−3.3
(Britain total)	(77.3)	(71.6)	(−5.7)

Source: British Parliamentary Constituencies, 1992–97.

parisons across time difficult, but a rough comparison of the regional deviation in the vote can be made from the 1979 general election up to 1997. For both the major parties, the regional polarization in the vote peaked at the 1987 election, when the mean deviation in the Labour vote across the English regions and Wales and Scotland was 9.3%, compared to 8.6% for the Conservatives (Figure 1). The Conservative pattern shows a consistent decline in regional polarisation through to 1997, and indeed, the 1997 figure is the lowest of the five most recent general elections. The mean deviation in the Labour vote in 1997, at 8.5%, is almost identical to the 1992 result, and still the third highest

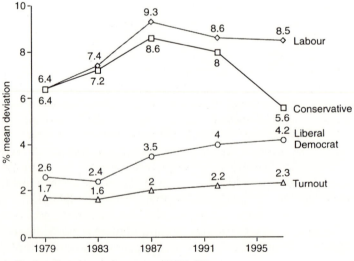

Figure 1. Regional voting and turnout, 1979–97

Note: Estimates are the mean deviation in the vote (or turnout) from the Britain-wide figure, by region.

Source: UK Ecological File, 1979–87; British Parliamentary Constituencies, 1992–97.

over recent general elections. By contrast, the mean deviation in the Liberal Democrat vote has increased since 1987, although the 1997 figure of 4.2% is still half the Labour figure for the same election. The regional deviation in turnout has gradually increased since 1983, standing at 2.3% in 1997.

Regionalism remained an important element in the British 1997 general election, albeit at a reduced level compared to the peak of 1987. The regional vote did, however, display a new characteristic between the major parties in 1997: rather than both parties being affected by regional voting in much the same way, as had occurred in the past, the Labour vote varied from region to region to a much greater extent than the Conservative vote. In part, this was a consequence of incumbency, with Conservative support being more evenly spread across the regions, Labour support less so. But it was also an indirect consequence of various socio-economic and political factors which were associated with particular regions; these factors are examined in the analyses that follow.

Social structure and regional voting

While the patterns of regional voting that have emerged in recent British general elections are undisputed, the explanations for these trends have generated much controversy. One explanation identifies the increasing socio-economic differences between regions as a cause of the change, which is in turn mediated by the changing relationship between the social structure and party alignment.[9] As particular regions have become poorer or more affluent, the social structure has changed, and that in turn has altered levels of support for particular parties. This explanation accords with the Thatcher government's economic policies throughout the 1980s, which caused major economic restructuring in the older industrialised regions, but left the prosperous South of England comparatively untouched. In other words, spatial discrepancies in economic conditions have made the South more affluent (at least relative to the North), creating electoral support for the Conservatives, while the North, Wales and Scotland have become poorer, which in turn has induced greater electoral support for Labour.

This explanation is also in line with conventional theories of class and partisan dealignment in Britain.[10] As the links between class and party and between voter and party have weakened, regional diversity has grown. Voters have become less subject to relatively stable, country-wide political influences that existed in the past and are instead prone to the influences of other forces such as regional economies and political cultures. Without a strong link to a party and to a social class, so the argument goes, voters are more likely to be influenced by factors in their more immediate social milieu.[11] The issue, of course, is what spatial area this social milieu operates at. Studies of compositional and contextual effects on voting have suggested that such milieu are often spatially small, while others have argued that economic factors are more likely to influence voters at a broader regional level.[12] The nine standard regions in England, plus the nations of Scotland and Wales are used here as the measure of social milieu. Although they are necessarily large,[13] they represent spatial units within which we might expect information flow, economic interaction and social exchange to operate most effectively.

Two modifications have been made to the basic argument concerning regional social structure and its potential influence on regional patterns of voting. First, several scholars have argued that a major implication of these increasing spatial discrepancies in socio-economic conditions has been the creation of differential economic expectations in the regions, and the interaction between these expectations and local political cultures.[14] This link between the local economy and political structures, it is argued, has been particularly strong in traditional Labour areas, where reinforcing social and political networks have underpinned political alignments. Second, distinctions between compositional and contextual influences on voting have been emphasised, the former representing a person's position in the social structure and the economic benefits they derive from that position, the latter a person's physical location, which relates to his or her socialisation and informational networks.[15]

The constraints of the aggregate constituency data that are available here make it impossible to take these various factors into account in detail in trying to estimate the net effect of regional voting. It is possible, however, to move some way towards examining the impact of differential regional socio-economic structures in generating regional patterns of voting. The first stage is to identify the main dimensions of regional social structure in England and Wales, and to ascertain to what extent regional voting persists after social structure is taken into account.[16] This is accomplished by taking a range of socio-economic characteristics from the census which are available by parliamentary constituency and subjecting them to factor analysis, a technique which identifies any underlying pattern of relationships that might exist between the characteristics.[17] The factor solution in Table 4 identifies four underlying factors, which together explain 85.2% of the variance.

These four factors represent the major dimensions of social structure of English and Welsh parliamentary constituencies and are broadly comparable with similar exercises that have been conducted in Britain and elsewhere.[18] The first factor identifies the occupational structure of parliamentary constituencies, discriminating between constituencies that have large proportions of skilled and partly skilled workers and small proportions of higher status workers, and constituencies at the other end of the scale which have few manual workers but large proportions of professional and managerial workers. The second factor identifies social deprivation, through the proportions who are economic-

4. Dimensions of social structure in England and Wales

	Factor loadings			
	I	II	III	IV
Manual occupation				
Skilled manual workers	.91	.10	−.06	−.24
Professionals	−.86	−.26	.10	−.03
Managers	−.85	−.44	−.07	−.09
Partly skilled workers	.82	.41	−.05	.06
Social deprivation				
Economically inactive	.15	.90	−.15	.10
On government scheme	.39	.81	−.25	−.03
Reported illness	.39	.81	−.25	−.03
Unemployment	.28	.77	−.21	.46
Familism				
Pensionable age	−.12	.13	−.90	−.11
Working age	−.25	−.25	.88	.00
House owned outright	−.07	−.20	−.82	−.29
Aged 25 to 39	−.15	−.02	.81	.43
Ethnicity				
Indian, Pakistani, Bangladeshi	.20	−.05	.05	.84
Other non-white	−.39	.11	.35	.78
Black	−.13	.19	.36	.75
Eigenvalues	5.6	4.4	1.8	1.0
Per cent variance explained	37.4	29.1	11.9	6.8

Note: Varimax rotated factor loadings from a principal components factor analysis.

Source: British Parliamentary Constituencies, 1992–97.

ally inactive, participating in government work employment schemes, and unemployed, and the proportions of households reporting frequent illness. Although these two factors are both economic, they represent different aspects of the economic character of constituencies: seats with high scores on the manual occupation scale do not necessarily generate a similar score on social deprivation.

The remaining two factors reflect the social characteristics of constituencies. Familism is a common aspect of social structure which identifies areas where there are younger families with children, often in smaller rented accommodation or in accommodation that is being purchased. While there were no measures of family structure available in the constituency file, the factor identifies constituencies with low proportions of persons of pensionable age, higher proportions of persons of working age and aged under 40 years, and low proportions of those who own their homes outright. These characteristics suggest young families, purchasing their homes, and living mainly in urban constituencies. Finally, the fourth factor, ethnicity, identifies the proportions of non-white persons in parliamentary constituencies.

These four dimensions of social structure are effective in discriminating between the constituencies. For example, the most socially deprived constituencies are Liverpool Riverside, the Rhondda and Manchester Central, while the least deprived are Wokingham, Aldershot and Spelthorne. Not surprisingly, these two groups of constituencies are some of the safest in the country: in Liverpool Riverside, for example, the Labour candidate, Louise Ellman, attracted 70.4% of the vote in the 1997 election, while the Conservative candidate polled just 9.5%; in Wokingham, John Redwood for the Conservatives polled 51.1%, the Labour candidate 16.8%. The parliamentary constituencies that come lowest on the manual occupation scale are not surprisingly in some of the most affluent areas of London, such as Kensington and Chelsea, Hampstead and Highgate, and Wimbledon. The most manual constituency in Britain is Pontefract and Castleford, whose Labour candidate, Yvette Cooper, was returned with a majority of over 25,000 of the vote.

There are also major differences between the constituencies in familism. The constituencies with low levels of familism tend to be found outside the major conurbations, in semi-rural areas where there are large numbers of relatively affluent retired persons, such as Devon East and Christchurch. The constituencies with the highest levels of familism are predominantly found in London, where there are comparatively low levels of owner occupation and high proportions of those of working age. At the top of this scale are Lewisham Deptford, Vauxhall and Battersea. Most constituencies with high levels of familism are Labour seats: the correlation between familism and the Labour vote in 1997 was .37, compared to $-.32$ for the Liberal Democrat vote and $-.18$ for the Conservative vote.

Although the average proportion of non-white persons across England and Wales is 5.7%, there is considerable variation across the country: six constituencies record 40% or more non-white persons, ranging from Brent North with 41.5%, to the highest, Brent South, with 55.2% (see Saggar this volume). Two of these six constituencies, Brent South and Ealing Southall, are held by non-white Labour MPs, Paul Boateng and Piara Khambra, respectively.[19] One other constituency, Tottenham, just falls below the 40% non-white figure, and is held by another non-white Labour MP, Bernie Grant. Almost all of the constituencies with significant proportions of non-white voters are Labour: the only non-Labour constituency with more than 15% of its residents who are non-white is Cities of London and Westminster, which was held by Peter Brooke for the Conservatives with a majority of 4,881.

How effective are these four measures of the social structure of parliamentary constituencies in predicting electoral participation and the vote? Table 5 suggests that they are strong predictors, explaining over 70% of the variance in the Conservative and Labour vote and 30% in the case of the Liberal-Democrat vote; the four measures also explain 63% of the variance in turnout in the election. Social deprivation is consistently the most important predictor in three of the four equations, the exception being the Liberal-Democrats. Constituencies with high levels of social deprivation were significantly more likely to

5. Predicting vote and turnout in the 1997 election

	Conservative		Labour		Lib Dem		Turnout	
	b	beta	b	beta	b	beta	b	beta
Manual occupation	−1.4*	−.22*	3.8*	.38*	−1.9*	.33*	−.40*	−.13*
Social deprivation	−4.5*	−.71*	4.7*	.48*	−.91*	−.16*	−1.7*	−.54*
Familism	−2.2*	−.27*	5.7*	.44*	−2.6*	−.34*	−1.0*	−.25*
Ethnicity	.01	.01	.03	.02	−.07	−.06	−.18*	−.28*
Constant	66.2		−23.2				85.6	
R-squared	.77		.73		.30		.63	
(N)	(568)		(568)		(567)		(569)	

Note: Ordinary least squares regression analyses showing partial (b) and standardized (beta) coefficients predicting vote and turnout in English and Welsh parliamentary constituencies. * statistically significant at p<.01, two-tailed.

Source: British Parliamentary Constituencies, 1992–97.

vote Labour and less likely to vote Conservative, as well as registering a lower turnout. Familism is second in importance, and constituencies with large proportions of younger families were more likely to support Labour. Perhaps surprisingly given its once dominant position in British voting, manual occupation comes third, although it remains a significant predictor, particularly of the Labour vote. Finally, net of other factors, ethnicity has no statistically significant effect on the party vote: constituencies with large numbers of non-white voters are disproportionately Labour,[20] but it is for reasons other than their ethnic composition. As Denver and Hands also found, ethnicity is, however, a major predictor of turnout.

How far does the different social structure found across Britain account for patterns of regional voting? Table 6 suggests that it has a substantial impact in explaining regional voting, particularly for the Conservatives. For example, the actual Conservative vote in the South East was 41.4%; once social structure is taken into account, the Conservative vote in the region drops to 29.9%. In other words, the South East's strong support for the Conservatives in the election was a consequence of the region's affluence and occupational structure rather

6. Regional voting and turnout, controlling for social structure

	Estimated 1997 vote (%)			
	Con	Lab	Lib Dem	Turnout
England				
North	26.7	58.0	13.3	77.6
North West	25.7	59.4	13.1	75.5
Yorkshire and Humberside	26.5	55.7	14.9	73.6
East Midlands	30.3	55.5	11.4	76.0
West Midlands	31.5	52.6	13.2	75.3
London	26.7	56.6	12.9	73.0
South East	29.9	49.8	15.9	73.3
South West	27.5	43.0	25.5	75.8
East Anglia	29.7	52.3	13.9	75.0
Wales	21.3	57.7	9.5	80.7

Note: Figures are estimates derived from ordinary least squares regression equations, using the variables described in Table 5.

Source: British Parliamentary Constituencies, 1992–97.

than of political factors. Indeed, across the England regions, the overall distribution of the Conservative vote drops from 19.2% to 5.8% once social structure is taken into account. For Labour, social structure is particularly important in explaining their low vote in the South West and South East; once this is taken into account, the distribution in the Labour vote drops from 34.5% to 16.4%.

In contrast to the two major parties, the Liberal Democrat vote is less explicable in terms of social structure. Even when social characteristics are taken into account, the Liberal Democrat vote in the South West remains at almost twice the level found in the rest of the country — 25.5% compared to between 11.4 and 15.9% for the other English regions. Regional differences in turnout are, however, substantially a consequence of social characteristics. The actual distribution in turnout across England falls from 7.3% to 4.3% once these characteristics are taken into account. Overall, then, while social structure is an important explanation for regional patterns of voting across England and Wales, it remains a partial one; the next section examines some of the political factors associated with the regions that help to account for these patterns.

Tactical voting, party competition and local campaigning

The different socio-economic characteristics of the regions were not the only important factor which influenced their voting patterns, political differences were important as well. These political characteristics included the patterns of tactical voting which emerged across the country, and which varied significantly by region, as Pippa Norris shows in her chapter. Other political factors which were significant in helping to explain regional voting were the patterns of local government control in each of the regions, as well as the different levels of activity among the party organisations. As this section shows, all of these differences contribute to an explanation why the regions voted differently in the 1997 election.

TURNOUT. One political factor which shaped regional voting was turnout. Although turnout is, like the vote, partly dependent on the socio-economic characteristics of a region, it also reflects the ability of local parties to mobilise voters, and the nature of the constituency contest. In Britain as elsewhere, changes in turnout are a significant determinant of electoral outcomes, nationally between elections as well as between different areas at the same election.[21] The 1997 general election was no exception. Predicting the party vote from social structure and turnout shows that constituencies with lower turnout benefited the Conservatives by about 0.35% of the vote for every one per cent that turnout fell, while the Liberal Democrat vote fell by 0.46%. Labour benefited by 0.4% of the vote for each one per cent increase in turnout in a constituency.[22]

How does this translate into patterns of regional voting? In some regions, differences in turnout benefited the parties, in others it proved a disadvantage. In Wales, for example, turnout was higher than the national average while the Conservative vote dropped by nine per cent compared to their 1992 result. If, however, turnout in Wales had been the same as the country as a whole, then the Conservative vote would have been 0.7% higher and their vote decline since 1992 in Wales reduced to 8.3%.[23] Similarly, in London Labour increased their vote by 12.3% compared to 1992; if the comparatively low turnout in London had matched the national average then the party would have gained about 1.5% more votes than they actually did.[24] Clearly, then, while differential turnout in the regions does not explain the regional patterns of voting that persist after social structure is taken into account, it was a factor which caused the party votes to rise or fall.

TACTICAL VOTING. Since the Liberal-Social Democrat Alliance contested its first general election in 1983, tactical voting has become increasingly important in shaping electoral outcomes. There were unprecedented levels of tactical voting in the 1997 election, which served to concentrate the nationwide swing against the Conservatives in the constituencies where it would cause them most harm. The net effect of tactical voting was to translate a modest decrease in the Liberal Democrat vote of –1.0% across the United Kingdom into a more than 100% increase in their seats. But the potential for voting tactically was regionally concentrated. As Table 7 shows, the regions where there were Conservative seats with either a Labour or a Liberal Democrat candidate in second place were disproportionately located in the South East (96%), East Anglia (87%) and the South West (77%). There were comparatively few such seats in either the northern regions of England or, because of the intervention of nationalist candidates, in Scotland or Wales.

Restricting the analysis to England, an estimate of the level of tactical

7. Types of constituency contests

	Constituency contest (%)			
	Con-Lab	Con-Lib	Other	(N)
England				
North	11	6	83	(36)
North West	24	10	66	(70)
Yorkshire and Humberside	23	16	61	(56)
East Midlands	57	11	32	(44)
West Midlands	37	15	48	(59)
London	45	11	44	(74)
South East	35	61	4	(117)
South West	14	63	23	(51)
East Anglia	46	41	13	(22)
Wales	15	5	75	(40)
Scotland	6	4	90	(72)

Source: British Parliamentary Constituencies, 1992–97.

voting can be made by subtracting the estimated vote for the Labour and Liberal Democrat parties—the vote they would have expected to receive based on the four dimensions of social structure identified in the previous section—from the actual vote that they received. An increase in the vote means that the parties were attracting more votes than they would otherwise have expected; a decrease indicates that they were performing worse than expected. Table 8 show this estimate for the two types of party contest where tactical voting was most likely (either Conservative versus Labour or Conservative versus Liberal Democrat) and by marginality. There is modest evidence of tactical voting in Conservative-Labour contests, with Labour candidates gaining more votes than they would otherwise have expected, and Liberal Democrat candidates losing votes. However, the vote varies little by the marginality of the contest.

8. Tactical voting, England

| | Actual minus predicted vote | | |
	Lab	Lib Dem	(N)
Con/Lab contests			
Very marginal	+6.7	−5.8	(27)
Fairly marginal	+7.7	−7.0	(29)
Semi marginal	+3.2	−4.7	(16)
Fairly safe	+6.8	−7.5	(24)
Very safe	+2.5	−6.3	(76)
Con/Lib Dem contests			
Very marginal	−18.6	+22.5	(5)
Fairly marginal	−18.0	+18.0	(8)
Semi marginal	−11.6	+14.3	(14)
Fairly safe	−7.2	+10.4	(23)
Very safe	−5.0	+2.1	(102)

Note: Figures are the actual minus the predicted vote in each constituency, the predicted vote being a regression estimate based on the four social structural variables defined in Table 5. Marginality is defined as follows: very marginal, 0.0 to 4.9%; fairly marginal, 5.0–9.9; semi marginal, 10.0–14.9; fairly safe, 15.0–19.9; very safe, 20.0 or more.

Source: British Parliamentary Constituencies, 1992–97.

By contrast, there were high levels of tactical voting in the constituencies where a Liberal Democrat candidate was running second to a Conservative incumbent, and most particularly where that contest was marginal. In the most marginal seats—where the Liberal Democrat challenger was within five per cent of the Conservative incumbent—the Liberal Democrat vote was over 22% higher than would have otherwise have been expected, while the Labour vote declined by nearly 19%. In fairly marginal constituencies the vote change between the parties was about the same—18%. Even in constituencies which could be considered only semi-marginal—requiring a swing of between 10 and 14.9% to change hands—the Liberal Democrat vote increased by over 14%, while Labour's declined by just under 12%. Tactical voting was, therefore, a very significant factor in the Liberal Democrat's success in winning their 46 seats. While the impact of tactical voting on regional patterns of voting is difficult to estimate precisely, it undoubtedly had a significant impact in the South West, where 12 of the 22 marginal Conservative-Liberal Democrat contests took place, and to a lesser extent in the South East, where eight of the contests were located.[25]

LOCAL GOVERNMENT. Local government has rarely surfaced in national British politics, except perhaps as an early indicator of shifting party fortunes. But local government elections also reflect party organisation and activity: parties that win local elections and control local councils are also much more likely to have an organisation and a skilled core of activists on the ground; parties can also argue that the successful management of local affairs gives them a greater claim to national political office. Assessing the influence of local government control on national electoral outcomes is always difficult, not least because local electoral boundaries are not contiguous with those of parliamentary constituencies. Similarly, local elections are held at different times in different parts of the country, and thus reflect different stages in a party's fortunes, as well as a variety of specifically local considerations (see Rallings and Thrasher this volume).

An estimate of the importance of local government control, and of its potential to impact on regional patterns of voting, can be made by examining local party control in the English counties, at the various local elections held before the May general election.[26] The main beneficiaries from a strong local government presence, in terms of the national vote, were the Liberal Democrats (Table 9). They gained 3.8% more votes than would otherwise be expected in the constituencies which were located in counties where they had a majority of councillors, and six per cent where they had a plurality of councillors. Labour also benefited where the Liberal Democrats were the largest local party, and they gained just over two per cent of the vote where they themselves had a local government majority. The Conservatives could only potentially gain where they possessed a plurality (since there were no counties where the Conservatives held a majority of council seats); where that

9. Local government control and the party vote, England

	Con	Lab	Lib Dem	(N)
		Actual minus predicted vote		
Majority				
Con	n/a	n/a	n/a	
Lab	−0.7	+2.3	−1.3	(289)
Lib Dem	−1.4	−2.6	+3.8	(17)
Plurality				
Con	+1.6	−2.6	−0.3	(32)
Lab	+1.0	−0.3	−0.8	(123)
Lib Dem	+0.8	+7.7	+6.0	(68)

Note: Figures are the actual minus the predicted vote in each constituency, the predicted vote being a regression estimate based on the four social structural variables defined in Table 5. Local control is defined as the number of council seats in the county within which the parliamentary constituency was located.

Source: British Parliamentary Constituencies, 1992–97.

occurred, the gain in their vote was a comparatively modest 1.6% than would otherwise be expected based on the constituency's social structural characteristics.

LOCAL CAMPAIGNING.　　All of the major parties made strenuous efforts to target marginal constituencies, and to ensure that their party leader visited each of these constituencies at least once. Labour identified about 55 constituencies for special attention, ranging from the Vale of Glamorgan, which required a swing of just 0.02% to displace the incumbent Conservative, to Leeds North East, where a swing of 4.29% was needed (*The Times*, 28.4.97). Of these 55 constituencies, Tony Blair visited 22 of them once, 12 of them twice, and he did not visit the remaining 21; 16 of these 55 constituencies were visited by John Major, all once only. Among the 16 seats targeted by the Liberal Democrats, Paddy Ashdown visited 13 of them and John Major just four. Continuing his high profile constituency campaign, Tony Blair visited all 16, eight of them twice, six of them three times, and two once only. This targeting and the associated activity by the party leaders also showed some regional disparity: all three leaders concentrated much of their special efforts in the South West, while Tony Blair also focused on the South East and Wales and Paddy Ashdown on the North West and Wales.

10.　The electoral impact of leader activity, Britain

	Actual minus predicted vote		
Constituency visit by:	Con	Lab	Lib Dem
Major	+1.1	+0.1	−1.4
Blair	−2.0	−0.9	+1.9
Ashdown	−4.1	−14.3	+17.8

Note: Figures are the actual minus the predicted vote in each constituency, the predicted vote being a regression estimate based on the four social structural variables defined in Table 5.

Source: British Parliamentary Constituencies, 1992–97.

The local party activity—for which a leader's visit acts as a proxy—appears to have reaped electoral rewards. If the predicted constituency party vote is subtracted from the actual vote and estimated separately by whether or not one of the party leaders visited the constituency, an estimate can be made of the impact of leader activity (Table 10). The Conservative vote in a constituency visited by John Major rose by 1.1% than would otherwise have been expected while a visit by the other two party leaders reduced the Conservative vote, by two per cent for a Blair visit and just over four per cent for an Ashdown visit. It is, however, the Liberal Democrats who were the substantial beneficiaries from this type of activity. An Ashdown visit reduced the Labour vote by over 14% and increased his own party's vote by nearly 18%. By contrast, a Blair visit apparently had little impact on Labour's vote.

Although these results are confounded to some degree by tactical voting—as the previous discussion showed, tactical voting was most likely to occur in marginal constituencies which were in turn also more likely to be targeted by the parties—it nevertheless suggests that targeting appeared to work, particularly for the Liberal Democrats. The negligible vote shifts occasioned by Labour targeting perhaps reflects the fact that Blair's efforts were spread around many constituencies, while the constituency visits by Ashdown were fewer (and perhaps) more intensive and public, which would in turn flow through to local party activity. Despite John Major's much publicised campaigning skills, he does not manage to increase his party's vote by more than one per cent. From the perspective of regional patterns of voting, these were undoubtedly affected by this targeting, since they were more likely to occur in some regions rather than in others. For example, about two per cent of the additional vote gained by the Liberal Democrats in the South West compared to the Britain-wide average can be attributed to the targeting of marginal constituencies in the region by the Liberal Democrats.[27]

Conclusion

As in previous British general elections, regional voting emerged as a major factor in shaping the outcome of the 1997 election. The Conservative vote across the South of England was almost double the vote that they attracted in the North, while the reverse was the case for Labour. With the notable exception of the South West, the Liberal Democrat vote varied less by region compared to the other two parties. But the 1997 election differed significantly from the regional voting that emerged in more recent general elections in one important respect. While the regionalization of the Labour vote remained at a high level, the regionalization of the Conservative vote declined. In part, this reflected the fact that Conservative fortunes in some regions had declined significantly before the 1997 election, so that there were simply fewer votes to lose. But there were also major political factors at work, the most notable of which was tactical voting.

Tactical voting against the Conservatives was highly effective and regionally specific, since the types of contests where it could be most effectively used were in the South and South West of England. It enabled the Liberal Democrats to more than double their share of parliamentary seats. The Liberal Democrats also benefited from the targeting of marginal constituencies, as they did from having a strong presence in local government within the region. While the different social structures of the regions once again help to explain a major part of regional patterns of voting, the 1997 election was notable for the emergence of these associated and often regionally specific political factors. Future British general elections may have to deal with highly sophisticated, regional electorates who vote instrumentally in order to achieve a very specific outcome.

My thanks to Andrew Russell for comments and suggestions, and to Colin Rallings for providing the local government results.

1   R.J. Johnson, C.J. Pattie and J.G. Allsopp, *A Nation Dividing? The Electoral Map of Great Britain 1979–87* (London: Longman, 1988); J. Lewis and A. Townsend (eds), *The North-South Divide* (London: Chapman, 1989).

2   E. Spencer Wellhofer, *Democracy, Capitalism and Empire in Late Victorian Britain, 1885–1910* (London: Macmillan, 1996).

3   W.H. Field, *Regional Dynamics: The Basis of Electoral Support in Britain* (London: Frank Cass, 1997).

4   J. Curtice and M. Steed, 'Electoral Choice and the Production of Government: The Changing Operation of the Electoral System in the United Kingdom Since 1955', *British Journal of Political Science*, 12 (1982); A.R. Bodman, 'Regional Trends in Electoral Support in Britain 1950–83', *Professional Geographer*, 37 (1985).

5   P.J. Taylor, 'The Changing Geography of Representation in Britain', *Area*, 11 (1979).

6   R.J. Johnston, C.J. Pattie and J.G. Allsopp, *A Nation Dividing* (Longman, 1988).

7   I. Crewe, 'The Electorate: Partisan Dealignment Ten Years On', *West European Politics*, 6 (1983).

8   There are, of course, other ways in which to define regions. Using the standard regions plus Scotland and Wales has the advantage of producing units that are sufficiently large for analysis, as well as making the results comparable with other research which has used similar definitions.

9   I. McAllister and D. Studlar, 'Region and Voting in Britain, 1979–87: Territorial Polarization or Artifact?', *American Journal of Political Science*, 36 (1992).

10   M.N. Franklin, *The Decline of Class Voting in Britain* (Oxford: Clarendon Press, 1985); R. Rose and I. McAllister, *The Loyalties of Voters: A Lifetime Learning Model* (London: Sage, 1990); B. Sarlvik and I. Crewe, *Decade of Dealignment* (Cambridge: Cambridge University Press, 1983).

11   R.J. Johnston and C.J. Pattie, 'Class Dealignment and the Regional Polarization of Voting Patterns in Great Britain, 1964–87', *Political Geography*, 11 (1992).

12   R. Huckfeldt, P.A. Beck, R.J. Dalton and J. Levine, 'Political Environments, Cohesive Social-Groups, and the Communication of Public-Opinion', *American Journal of Political Science*, 39 (1995); R.J. Johnston and C.J. Pattie, 'The Regional Impact of Thatcherism: Attitudes and Votes in Great Britain in the 1980s', *Regional Studies*, 24 (1990).

13   The numbers of constituencies in each of the regions and nations is as follows: South East, 117; East Anglia, 22; London, 74; South West, 51; West Midlands, 59; E. Midlands, 44; Yorkshire and Humberside, 56; North West, 70; North, 36; Wales, 40; Scotland, 72.

14   Johnston, Pattie and Allsopp, *A Nation Dividing*; C.J. Pattie and R.J. Johnston, 'It's Not Like That Round Here: Economic Evaluations and Voting in the 1992 British General Election', *European Journal of Political Research*, 28 (1996).

15   E.A. Fieldhouse, 'Thatcherism and the Changing Geography of Political Attitudes', *Political Geography*, 14 (1995).

16   The census variables used here were not available for the Scottish constituencies, which had to be excluded.

17   I. McAllister and R. Rose, *The Nationwide Competition for Votes* (London: Frances Pinter, 1984); I. McAllister and J. Kelley, 'Social Context and Electoral Behaviour in Britain', *American Journal of Political Science*, 29 (1985).

18   McAllister and Rose, *The Nationwide Competition for Votes*; I. McAllister and J. Kelley, 'Contextual Characteristics of Australian Federal Electorates', *Australia and New Zealand Journal of Sociology*, 19 (1983).

19   The six constituencies are: Brent North (41.5% non-white), Ealing Southall (47.3%), East Ham (48.5%), Birmingham Sparkbrook and Small Heath (52.1%), Birmingham Ladywood (53.6%) and Brent South (55.2%). Bernie Grant's constituency of Tottenham records 38.3% non-white.

20   Z. Layton-Henry, *The Politics of Immigration* (Oxford: Blackwell, 1992).

21   I. McAllister and A. Mughan, 'Differential Turnout and Party Advantage in British General Elections, 1964–83', *Electoral Studies*, 5 (1986).

22   The partial regression coefficients for the three party equations were as follows:

	Con	Lab	Lib
Turnout	$-.35$	.40	.31
Ethnicity	$-.04^{ns}$	$.09^{ns}$	$-.15^{ns}$
Familism	-2.7	6.1	-3.2
Deprivation	-5.6	5.8	-1.9
Manual	-1.2	3.3	-2.0
R-squared	.77	.70	.31

23 The calculation is the difference in turnout between Wales and Britain as a whole (71.6–73.5 = −1.9) multiplied by the impact of turnout on the Conservative vote (0.35* −1.9 = 0.67).

24 The calculation is 67.8–71.6 = 3.8. 3.8 * 0.40 = 1.52%.

25 Of the 22 constituencies where there was a Conservative incumbent and a Liberal Democrat candidate second and which fell into either the very, fairly or semi-marginal category, 12 were in the South West, 8 in the South East, 4 in the North West, 2 in London and 1 in the West Midlands.

26 The local election dates were as follows: London, 1994; Scotland and Wales, 1995; Metropolitans one-third each in 1994, 1995 and 1996; Counties, 1997; Districts and Unitaries were spread over 1994, 1995, 1996 and 1997.

27 The estimate is from a regression equation predicting the over or underprediction in the Liberal Democrat vote from variables measuring the leaders' visits, and dummy variables for region.

Scotland: Paving the Way for Devolution?

BY ALICE BROWN*

IN SCOTLAND the contrast between the morning after the general election in 1992 and that of 1997 could not be more stark. After a campaign that seemed to have lasted for the intervening five years, people in Scotland woke up to the news on the morning of 2 May 1997 not just of a Labour government with a record majority in the House of Commons, but also to the fact that not one Conservative candidate had been elected to represent a Scottish constituency. While a Tory wipe out was predicted by a few foolhardy commentators in 1992, no such speculation was being made in 1997 in spite of evidence from the opinion polls showing the Conservatives in a very weak position and the fact that the party had performed badly in the European and local elections in 1995. Indeed there was an extremely cautious air about the pre-election predictions in Scotland. The memory of 1992 when the Conservatives actually increased their vote and seats in Scotland, still haunted those who had anticipated a change of government. The reason for this caution can be explained partially by the belief that so much was at stake in the constitutional question in Scottish politics. For political opponents of the Conservatives, the object was not just to replace the government, but also to fulfil aspirations for home rule in Scotland. This paper, therefore, places the results of the general election in Scotland in the context of the campaign for constitutional change both before and after 1 May 1997. Developments following the return of the Conservative government in 1992 and conditions in the pre-election period are outlined before the key features of the campaign and the election results are analysed. It is argued that the results may provide evidence of a narrowing of the so-called north/south divide, but that the constitutional question continues to have a major influence on politics in Scotland.

Scottish developments 1992–97

For supporters of constitutional change the results of the 1992 general election and the return of the Conservative government were a signific-ant setback. James Mitchell argues that it had the same impact as the referendum of 1979 in that 'though a numeric majority voted for change, the failure to realise expectations was a psychological blow to the opposition parties'.[1] The immediate reaction of the opposition was

---

* Professor of Politics at Edinburgh University.

not edifying as they sought to find an explanation for the result. Initial efforts by Campbell Christie, the General Secretary of the STUC and key player in the Scottish Constitutional Convention, to bring the opposition parties together failed. A mood of depression engulfed the Scottish Labour Party. The leader of the Scottish Liberal Democrats, Malcolm Bruce, argued that their party's stance on devolution and involvement in the Scottish Constitutional Convention had been electorally damaging. The Scottish National Party referred back to their pre-election warning that the Labour Party could not win the general election and that supporters of constitutional change had no alternative but to vote for the SNP. In contrast, members of the Conservative Party who had anticipated at least some losses in the general election, were perhaps the most surprised of all to have witnessed a marginal increase in electoral support from 24% to 25.7% and the return of 11 MPs to Westminster, one more than in 1987.[2] Although the Conservative Party enjoyed a modest recovery, the claim that the majority of Scots still voted for parties in favour of constitutional reinforced arguments concerning a 'democratic deficit' in Scotland.[3]

In recognition that the demand for constitutional change had not evaporated with their return to office, the Conservative Party announced modest constitutional changes following its 'taking stock' exercise, including the decision in 1995 to hold meetings of the Scottish Grand Committee in different venues throughout Scotland. For their political opponents, however, such measures were no more than a cosmetic exercise, although the meetings of the Grand Committee were used, particularly by groups and organisations, as a way of lobbying and protesting about government policy in Scotland.

The immediate post-election period saw the setting up of a number of organisations with the aim of keeping the constitutional question high on the political agenda including democracy for Scotland, Scotland united and common cause. The Women's Coordination Group was also established to continue pressing the case for equal representation of men and women in a future Scottish parliament. Although the different groups continue to exist, an umbrella organisation, the Coalition for Scottish Democracy, was established in 1995 and has been instrumental in setting up a Scottish Civic Assembly. The Assembly has representatives from a wide range of non-party organisations in Scotland and has played a role in articulating an alternative to the government's approach to policy issues in Scotland. Despite predictions to the contrary, the Scottish Constitutional Convention also survived and established a Scottish Constitutional Commission to take forward the Convention's scheme. The Convention was established in 1989 as cross-party and non-party organisation following recommendations by the Campaign for a Scottish parliament (formerly known as the Campaign for a Scottish Assembly). It has proved a useful vehicle which allows the Scottish Labour Party and the Scottish Liberal Democrats to be seen to be doing something on the constitutional issue while at the same time it provided them with some political distance from the home rule question.

A certain urgency pervaded the work of the Convention, and there was a desire to have an agreed scheme in place in good time for the 1997 general election. This sense of urgency was precipitated by the view that the Prime Minister was vulnerable following the events of Black Wednesday (discussed by Pippa Norris) and it continued as pressure on the government built up over the years and some anticipated an early election. The launching of the Scottish Constitutional Convention's final document, *Scotland's Parliament, Scotland's Right*, on St Andrews Day in November 1995 was significant because it represented a consensus of view between two of Scotland's main political parties and a wide range of organisations in Scottish civil society on a scheme for a future Scottish Parliament, and because of the reaction is provoked from the Prime Minister. Accusing the members of the Convention of indulging in 'teenage madness' (a strange description given the average age of Convention activists), John Major launched his attack against constitutional change warning of the break-up of the United Kingdom.[4] This was one issue where there was clear blue water between the Conservatives and every other major party in Britain.

The Convention proposed a Scottish parliament of 129 members to be elected by an additional member system. Under this electoral system 73 members would be elected from individual constituencies on the basis of first-past-the-post, while another 56 members would be elected from top-up lists based on Scotland's eight European constituencies. Parties in the Convention also signed an Electoral Agreement in which they committed themselves to the principle of equal representation in the first parliament and to field an equal number of men and women in winnable seats in order to achieve this aim.[5] The Convention's document outlined the powers and functions of a Scottish parliament and what turned out to be the most controversial aspect of the scheme, the power to vary the basic rate of income tax by a maximum of 3p in the pound.[6]

While the campaign for constitutional change continued, mid-term elections provided indicators of party fortunes. By-elections were called as a result of the deaths of two MPs, John Smith in 1994 and Nicholas Fairbairn in 1995. The death of John Smith, the Labour leader, came as an enormous blow, for personal and political reasons, to the campaigners for change. In addition to his qualities as leader of the Labour Party, John Smith was viewed as a guardian of the constitutional question and was trusted to work effectively towards the establishment of a Scottish Parliament and to complete what he described in his own words, as 'unfinished business'. The by-election that followed in Monklands East was held within the context of accusations of religious sectarianism and provided another opportunity for intense partisan conflict between the

Labour Party and the SNP. The seat was won by Helen Liddell, former general secretary of the Labour Party in Scotland, although the SNP were to be rewarded in a second by-election the following year when they took Perth and Kinross from the Conservatives. The election of Roseanna Cunningham for the SNP, a nationalist, republican, socialist, feminist in place of one of Scotland's more traditional and flamboyant Conservative MPs did not go unnoticed by commentators.

Prior to the 1994 European election, Labour held seven of Scotland's eight European constituencies, with the SNP holding one. While Labour regained six of its seats at the 1994 election with 42.5% of the vote, the SNP was successful in winning North East Scotland from Labour and in achieving 32.6% of the vote across Scotland, an increase of seven per cent on the 1989 European election results. As David Denver reports, the Conservatives lost support in every euro-constituency in Scotland and experienced a decline of 6.4% of their overall electoral support.[7] The period also witnessed three other contests, the district elections which quickly followed the 1992 general election, the regional elections in 1994, and the elections for the shadow unitary authorities in 1995. The latter followed a major restructuring of local government in Scotland. The decision to move from a two-tier local government system of nine regions and 53 districts to a unitary system of 29 new authorities on the mainland and to retain the three island councils was taken following limited consultation and in the absence of a Commission to examine the case and the proposals for change.[8] Ian Lang, then Secretary of State for Scotland, answered the criticism that the case for reform had not been made by citing the benefits of a single-tier structure as efficiency, effectiveness and an improvement in local democracy.[9] The government was also accused of gerrymandering the boundaries of the new authorities in an attempt to gain political advantage. As David Denver and Hugh Bochel comment, if this was the intention then it failed miserably, as the election results can only be interpreted as a catastrophe for the Conservatives.[10] The Conservatives' share of the vote dropped to 11.3% leaving the government in office without control of any of Scotland's local authorities. This reinforced the view that the party did not have a mandate to rule in Scotland and that the democratic deficit had been exacerbated. In contrast, Labour reasserted its dominance of Scottish local government winning control of 20 of the 29 new authorities. In hindsight it can be seen that both the European and the local elections helped pave the way for the defeat of the Conservatives on 1 May 1997 (see also Rallings and Thrasher this volume).

The long campaign

As pressure on the government mounted, and their majority in the House of Commons was gradually depleted, the political parties in Scotland prepared for the general election. In November 1995 the Scottish Labour Party and the Scottish Liberal Democrats consolidated and articulated their support for the blueprint agreed in the Scottish Constitutional Convention. The SNP put forward their own proposals for 'Independence in Europe' and the establishment of a 200-member Scottish parliament elected by a single transferable vote electoral system. Meanwhile the Conservative Party in Scotland, under the leadership of the new Secretary of State, Michael Forsyth, began a concerted campaign against the Convention's scheme, especially the decision to give the Scottish parliament tax-varying powers. Iain MacWhirter likened the appointment of Michael Forsyth to the post to 'trying to put out a house fire by throwing petrol over it'.[11] The new Minister dubbed this proposal the 'Tartan Tax' and the effectiveness of this attack, particularly on the Labour Party, was demonstrated by events that followed.

Attempts by the Scottish Labour Party to gain more autonomy of decision-making were affected by the election of the new leader, Tony Blair, and the injection of 'new Labour' policies and ideas north of the border. Political differences were evident over controversial issues such as the reform of Clause IV of the party's constitution and other aspects of policy such as education, and, most crucially, taxation and spending. To the surprise of many, not least members of the party in Scotland and their Convention partners, the Scottish Liberal Democrats, on 27 June 1996 the Labour Party announced its plans to hold a Referendum on the constitutional question.

Before this announcement, the line of argument advanced by the Scottish Labour Party and by its leader, George Robertson, was that the mandate for constitutional change had already been given by the fact that around 75% of the Scottish electorate consistently voted for parties who supported reform. In the event of Labour winning the election on a platform that included plans to set up a Scottish parliament, this was argued to be a sufficient mandate to implement the policy. In these circumstances, the reaction from political activists to the party leadership's decision to hold a referendum on the issue was somewhat predictable and Labour was accused of once again betraying the hopes and aspirations of the Scottish people for home rule. It was interesting to compare the response of the media and commentators north and south of the border to the change of policy. For those in England, the decision seemed politically sensible and a way of endorsing and strengthening the plans for a Scottish parliament. On the other hand, the initial Scottish reaction was to interpret the decision as potential political suicide, leaving Labour open to losing electoral ground to the SNP, and one that could seriously endanger the setting up of a parliament in Scotland. To understand the mood that followed the decision to hold a referendum in Scotland, one has to place it within the context of memories of the referendum experience in the 1970s. For those who had been part of the 'Yes' campaign in the late 1970s, it was interpreted as another obstacle in the long road to home rule and anxieties were raised that history would repeat itself especially if the referendum was subject to a 40% rule or other condition.[12]

The debate became more heated when it became clear that there was not just going to be one question but two, the first asking the Scottish people if they wanted a Scottish parliament and the second question directed at the tax-varying powers. The split over the referendum was rehearsed at executive meetings of the Scottish Labour Party where attempts were made to restrict the referendum to the single question of whether or not to establish a parliament. At one stage, following a particularly difficult executive meeting, a so-called compromise of three questions was proposed, a decision that only added fuel to the debate. In the event, a final decision was made for a two-question referendum — one on the parliament and one on the tax question — and Tony Blair arrived in Scotland to explain why the decision had been taken, at one stage saying that it had originated from a proposal from George Robertson. The argument was made that without a referendum, the plans for a parliament were open to attack from supporters of the status quo and especially the decision over tax-raising powers that had been the subject of criticism from Michael Forsyth and others. The latter point was, of course, related very directly to the Labour Party's policy on taxation and its determination to rid itself of the image of a tax raising party. The argument was also put by the Labour leadership that a 'Yes' vote in the referendum would ease the passage of a Scotland Act through the House of Commons and help entrench the Scottish parliament and make it less vulnerable in the future should the Conservatives return to power at Westminster.

Not surprisingly, the SNP jumped at the opportunity handed to it to make political capital from the decision accusing George Robertson of being a puppet of Tony Blair and stating that once again policy in Scotland was being driven from south of the border. Tony Blair was even compared by some to Margaret Thatcher in that he was accused of being insensitive to the political situation in Scotland. The storm mounted as the SNP got hold of a research report, carried out on behalf of the Scottish Labour Party, and based on evidence from focus groups which showed that Blair was identified with moving Labour to the right and that Labour was seen to be back-tracking on the commitment to home rule. For their part, the Scottish Liberal Democrats reiterated their strong opposition to the holding of a referendum on the grounds that the mandate for such constitutional change had already been demonstrated by the Scottish electorate. They were particularly opposed to the second question on taxation fearing that a parliament without the ability to raise revenue would not have the type of powers envisaged in the Scottish Constitutional Convention plans.

Those within the Scottish Labour Party who opposed the referendum decision found their positions under threat as the party moved closer to the general election and demonstrated its willingness to impose party discipline. One casualty of this trend was the departure of Tommy Sheppard who had held the position of Assistant General Secretary at Keir Hardie House and was responsible for the election campaign. Suspicions within the party mounted and were fuelled by the news that a group of senior Labour activists broadly sympathetic to Mr Blair and the policies of new Labour has formed a group called the Network (*The Scotsman*, 29.1.97). At the elections for the Scottish executive which followed in March 1997, a number of well-known members on the left lost their positions, reflecting the change in the balance of power in the party in Scotland.

The official campaign

These developments meant that many Labour activists in Scotland entered the campaign with mixed feelings. They desperately wanted a change of government, but the shift away from the type of policies they supported and the referendum issue severely damaged morale. With an election imminent, however, the majority view was to accept the decisions and move into the campaign. Commentating on the disillusionment of some supporters of the party, the journalist, Lesley Riddoch, argued that if the object was to get a change of government, then the Labour Party was 'the only show in town'.

It was not only the Scottish Labour Party that was facing difficulties. The Scottish Conservative and Unionist Party encountered its own problems following the sudden resignation of Alan Stewart, sitting MP for Eastwood, in the spring of 1997. Sir Michael Hirst, tipped as a possible successor to Alan Stewart, caused further confusion when he dramatically withdrew his candidacy and resigned as chair of the party. The latter event was precipitated by threats made by political opponents within the party to reveal evidence about Michael Hirst's private life. The disarray and divisions within the Conservative Party were also exposed in their response to the constitutional question. While the Health Secretary, Stephen Dorrell, warned that a future Tory government would abolish a Scottish Parliament should it be established, the Secretary of State, Michael Forsyth, repeated his view that a Scottish Parliament which had the endorsement of the people of Scotland would not be abolished easily stating 'A Scottish parliament is not just for Christmas, it's for life' (*The Scotsman*, 11.2.97).

Given the criticism of the accuracy of opinion polls in predicting the outcome of the 1992 general election, the evidence from the polls in the run-up to the 1997 election was treated with some caution (see Crewe this volume). Learning from the 1992 experience, the pollsters had changed their methods, and as David McCrone reports 1997 was 'the year when the opinion polls got the election result more or less correct.[13] Polls conducted by ICM throughout the election campaign estimated Labour's vote in Scotland at under 50% and the poll conducted just two days before the election came within one percentage point of the

Scottish result. The poll indicated that there was virtually no gender gap in the voting intentions of men and women with the exception of a split in the male/female support for the Liberal Democrats. Polls conducted by System Three had recorded a reasonably consistent pattern of support for constitutional change with 40% of potential voters supporting the devolution option and 30% preferring independence, leaving just 20% in favour of the status quo. However, evidence from the ICM polls during the election itself showed an improvement in the support for the status quo. Asked about how they would vote on a two-question referendum for a Scottish parliament, 69% of respondents to the Scotsman/ICM poll said they wanted a Scottish parliament within the UK and some 59% also ageed with the statement that a devolved parliament should have the power to vary income tax by up to three pence in the pound (*The Scotsman*, 22.1.97). Testing the opinion of voters outside Scotland on constitutional change, ICM conducted a poll of a representative sample of people across Britain (*The Scotsman*, 28.1.97). Almost 50% of those polled supported constitutional change (15% of them preferring independence in Europe and 33% devolution within the UK). A minority, some 38%, noted their preference for the status quo. The evidence from this poll at least gave little credence to the government's claim that there was strong opposition in England to the establishment of a Scottish parliament.

The main activity in the campaign was concentrated in key marginals. A surprising number of the issues remained remarkably absent from the debates. Unlike the campaign south of the border, the European question did not have the same impact in Scotland. Instead the constitutional question dominated the media coverage. Again Tony Blair hit the headlines in the now infamous interview with a journalist from *The Scotsman* when he made his controversial remark that even with the establishment of a Scottish parliament, 'sovereignty rests with me as an English MP and that's the way it will stay'. Responding to a questions on the Scottish parliament's ability to exercise tax powers, the Labour leader was accused of comparing a parliament in Scotland to a 'parish council' in England (*Scotland on Sunday*, 6.4.97). Much was made of these comments during the campaign, even although they had been taken out of context, and questions were asked about Labour's commitment to its home rule plans. As has been discussed elsewhere,[14] one of the key issues in Scottish politics is 'who speaks for Scotland?' by which is meant which party can be most trusted to represent Scottish interests in the parliamentary system. In the run-up to the election, the SNP leader, Alex Salmond, made much of Tony Blair's comments accusing Labour of being a single issue party, 'that issue being the pursuit of power by Tony Blair in Middle England, regardless of what Scotland needs and wants'. Stating that Scotland itself was at the heart of the concerns of people in Scotland, he argued that one question summed up the position at the election: 'who will speak for Scotland?' (*Herald*, 30.4.97). On election day itself, as the results suggest, another key question that appears to have exercised most voters minds, is 'which party is most likely to defeat the Conservatives?'

One of the surprising features of the campaign was the low profile played by the Conservative Party and some of its main players like Michael Forsyth. The Labour Party expected the attack on the constitutional question and the 'Tartan Tax' to continue, and although John Major could be relied upon to make speeches warning against the break-up of the United Kingdom if Scotland went down the devolution road, the Secretary of State for Scotland was often conspicuous by his absence. Could it be that the 'Tartan Tax' campaign had peaked too early, and/or had Tony Blair adopted the correct political tactics by deciding to hold a referendum? The weekend before the election, *Scotland on Sunday*'s front page featured Michael Forsyth (Secretary of State), Malcolm Rifkind (Foreign Secretary) and Ian Lang (Trade Secretary) with the headline 'Yesterday's men'. They publicised the results of an ICM poll which predicted that all three would lose their seats in Stirling, Edinburgh Pentlands, and Galloway and Upper Nithsdale respectively, the first two to Labour and the third to the SNP (*Scotland on Sunday*, 27.4.97). There was also little comfort for the Conservatives from the business community. Although some companies had come out strongly against a parliament in 1992 threatening to pull out of Scotland if Labour won the election, few views of this nature were being articulated publicly in 1997.[15] Some attempts were made to highlight the potential negative effects of levying higher taxes in Scotland with evidence for and against being advanced by different accountancy experts. Michael Forsyth's last-minute claim that the Treasury would use the opportunity of constitutional change to slash Scotland's budget by £2.5b, met with little support (*Herald*, 30.4.97).

The outcome in Scotland

The results confirmed the writing on the wall for the Conservatives. At the 1992 general election, Labour won 49 seats with 39% of the vote, the Conservatives won 11 seats with 25.7%, the Liberal Democrats returned nine MPs with 13.1% and the SNP had just three seats with some 21.5% of the vote.[16] On 1 May 1997 history was made when, in spite of receiving 17.5% of the vote, the Conservatives lost all their seats in Scotland, including the Tory stronghold of Eastwood. Labour again benefited as the front-runner from the first-past-the-post system by achieving 56 seats (77.7%) with 45.6% of the vote, a seats:votes ratio of 1.38. They were followed by the Liberal Democrats who were roughly proportional with ten seats (13.8%) and 13% of the vote. In contrast, the SNP were heavily penalised in third place by winning six seats (8.3%) with 22.1% of the vote. One question that arises from these results is 'who is the opposition party in Scotland?' At the Westminster level it is clearly the Conservative Party, but in Scotland with no MPs, who is to be the Shadow Secretary of State? The position is claimed by both the SNP and the Scottish Liberal Democrats, the former on the basis that they have the largest share of the vote at 22% and the latter on the grounds that they have the largest share of the seats with ten MPs.

1. Percentage share of the vote in Scotland, 1992–97

	1992	1997	Change
Conservative	25.7	17.5	−8.2%
Labour	39.0	45.6	+6.6%
Liberal Democrats	13.1	13.0	−0.1%
SNP	21.5	22.1	+0.6%
Others	0.8	1.9	+1.1%

Source: British Parliamentary Constituencies, 1992–97.

Party fortunes clearly varied significantly with an 8.2% reduction in support for the Conservatives as against a 6.6% increase in the votes for the Labour Party. While the Conservatives lost all of their seats, Labour gained Aberdeen South, Ayr, Eastwood, Edinburgh Pentlands, Dumfries and Stirling; and was also successful in winning the four-way marginal in Inverness East, Nairn and Lochaber. The votes for the Scottish Liberal Democrats were almost static but, because of its distribution, had the result of increasing the party's seats from nine to ten. The Liberal Democrats held Gordon despite boundary changes that made it vulnerable to a challenge from the Conservatives, and they held Tweeddale, Ettrick and Lauderdale following the retirement of Sir David Steel. The party also gained two seats from the Conservatives, Edinburgh West, and West Aberdeenshire and Kincardine. Votes for the SNP increased modestly by just 0.6%, but their seats doubled from three to six, as the party retained Perth and Kinross, and won Tayside North, and Galloway and Upper Nithsdale from the Conservatives. The SNP, however, failed to win Glasgow Govan with Mohammed Sarwar being elected to represent Labour and holding-off a strong challenge from the SNP candidate, Nicola Sturgeon.[17] This was a disappointing result for the party which hoped to mount a greater challenge to Labour's dominance of seats in Scotland. The first-past-the-post electoral system and the relatively even spread of their vote across the country worked against the SNP. This can be contrasted with the concentration of support for the Liberal Democrats and their success in terms of seats with a lower percentage of the vote.

The turnout of electors dropped in Scotland from an average of 75.4% in 1992 to 71.4% in 1997, although the drop was smaller than in Britain as a whole (see Denver and Hands this volume).[18] Changes in support for the four main political parties varied in different parts of Scotland and reflected the willingness of the electorate to vote tactically, most obviously by voting for the party most likely to deny the Conservatives. As a result, Conservative support fell more heavily in the seats they were defending. In a four-party system, it is difficult to make direct comparison with the results of the election in England. For example, although the swing against the Conservatives was an average of 10.5% across the whole of Great Britain, it was just 7.5% in Scotland. The difference in the swing has to be analysed within the context of Labour's dominant position in Scottish politics and the fact that it is operating in a four-party system. A similar situation exists in Wales where the swing was 7.4% against the Conservatives, enough to result in a wipe out for the party in both countries (see Norris this volume).

Some eighteen new MPs were elected to represent Scottish constituencies, including fourteen from the Labour Party. The gender balance of MPs also altered significantly with the increase in the number of women MPs from five in 1992 to twelve in 1997, more than doubling the representation rate from 6.9% to 16.6%. The new Labour government at Westminster also reflects the influence of Scottish MPs with a number holding ministerial posts, including Gordon Brown as Chancellor, Robin Cook as Foreign Secretary, George Robertson as Defence Secretary, Alastair Darling as Chief Secretary to the Treasury and Gavin Strang as Transport Minister. Helen Liddell, the MP for Airdrie and Shotts, was also promoted to the Treasury team.

The longer term effect of events on the night of 1 May will take some time to absorb and assess, yet the impact on the Conservative Party in Scotland was immediately felt as the party has struggled to come to terms with their wipe out. The new government lost little time in moving to implement some of its manifesto commitments. As the new Prime Minister, Tony Blair, appointed Donald Dewar, MP for Anniesland, as the Secretary of State for Scotland to be supported by the Scottish Office ministerial team including Malcolm Chisholm, Sam Galbraith, Henry McLeish and Brian Wilson. Those involved in the campaign for a Scottish Parliament and a 'Yes/Yes' vote in the referendum immediately reacted to Labour's victory by putting into place an umbrella organisation—Partnership for a Parliament. Funding for the campaign was raised prior to the election, largely at the instigation of a pro-home rule businessman, Nigel Smith.[19] The campaign was formally named *Scotland Forward* and launched on 15 May 1997, the same day as the government introduced its Referendum Bill to the House of Commons. The Minister for State at the Scottish Office responsible for overseeing the devolution plans, Henry McLeish, gave his assurance that Labour would move quickly in proceeding with its plans for a referendum. The holding of the referendum in the early days of the government can be contrasted with the experience in the 1970s. Henry McLeish was also present to launch the campaign on behalf of women activists in Scotland organised by the Scottish Women's Coordination Group on 7 June, in his capacity not only as Minister with responsibility for devolution but as the Minister responsible for women's issues in the Scottish Office. A major aspect of the women's campaign is to ensure that the commitment to gender balance in a future Scottish Parliament is honoured by the political parties.

The Minister reinforced the government's commitment to change stating that the Referendum Bill was 'the first Bill to be published, the first Bill to have a second reading and the first Bill to go through the House of Commons.' The government has faced some criticism, however, from opponents for subjecting the passage of the Bill to a guillotine motion in the House of Commons, and for noting its intention to hold a referendum on the basis of a White Paper rather than the actual Scotland Bill to be put to Parliament. The next stage, the introduction of the Referendum Bill into the House of Lords, could cause further difficulties for the government, although it is not considered a serious proposition. Assuming a smooth passage through the House of Lords, the government propose to publish its White Paper in July 1997. The referendum is expected to follow in the autumn and, if a mandate is received, the Scotland Bill will then go before Parliament. Assuming that the Bill receives Royal Assent in 1998, elections for the first Scottish parliament since 1707 could then be held in 1999.

Although criticisms of the government's approach have been made, what is less easy to identify is a credible 'No' campaign. The *Think Twice* campaign has attempted to coordinate opposition but has had little impact. Again this provides a marked contrast to the 1970s when the 'No' campaign was well financed and organised and the 'Yes' campaign was divided. The most recent opinion polls, however, show that there is little room for complacency on the part of those in favour of a Scottish parliament, especially one with tax-varying powers. Some 64% saying they were in favour of a Scottish parliament, while only 53% were in favour of a Scottish Parliament with tax-varying powers (*Herald*, 4.6.97). If we refer back to the support for the different parties at the general election, and the fact that Labour won the majority of seats in Scotland with less than 50% of the vote, it is clear that the Labour Party cannot rely on its own supporters alone to deliver a Scottish parliament with tax-varying powers.

Given the speed with which the Labour government has moved to implement its manifesto promises on constitutional change, what has been the impact on the other parties? The Scottish Liberal Democrats have maintained their opposition to a referendum, particularly to the second question. They have, however, given their commitment to the *Scotland Forward* campaign. A commitment has been given by the SNP, although they had earlier proposed that the referendum should include a question on the options for constitutional change relating to 'independence in Europe'. Following the publication of the government's White Paper the SNP has agreed to lend its support and campaign for a double 'yes' vote.

The result of the election and the prospect of a Scottish parliament has had a devastating impact on the Conservative Party in Scotland. The pro-devolution wing have accused the party leadership of losing the election because of their failure to respond to pressure for constitutional change in Scotland. Some prominent members of the party have proposed setting up a separate Scottish party. Given that they have no seats in Scotland, the party has been unable to participate in the elections for a new leader of the Conservatives. Although many within the Conservative Party still maintain their opposition to home rule in Scotland, the paradox is that they stand to gain from a Scottish Parliament with proportional representation. In this sense the parliament could be the midwife for a renewed Conservative Party in Scotland. Some have argued that the party stands to gain most by electing its own leadership and devising its own devolution policy in order to mount a credible opposition to the plans for home rule.[20]

There is clearly much to play for in politics in Scotland in terms of the referendum but also the prospect of the first elections for the new Scottish parliament being held in 1999. Much can happen before 1999, not least that the popularity the Labour government may decline (see Rose this volume). In mid-April 1997, a NOP poll asked respondents which party they were likely to vote for in a Scottish parliament. David McCrone notes that although the stated voting intentions for the forthcoming general election put Labour ahead of the SNP by 47% to 28%, the predicted vote in a Scottish Parliament narrowed from 39% to 38%.[21] This poll perhaps helps explain why the SNP did not do as well as anticipated in the general election itself where the first step was to ensure the defeat the Conservative government. Another consideration is, of course, that members of the Scottish parliament will be elected by the electoral system of AMS agreed in the Scottish Constitutional Convention and subsequently endorsed in the government's White Paper on Devolution. Given that the electorate will be allowed two votes, we will have to see how far they split their vote between two different parties.

Conclusions

As Pippa Norris has discussed, the 1997 general election will have a special place in history for the number of records broken on election night. In Scotland, it will be remembered particularly because of the wipe out of seats held by the Conservative Party. If there is a 'Yes' vote in the referendum, it will also be seen as the election that paved the way for a Scottish Parliament. While the results show a slight narrowing of the north/south divide in support for the Labour and Conservative parties, the constitutional debate in Scotland and the four-party system means that politics in Scotland continues to have a distinctive character. Much hangs on the referendum result and paradoxically the establishment of a parliament could aid the recovery of the Conservative Party in Scotland. However, it is also a major test for the Labour Party. With a double 'Yes' vote, Tony Blair's strategy will be vindicated. But should the result be 'Yes/No', then it will prove difficult to hold the broad consensus for change together. In the unlikely event of a 'No/No' result, then Labour will be blamed for wasting Scotland's best chance ever to have a parliament. With proportional representation and more equal representation of men and women, the political and gender balance of the new parliament could look quite different. Perhaps the key danger for the referendum and for the parliament itself is complacency. Much needs to be done by the campaign organisations and the political parties themselves in making the case and getting out the vote for the parliament, and in shifting the debate away from the negative aspects of taxation towards a more positive vision of what a parliament could actually achieve. Although the political outcome is uncertain, what can be predicted is that Scottish politics is going to be anything but dull in the next few years.

1   J. Mitchell, 'The 1992 Election in Scotland in Context', *Parliamentary Affairs*, October 1992.
2   I. MacWhirter, 'The Disaster That Never Was: The Failure of Scottish Opposition After the 1992 General Election', *Scottish Affairs*, Autumn 1992.
3   The term 'democratic deficit' was used by supporters of constitutional change to describe the situation where the Conservative government had a minority of MPs in Scotland and where the majority of voters supported parties who are in favour of constitutional change. The claim that the party had no mandate to rule in Scotland was rejected by the government.
4   P. Lynch, 'The Scottish Constitutional Convention 1992–95', *Scottish Affairs*, Spring 1996.
5   A. Brown, 'Women and Politics in Scotland' in J. Lovenduski and P. Norris (eds), *Women in Politics* (Oxford University Press, 1996).
6   *Scotland's Parliament, Scotland's Right* (Scottish Constitutional Convention, 1995).
7   D. Denver, '1994 European Elections: Results', *Scottish Affairs*, Autumn 1994.
8   D. McCrone, L. Paterson and A. Brown, 'Reforming Local Government in Scotland', *Local Government Studies*, 19, 1993.
9   I. Lang, 'Local Government Reform: Change for the Better', *Scottish Affairs*, Autumn 1994.
10 D. Denver and H. Bochel, 'Catastrophe for the Conservatives: the Council Elections of 1995', *Scottish Affairs*, Autumn 1995.
11 I. MacWhirter, 'Doomsday Two: the Return of Forsyth', *Scottish Affairs*, Autumn 1995.
12 P. Jones, 'Labour's Referendum Plan: Sell-out or Act of Faith?', *Scottish Affairs*, Winter 1997.
13 D. McCrone, 'Opinion Polls in Scotland, July 1996–June 1997', *Scottish Affairs*, Summer 1997. A summary of opinion polls for 1993, 1994 and 1995 can be found in nos. 4, 8 and 12 of the journal respectively.
14 A. Brown, D. McCrone and L. Paterson, *Politics and Society in Scotland* (Macmillan, 1996).
15 N.R. Smith, 'The Business Case for Devolution', *Scottish Affairs*, Summer 1996.
16 J. Bochel and D. Denver, 'The 1992 General Election in Scotland', *Scottish Affairs*, Autumn 1992.
17 Mohammed Sarwar was elected as the first Muslim MP. Since elected, he has been the subject of controversy and allegations that he attempted to bribe another candidate in the election.
18 D. Denver, 'The 1997 General Election in Scotland: An Analysis of the Results', *Scottish Affairs*, Summer 1997.
19 Nigel Smith had been active in the campaign for devolution in the 1970s and was a member of the Scottish Constitutional Commission. He was successful in securing funding from some of Scotland's trade unions, including the EIS and UNISON, and in working with the Scottish Constitutional Convention in planning the post-election referendum campaign.
20 P. Jones (*The Scotsman*, 6.5.97) and M. Fry (*Herald*, 7.5.97).
21 D. McCrone, op.cit.

Northern Ireland: La Fin de Siècle, The Twilight of the Second Protestant Ascendancy and Sinn Féin's Second Coming

BY BRENDAN O'LEARY* AND GEOFFREY EVANS†

LET US begin with a confident but falsifiable prediction. The 1997 Westminster election is likely to be the last of such elections in which the Unionist (with a capital 'U') bloc wins an overall majority of the votes cast in Northern Ireland—even if there is no reform of the electoral system for the United Kingdom parliament. Our prediction is based on the results displayed in Table 1. They show that in three region-wide elections held in Northern Ireland within one year (May 1996–97) the average share of the vote of the Unionist bloc—the Ulster Unionist Party (UUP), the Democratic Unionist Party (DUP), the United Kingdom Unionist Party (UKU), the Progressive Unionist Party (PUP), the Ulster Democratic Party (UDP) and the Conservative and Unionist Party (Con)—was 50.3%. The Unionist (U) bloc has been distinguished by its unionism, its ethnic Protestantism, and its reluctance to share significant political power with nationalists, which is why supporters of the Alliance Party of Northern Ireland (APNI) should not be defined as part of the U bloc. The APNI supports the Union, but draws albeit small-scale electoral support (averaging 7%) from both Protestants and Catholics. It also promotes power-sharing between nationalists and unionists, favours cooperative relations between Northern Ireland and the Republic, and therefore presents itself as a bridge-builder. Provided one condition is met, Table 1 suggests that the APNI will have a social base for its self-professed role at the beginning of the next century because it will hold a pivotal electoral share of votes. The condition is that the proportion of the Northern Irish electorate which belongs to cultural Catholic families continues to rise—a condition that will be met.[1]

Our prediction does not imply an immediate and complete reversal of fortunes for unionism (with a lower case 'u'). The U bloc's loss of an overall majority of the future electorate will not mean that the Nationalist (N) bloc will enjoy exactly what the U bloc loses. That is because although the N bloc is growing, as visibly demonstrated in Figure 1, it cannot, ceteris paribus, become a majority bloc for another two decades; and it is that fact that will give the APNI its bridge-building opportunity.

* Professor of Political Science at the London School of Economics and Political Science.
† Fellow of Nuffield College, Oxford.

1. Bloc performances in Northern Irish elections 1996–97. Parties' share of the vote (in %)

Party	Westminster '97	Local government '97	Forum '96
UUP	32.7	27.8	24.2
DUP	13.6	15.6	18.8
UKU	1.6	.6	3.7
PUP	1.4	2.3	3.5
UDP	–	1.2	2.2
Con	1.2	*	.5
Total U bloc	50.5	47.5	52.9
Average: 50.3			
SDLP	24.1	20.7	21.4
SF	16.1	16.9	15.5
Total N bloc	40.2	37.6	36.9
Average: 38.2			
APNI	8	6.5	6.6
Average 7			
Total: U + N + APNI	98.7	91.6	96.4
Other	1.3	**8.4	3.6

Notes: (i) Key to Parties: UKU = United Kingdom Unionist Party; Con = Conservative and Unionist Party; DUP = Democratic Unionist Party; PUP = Progressive Unionist Party; UUP = Ulster Unionist Party; SDLP = Social Democratic and Labour Party; SF = Sinn Féin; Others = Workers' Party, Natural Law Party, NI Women's Coalition, Independents etc. (ii) * Figure for Conservatives is not yet available, but is less than .5. (iii) ** The high proportion of Others in local government masks the presence of some successful independent nationalist and unionist candidates.

Table 1 shows that in the three region-wide elections held in Northern Ireland within the last year the average share of the vote of the N bloc — the Social Democratic and Labour Party (SDLP) and Sinn Féin (SF) — was 38.2%; and that in the 1997 Westminster elections it was, for the first time, above 40%. We see no reason to believe that this growth will be arrested — differential abstentionism and alienation amongst unionist voters are not the major causes of the growth of the N bloc.

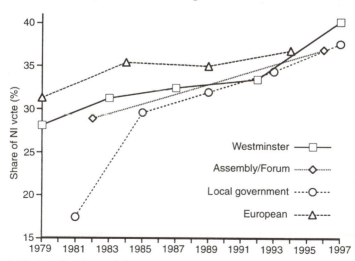

Figure 1. Nationalist share of the NI vote in Westminster, assembly, forum, local government and European elections, 1979–97

Beneath the headline news of electoral victories for the leading lights in Sinn Féin, Gerry Adams in West Belfast and Martin McGuinness in Mid-Ulster, a slow but seismic shift is taking place in the balance of electoral power in Northern Ireland. The proportion of cultural Catholics in Northern Ireland was at least 42% in the 1991 census,[2] and since then it has continued to expand. This demographic shift, in a population in which bloc and party identification are much stronger than in Great Britain and Ireland, is now making itself felt, and is especially evident amongst younger cohorts of voters. The fact is commented on by observers watching the expansion of the electoral register in nationalist districts. All nationalists are the beneficiaries of this changing demography; although Sinn Féin, so far, is benefiting more than the SDLP. In a survey we conducted in May 1996 almost 60% of Sinn Féin's support came from the 18–34 age cohort, three times the level of support the party enjoyed amongst respondents aged 55 or over,[3] a pattern consistent with evidence from the Northern Ireland Social Attitudes Survey data in the early and mid 1990s.[4] Moreover, in the last year Sinn Féin has experienced a second coming, averaging 16.5% of the vote in three elections, compared with its 1982–94 average of 11.3%. The party first erupted into electoral politics in 1982, but soon seemed trapped in a ten per cent electoral ghetto, especially after the Anglo-Irish Agreement of 1985 had appeared to staunch its growth-prospects.[5] Its recent and second wave of growth therefore has two primary sources: one is the demographic factor just discussed; the second is political. Sinn Féin has gained from its identification with what is optimistically called the first peace process, and it has won votes that might otherwise have gone to the SDLP, a fact which SDLP canvassers conveyed with dismay to one of the authors[6] and which was predicted some time ago by the other on the basis of analyses of the bases of competition among the nationalist parties in the early 1990s.[7]

The Westminster elections of 1 May 1997 were largely and understandably reported as the tale of Sinn Féin's second coming, but the broad changes the election signified were first highlighted in the elections to the Northern Ireland Peace Forum in May 1996.[8] The latter, conducted in the same newly drawn 18 constituencies as those used for the Westminster elections, revealed a significant fragmentation in the unionist vote as well as a significant leap in support for Sinn Féin. Despite the complaints of David Trimble, the leader of the UUP, the fragmentation or 'shredding' of the U bloc is only partly explained by the mechanics of the Forum's electoral system—a party list-system using a combination of the Droop formula and the d'Hondt divisor (but equivalent to pure d'Hondt).[9] 'Other Unionists', by comparison with the mid-1980s, are now attracting an increasing share of the vote in the region, even though none of these fragments can as yet hope to displace the UUP or the DUP as the major unionist parties. In the Westminster elections there was less fragmentation of the unionist vote than in the

Forum election, and that, of course, is partly explained by the well-known mechanical effects of plurality rule (see Tables 1 and 2), but the local government elections held three weeks after the Westminster election, under the single transferable vote, suggest that there are political as well as mechanical reasons for the fragmentation of the U bloc.

2. Party performances in the Westminster election in Northern Ireland. Parties' share of the vote (in %)

Party	UKU	Con	DUP	PUP	UUP	APNI	SDLP	SF	WP	NL	Oth
Seats	1	–	2	–	10	–	3	2	–	–	–
Seats %	5.6	–	11.1	–	55.6	–	16.7	11.1	–	–	–
Votes %	1.6	1.2	13.6	1.4	32.7	8	24.1	16.1	.3	.3	.7

Notes: (i) Deviation from proportionality (D = (1/2) $\Sigma |S_1 - V_1| = 26.2$. (ii) Key to Parties: As in Table 1, except that WP = Workers Party; NL = Natural Law Party; Oth = Others, Independents and Northern Ireland Women's Coalition.

There are two key political reasons for this. First, the uncertainty amongst unionists about the best political strategy to pursue in the face of the British and Irish inter-governmentalism established by the Anglo-Irish Agreement of 1985, re-expressed in the Joint Declaration for Peace in 1993, and given detailed institutional form in the joint framework documents of February 1995.[10] And second, the electoral emergence of two small loyalist parties, the Progressive Unionist Party (PUP) and the Ulster Democratic Party (UDP), as the political fronts of the loyalist paramilitaries in the wake of their official cease fires in October 1994. The first reason explains the rise and fall in support for the Conservatives between 1989 and 1994 (from 0% to 5% and back to just about 0%), and the vicissitudes of the political career of Robert McCartney MP who originally proffered his United Kingdom Unionist Party (UKU) as an alternative to conventional unionism, especially as articulated by Ian Paisley's DUP, but who now wins his seat in North Down with the support of Paisley's party. The second reason explains why urban working class Protestant voters are leaving the UUP and the DUP, albeit so far in small numbers. These uncertainties amongst unionists must not all be read in an entirely negative light — suggesting that moderate unionists in the UUP are faced by multiple forms of extremist 'outflanking'. The internal possibilities and complexities of the divisions and uncertainties amongst unionists need to be emphasised, e.g. it is not widely appreciated in Great Britain that the leaders of the PUP are far more constitutionally flexible than for example the leadership of the DUP.

It may seem odd to maintain that there is a political crisis amongst unionists when the UUP alone took 10 of the 18 Westminster seats, and when the U bloc as a whole took 13 (see Table 2). But the U bloc's success in seats is superficial, as we shall argue below. The success is, of course, in part the outcome of the absurdities of plurality rule (see Dunleavy and Margetts in this volume): deviation from proportionality was a staggering 26.2; and with merely 32.7% of the vote the UUP won

3. 'Safe' unionist seats. Order of placement of parties and per cent share of vote (%)

Seat	1		2		3		4		5	
Antrim E	UUP	(38.8)	APNI	(20.2)	DUP	(19.5)	Con	(6.8)	PUP	(5.1)
Antrim N	DUP	(46.5)	UUP	(23.7)	SDLP	(15.9)	SF	(6.3)	APNI	(6.2)
Antrim S	UUP	(57.5)	SDLP	(16.2)	APNI	(11.6)	PUP	(8.7)	SF	(5.6)
Bann U	UUP	(43.6)	SDLP	(24.2)	SF	(12.1)	DUP	(11.5)	APNI	(6.3)
Belfast E	DUP	(42.6)	UUP	(25.3)	APNI	(23.8)	Con	(2.4)	SF	(2.1)
Belfast N	UUP	(51.8)	SDLP	(20.4)	SF	(20.2)	APNI	(5.4)	GP	(1.3)
Belfast S	UUP	(36)	SDLP	(24.3)	PUP	(14.4)	APNI	(13)	SF	(5.1)
Derry E	UUP	(35.6)	DUP	(25.6)	SDLP	(21.7)	SF	(9.1)	APNI	(6.4)
Down N	UKU	(35.1)	UUP	(31.1)	APNI	(20.7)	Con	(5)	SDLP	(4.4)
Lagan V	UUP	(55.4)	APNI	(17.2)	DUP	(13.6)	SDLP	(7.8)	Con	(2.7)
Strangford	UUP	(44.3)	DUP	(30.2)	APNI	(13.1)	SDLP	(6.7)	Con	(4.2)

Notes: (i) Key to Parties: As in Table 1. 'Safe' refers to seats where support for unionist parties (UUP, DUP, PUP, UKU, Con) is over 50%. (ii) The seats most vulnerable to a nationalist pact are Belfast North and Belfast South, but for nationalists to win these seats the unionist vote must be divided. (iii) In Tables 3–5 we employ the mode of presentation first used by P. Mitchell, 'Party Competition in a an Ethnic Dual Party System', *Ethnic and Racial Studies*, 18 October 1995, p. 773.

55.6% of the seats. Northern Ireland's results should therefore be added to the arsenal of those who suggest the case for a reformed and proportional representation electoral system for Westminster. But the success of the U bloc in seats is also the outcome of greater coordination by unionist parties in competition against nationalist parties. The ethno-national imperative, uniting when necessary against the ethnic competitor, is for the moment felt more keenly by unionists than nationalists. In 'safe unionist' seats (see Table 3) and in 'safe nationalist' seats (see Table 4) the number of effective unionist candidates reflected their bloc's chances, while the two nationalist parties competed with one another in seventeen of the eighteen seats (Sinn Féin did not run a candidate in North Down, a unionist haven if not heaven). The DUP chose not to run candidates against the UUP where to do so might have facilitated a nationalist victory (notably in West Tyrone, Belfast North, and Belfast South). The UDP, the less successful of the smaller loyalist parties in the Forum elections, decided not to compete in any Westminster seats; while the PUP decided not to endanger the sitting UUP MP in Belfast North, Cecil Walker, where its intervention just might have led to a nationalist victory, or to run against the sitting DUP MP, Peter Robinson, in Belfast East, where its intervention might conceivably have

4. 'Safe' nationalist seats. Order of placement of parties and per cent share of vote (%)

Seat	1		2		3		4		5	
Belfast W	SF	(55.9)	SDLP	(38.7)	UUP	(3.4)	WP	(1.6)	HR	(0.2)
Down S	SDLP	(52.9)	UUP	(32.8)	SF	(10.4)	APNI	(3.5)	NLP	(0.4)
Foyle	SDLP	(52.5)	SF	(23.9)	DUP	(21.5)	APNI	(1.7)	NLP	(0.3)
Mid Ulster	SF	(40.1)	DUP	(36.3)	SDLP	(22.1)	APNI	(0.9)	WP	(0.5)
Newry & Armagh	SDLP	(43)	UUP	(33.8)	SF	(21.1)	APNI	(1.9)	NLP	(0.2)
Tyrone W	UUP	(35.6)	SDLP	(32.1)	SF	(30.9)	APNI	(1.8)	WP	(0.5)

Notes: (i) Key to Parties: As in Table 1. 'Safe' refers to seats where support for nationalist parties (SDLP, SF) is over 50%. (ii) The seats most vulnerable to a unionist pact are Newry and Armagh, Mid Ulster and Tyrone West, but for unionists to win these seats the nationalist vote must be evenly split (as occurred in 1997 in Tyrone West).

let the APNI candidate win. Unionist cooperation can be seen most clearly in Fermanagh and South Tyrone where the sitting UUP MP, Ken Maginnis, faced no rival unionist (see Table 5), and in West Tyrone where the UUP won a seat despite a combined nationalist vote of 63% (see Table 4).

5. Unionist-Nationalist marginal(s). Order of placement of parties and per cent share of vote (%)

Seat	1		2		3		4		5	
Fermanagh & S Tyrone	UUP	(51.5)	SF	(23.1)	SDLP	(22.9)	APNI	(2)	NLP	(0.5)

Note: 'Marginals' refers to seat where the difference between support for unionist and nationalist parties is less than 6%.

Unionist coordination and nationalist competition can be seen clearly in the contrast in the nature of party competition in safe unionist and safe nationalist seats. In the latter (Table 3) unionists unite behind the unionist candidate most likely to win; in the former they allow themselves the luxury of limited competition (Table 4). As Table 6 shows, by comparison with the Forum election the UUP enjoyed major increases in its share of the vote in the Westminster election in safe unionist (an average of 12.8%), safe nationalist (an average of 9.6%)

6. Comparing party performances in 1997 Westminster and 1996 Forum elections.
(% Westminster − % Forum)

Seat	Con	UKU	UDP	PUP	DUP	UUP	APNI	SDLP	SF
Antrim E	6	*	*	−1.7	−9.2	8.7	8.3	−2.1	−.3
Antrim N	*	*	*	*	9.5	−1.6	.5	−.3	.5
Antrim S	*	*	*	4.4	*	27.3	3.2	1.1	.1
Bann U		*	*	*	−4.1	7.3	1.6	2.7	−.2
Belfast E	1.7	*	*	*	13.2	2.8	5.2	−1.8	−.2
Belfast N	*	*	*	*	*	34.6	1.3	1.9	1.2
Belfast S	1.7	*	*	8.3	*	13.2	.5	5.8	−1.4
Derry E		*	*	*	1.8	4.7	.7	1.4	−.2
Down N	3.8	14.3	*	*	*	5.5	3.6	−.1	*
Lagan V	*	*	*	*	−8.5	17.7	6.8	−1.4	−.1
Strangford	1.5	*	*	*	1.3	13	1.6	−.6	.6
Average increase in 'safe' unionist seats contested	2.9	14.3	*	3.6	.6	12.8	3	.6	0
Belfast W	*	*	*	*	*	−.2	*	12.2	2.5
Down S	*	*	*	*	*	10.6	−.1	9.6	−2.7
Foyle	*	*	*	*	10.3	*	−.1	8.3	−1.8
Mid-Ulster	*	*	*	*	19.8	*	−.4	−6.4	10.4
Newry & Armagh	*	*	*	*	*	11.3	−.2	8.9	−4.5
Tyrone West	*	*	*	*	*	16.7	−.8	3.7	2.8
Average increase in 'safe' nationalist seats contested	n/a	n/a	n/a	n/a	15.1	9.6	−.3	6.1	1.1
Fermanagh & S Tyrone	*	*	*	*	*	19.2	.3	1.3	−1.1
Increase in marginal	*	*	*	*	*	19.2	.3	1.3	−1.1

Notes: (i) Figures in cells are share of the vote in (1997) Westminster elections minus share of the vote in (1996) Forum election. (ii) * signifies that no candidate from this party ran in the relevant Westminster constituency.

and safe marginal seats (up 19%). The behaviour of the local branches of the Conservative party is perhaps most revealing of Northern Ireland's dual party system. It was set up in 1989 in a wave of enthusiasm for 'electoral integration' that maintained that votes for British parties would transcend traditional divisions within the population.[11] But in the 1997 Westminster election the party ran no candidates in safe nationalist seats, suggesting that its integrationist ambitions count less than saving deposits.

Nationalist competition, by contrast, was fierce, but not violent, throughout Northern Ireland. Sinn Féin's Gerry Adams won back West Belfast, benefiting from redrawn electoral boundaries, and won comfortably despite evidence of tactical voting by loyalists and unionists for the SDLP's Joe Hendron and the decision of the APNI not to run a candidate. Martin McGuinness of Sinn Féin won the re-structured seat of Mid-Ulster from the DUP's Reverend William McCrea, and also comfortably beat his SDLP challenger, Denis Haughey — even though the SDLP and Sinn Féin had been level-pegging in the same constituency in the Forum election of 1996. McCrea's outspoken support for a loyalist who was subsequently jailed helped unite local nationalists behind McGuinness, who as Sinn Féin's Chief Negotiator also enjoyed the benefits of a much higher media profile than Haughey. In Foyle, Newry and Armagh, and South Down the SDLP's John Hume, Seamus Mallon and Eddie McGrady, comfortably held off their Sinn Féin challengers. But in West Tyrone a dead-heat in the nationalist race between the SDLP and Sinn Féin enabled the UUP's William Thompson to win with less than a third of the total vote.

This pattern of unionists being more disciplined within their bloc and nationalists being more competitive within theirs is not, however, likely to continue into the next century. One of the repercussions of a second peace process is likely to be an agreement amongst nationalists to have electoral pacts for Westminster elections, in which case under the present arrangements nationalists would win at least six and possibly up to eight seats. A pact was promoted by Sinn Féin during late 1996 and early 1997 but it was turned down by the SDLP because of the IRA's resumption of violence in February 1996. Moreover, if the Labour Government, as seems possible, introduces proportional representation for Westminster elections then nationalists will not need to cooperate to deprive the UUP of its 'surplus' seats; and the share of seats won by nationalists will rise in proportion with their votes, with or without a second peace process. Unionism does therefore face an electoral crisis. Come what may the U bloc will soon be an electoral minority in the region, albeit the biggest one; and it is conceivable that all Northern Ireland elections will soon be by proportional representation (various permutations of PR are already used for local government districts, Northern Ireland assemblies/forums and the European parliament). We are therefore witnessing the twilight of the second Protestant ascendancy in Irish history—the first was that enjoyed by the Anglo-Irish from the end of the seventeenth until the nineteenth century.

The electoral crisis of the U bloc has been less noticed than the other outcome of the Westminster election with implications for the unionists: the loss of the UUP's grip on a Conservative Government with no parliamentary majority and its replacement by a Labour Government with an overwhelming parliamentary majority. The new Government is committed by its manifesto to the agenda of the Framework Documents—which envisage the creation of a power-sharing Northern Irish assembly; elaborate North-South institutions with consultative, harmonising and executive powers; the modification and expansion of the institutions of the Anglo-Irish Agreement; and the possible establishment of identical legal protections of individual and collective rights on both sides of the border in Ireland.[12] Throughout her time as Shadow Secretary of State for Northern Ireland Dr Marjorie Mowlam MP was unwavering in her support for the Framework Documents, more disposed than the Conservatives to being flexible on facilitating Sinn Féin's entry into all-party negotiations, warmer towards the reform of the police force, the predominantly Protestant RUC, and keener to implement the North Report on the control of marches and parades—the desire of the Orange Order to assert its traditional supremacist prerogatives is the most frequent source of unarmed public disorder in the region. Dr Mowlam's appointment as Secretary of State, and the willingness of the new Prime Minister, Tony Blair, to have his first heads-of-government meeting with the Irish prime minister, and to sanction meetings between Sinn Féin and civil servants even before a restoration of the IRA cease fire, spell out a simple message, albeit one already embedded in the Anglo-Irish Agreement. The message to unionists is this: Northern Ireland remains part of the United Kingdom for as long as a majority wants, but the U bloc has no veto on the reform of Northern Ireland, or indeed on its relations with the Republic of Ireland, other than those which a Westminster Government considers it prudent to yield.

Unionists face a very difficult transition as the second millennium beckons: a Labour Government and its allies could be in power at Westminster for a decade; the dominant party in Dáil Eireann may once again be Fianna Feil; an IRA cease fire will guarantee Sinn Féin a place at negotiating tables; the Irish, British and American governments will be keen to keep Sinn Féin in such negotiations in which the agenda is based on the Framework Documents; and against this background the demographic and electoral power of unionists is slipping. Time will tell whether in the twilight of the second Protestant ascendancy sufficient reformers emerge from the ranks of unionists to carve out a political settlement with their nationalist rivals. It is not impossible, and is eminently desirable, but it will have to be the subject of another article.

1   For further discussion of demography and its political implications in Northern Ireland see B. O'Leary, 'Appendix 4. Party Support in Northern Ireland, 1969–89' in J. McGarry and B. O'Leary (eds), *The Future of Northern Ireland* (Oxford University Press, 1990), p. 342 and B. O'Leary, 'Introduction: Reflections on a Cold Peace' *Ethnic and Racial Studies* 18, 1995.

2   See J. McGarry and B. O'Leary, *Explaining Northern Ireland: Broken Images* (Basil Blackwell), p. 502, fn. 24.

3   For details see G. Evans and B. O'Leary, 'Frameworked Futures: Intransigence and Flexibility in the Northern Ireland Elections of 30 May 1996', *Irish Political Studies*, 12, 1997.

4   See, inter alia, M. Duffy and G. Evans, 'Class, Community Polarisation and Politics', in L. Dowds, P. Devine and R. Breen (eds), *Attitudes in Northern Ireland: the 6th Report* (Gower, 1997), p. 102; and G. Evans and M. Duffy, 'Beyond the Sectarian Divide: The Social Bases and Political Consequences of Nationalist and Unionist Party Competition in Northern Ireland', *British Journal of Political Science* 27, 1997.

5   See B. O'Leary and J. McGarry, *The Politics of Antagonism: Understanding Northern Ireland* (Athlone, 1996, 2nd edn).

6   We know of no good administrative or logistical argument to suggest that Sinn Féin has become more proficient in 'vote-stealing', as some of its opponents declare. Electoral manipulation has been a constant feature of Northern Irish politics, within and across both blocs and most parties, but we think that the scale of Sinn Fein's recent expansion cannot be attributed to this factor.

7   See G. Evans and M. Duffy, 'Beyond the Sectarian Divide: The Social Bases and Political Consequences of Unionist and Nationalist Party Competition in Northern Ireland, *British Journal of Political Science* 27, 1997.

8   Supra n. 3.

9   Ibid.

10 See B. O'Leary, 'Afterword: What is Framed in the Framework Documents?', *Ethnic and Racial Studies* 18, 1995.

11 A belief which has been shown to be mistaken: see M. Duffy and G. Evans, 'Building Bridges: The Political Implications of Electoral Integration for Northern Ireland', *British Journal of Political Science* 26, 1996.

12 See n. 3.

The Local Elections

BY COLIN RALLINGS* AND MICHAEL THRASHER†

EIGHTEEN YEARS of Conservative government ended as it had begun—on the first Thursday in May, local election day. Only twice in history have the general and local elections been held simultaneously. On the first occasion in 1979 the Labour Prime Minister, James Callaghan, had little choice over the election date. His party's pact with the Liberals had crumbled, leaving a minority government vulnerable to an opposition vote of no confidence. The Conservatives under Mrs Thatcher swept to power, winning not only a Commons majority but also political control of many local authorities across Britain. Now, with a pleasing symmetry the wheel has turned full circle. John Major decided that local election day 1997 offered the Conservatives their best chance of securing a fifth successive term, but instead it proved to be their electoral nemesis. Inevitably, in both 1979 and 1997 the local election campaign was overshadowed by the general election. Yet these 'forgotten elections' provide unique opportunities to further our understanding of electoral behaviour and the development of party competition in Britain.

In this article we shall examine a number of different aspects of the 1997 local elections. First, we review the results and, crucially, frame our discussion within the context of what has been a decade long Conservative decline in local government. The party now begins a period in opposition in far worse shape in local government than ever before. Second, we will use the fact of simultaneous elections to look for evidence of differential voting. Did some parties perform better in one form of election than another? Was there a consistent pattern of voting or were there local variations? Did voters turn out to vote in equal numbers for both types of election? Although only parts of Britain had local elections the contests were sufficiently widespread to allow such comparisons. Finally, we shall identify the main changes in the pattern of voter behaviour between 1979 and 1997, and assess what they might tell us about political attitudes and party loyalties.

The local election results in 1997

Ordinarily the seats up for re-election in 1997 would have been in the shire counties, last fought in 1993. But the electoral cycle has been

* Professor of Politics at the University of Plymouth.
† Professor of Politics at the University of Plymouth.

severely dislocated by structural changes to some local authorities. There were, for example, no elections in Wales because there the former two tier system of eight county and 37 district authorities was wholly replaced in 1996 by 22 new unitary councils. In England the process of change has been piecemeal. At the same time the administrative counties of Avon, Cleveland, Humberside and Isle of Wight were abolished and replaced with unitary authorities. Since then the body charged with reviewing structure, the English Local Government Commission, has made further recommendations resulting in the abolition or alteration of further counties. The administrative county of Berkshire no longer exists while Hereford and Worcestershire, an amalgamation forged in 1973, has been replaced by a separate unitary authority of Hereford-shire and a two-tier county of Worcestershire. The creation of other unitary authorities in largely urban areas such as Derby, Leicester, Portsmouth, and Stoke-on-Trent has had an equally significant impact on other counties. The scale of this quiet revolution can be gauged from the fact that in only 14 of the original 39 English counties did the electoral battle in 1997 reflect precisely the previous contests of four years before. Overall, 1997 brought elections for 34 shire counties, 19 new unitary authorities and one substantially revised district council (Malvern Hills). Additionally, there were partial council elections in the unitary authorities of Bristol and Kingston upon Hull.

Local elections in Britain have never been easy to understand but the process of piecemeal structural change has complicated matters still further. These changes and the redrawing of some local ward boundaries meant it was difficult to estimate how many seats and councils each party was defending going into the elections. Direct comparisons with previous contests were not always feasible and so adjustments had to be made to take account of the reconfiguration of some county councils and the creation of new unitary authorities. Only after making such adjustments could we provide a benchmark from which to judge the outcome of the 1997 local elections. Before the elections took place it was felt that while the Conservatives might lose the general election the party would make gains in the local contests. Most seats and councils were last contested in 1993 or 1995 and on both occasions the Conservatives performed badly, polling a projected 31% national equivalent vote in 1993 and a record low 25% in 1995. It followed that should the Conservatives do better in 1997 then that would bring its reward in additional seats and more council control. Furthermore, the coincidence of the local elections with the general election was thought to be to the Conservatives' advantage because one explanation for previous local election disappointments was that the party's supporters had chosen to abstain.

Table 1 shows, however, that Conservative gains, in what was once regarded as the party's heartland, were extremely modest. Across the counties, there was a net gain of only 121 seats, although a number of

1. The 1997 local election results

Seats*

	Counties			Unitaries			
	Before	After	Net +/−	Before	After	Net +/−	Total +/−
Conservative	760	881	+121	126	226	+100	+221
Labour	739	746	+7	575	541	−34	−27
Lib Dem	678	495	−183	216	195	−21	−204
Ind/Other	101	81	−20	18	15	−3	−23

Note: * Figures are approximate and net changes do not sum to zero because of alterations to boundaries/councillor numbers.

Council control*

	Counties		Unitaries	
	Before	After	Before	After
Conservative	2	9	0	2
Labour	7	8	12	10
Liberal Democrat	6	2	4	2
No overall control	19	15	1	3

Note: * Figures refer to situation when new authorities assume responsibilities in April 1998.

county councils, including Cambridgeshire, Kent, Surrey and West Sussex returned to Conservative control. In the new unitary authorities, where the disastrous elections of 1995 were the base for comparison in most cases, the number of Conservative councillors increased by just 100. Only in Bracknell Forest and Wokingham were the gains sufficient to give the Conservatives an overall council majority. Labour lost overall control in two unitary authorities but was compensated by victory in Cumbria. Conservative advances, such as they were, drew mainly from the Liberal Democrat party which lost just over 200 seats overall and saw its majority evaporate on four county councils and two unitary councils. But the outcome might have been much worse for the Liberal Democrats. In recent years Liberal Democrat candidates have performed well in local elections. Indeed, throughout the 1990s the party has consistently polled about a quarter of the national equivalent vote in such elections. In 1997 the special circumstances thought to favour the Liberal Democrats in local elections were missing. Turnout, particularly amongst Conservative-leaning voters, was expected to be higher than normal because of the general election. Resources, always a problem, would be stretched as the party struggled to make a breakthrough at Westminster and Liberal Democrat activists, normally canvassing for the local vote, were concentrated in the national party's key target seats. Finally, the party was not expected to improve on its 1992 general election share and its expected local vote would certainly be lower than that achieved in the mid 1990s. Indeed, those three conditions were met but the Conservative party did not benefit. Turnout in the local elections did rise considerably, above 70% compared with less than 40% for the two previous sets of county elections. The Liberal Democrats did concentrate resources on its key seats and the party's overall support did decline. Yet the Conservatives were unable to capitalise on those circumstances and to understand why we need briefly to examine recent critical changes in the nature of party competition and local voting behaviour.

The long-term decline in Conservative support 1990–97

While in opposition between 1974 and 1979 the Conservatives benefited from the pattern of protest voting characteristic of local elections. Once in power the party found itself exposed to those same forces, but managed to limit losses in both seats and council control from 1979 to 1989. The 1990 local elections, popularly known as the 'poll tax' elections, changed all that and, although the party recovered sufficiently to win the 1992 general election, significant damage had already begun to be inflicted on its local government base. The process of decline accelerated from 1993 onwards. That year saw the party lose almost 500 seats and political control of county councils which had been in Conservative hands for a century. The decline was greatest in southern England with an average fall of nine per cent in the Conservative vote. Senior party figures, including the party chairman, anticipated gains not losses at the 1994 local elections. The reason for this optimism was the belief that the equivalent elections in 1990 had been so awful that Conservative fortunes could only improve. That view was misplaced and the party went on to sustain further heavy losses in seats and control of no fewer than another 21 local authorities, including nine London boroughs. Ominously, the decline in Conservative support was, once again, greatest in the south of England.

These results were poor for the Conservatives but they could not compare with what happened to the party in 1995. Conservative councillors seeking re-election in this year had formerly been regarded as the most fortunate in electoral terms. This was because of the national party's past willingness to use this phase of the electoral cycle, when the largest single number of council seats fell vacant, to signal both in 1983 and 1987 the imminence of a general election which, in turn, brought a corresponding increase in party support. It was expected in 1995 that the anti-government protest vote would begin to scale down and that the elections might mark the beginning of the Conservatives' long-awaited recovery. Instead, the reverse happened as the Conservatives lost a further 2,000 council seats and political control of another 61 local authorities. The party's national equivalent vote, just 25%, represented its lowest ever poll share. Local elections were also held that year for the new unitary authorities in Scotland and Wales. In both countries Conservative candidates fared badly and, significantly, the party failed to win control of a single council. With hindsight we should view these elections as a dress rehearsal for the general election. Conservative support had fallen to dangerous levels, to the point where it became penalised by Britain's first-past-the-post electoral system. The party lost many more seats than had uniform swing been in evidence.

The explanation for this lies with the impact of tactical campaigning by Labour and Liberal Democrat parties in different wards. Each of those parties has, in recent years, developed a more efficient strategy of targeting vulnerable Conservative controlled wards.[1] As a result the party best positioned locally to unseat the Conservatives saw its candidate's vote share rise the most. In effect local Conservatives found themselves caught in a pincer movement which had a devastating impact.

Further Conservative losses occurred in the 1996 local elections and although this slide was halted in 1997 there is no doubting the damage incurred. Table 2 contrasts party representation in local government between 1979 and 1997. There has been a three-fold collapse in the number of Conservative councillors and an eleven-fold reduction in the number of councils controlled. Labour has benefited, now controlling almost half of all councils and council seats in Great Britain but the Liberal Democrats have also advanced with more councillors and controlling more than twice as many local authorities as the Conservatives. Closer inspection of the Conservative retreat from local government reveals that currently there are more than 50 councils administering services for some six million electors where not a single Conservative sits in the council chamber. In many other local authorities responsibility for arguing the Conservative position lies with a single councillor. Quite simply, the Conservative voice in local government has become muted following a decade of electoral decline.

2. Seats and council control in Great Britain, 1979 and 1997

	1979				1997			
	seats	%	councils	%	seats	%	councils	%
Conservative	12,222	48.2	244	47.2	4,449	19.9	23	5.2
Labour	7,410	29.2	109	21.1	10,643	47.7	206	46.8
Lib Dem	1,059	4.2	2	0.4	4,756	21.3	50	11.4
Nationalists	301	1.2	4	0.8	301	1.4	4	0.9
Ind/Other	4,388	17.3	82	15.9	2,153	9.7	24	5.5
No overall control	–	–	76	14.7	–	–	133	30.2

Note: The overall number of seats and councils has altered because of local government reorganisation.

The Conservatives' decline as a force in local government has been truly dramatic, particularly in urban areas. For example in 1945, the only previous occasion on which Labour has achieved a parliamentary majority of over 100, Birmingham council was hung with no single party having overall control but with the Conservatives still a major force. Following recent elections Britain's second city has just 13 Conservative councillors, with a Labour administration and Liberal Democrats making up the official opposition. Liverpool, Conservative controlled between 1945 and 1954, now has a solitary Conservative councillor. The Conservative position is much worse now than in the early 1960s when the party was coming to the end of another long period of office. In the more urban borough councils, for example, at the end of the

Macmillan government the Conservatives still averaged around 30% of seats. In contrast at each of the last three elections in the metropolitan boroughs the party share of seats has not risen into double digits. The Conservatives control no councils in Scotland and Wales and the party has also disappeared from some of the English regions. In the North, Yorkshire and Humberside, East and West Midlands there is currently no local authority with a majority Conservative administration and in two other regions, North West and South West, the party's presence is limited to a single authority. In effect, the party has seen its local government base narrowed to the point where almost one in five of Conservative councillors sits on the 23 authorities it controls.

Split-ticket voting 1979 and 1997

How far do British electors 'vote the party ticket' at local and national elections? As we have noted the only previous chance to compare votes cast simultaneously at local and general elections occurred in 1979. In a study of the two types of election in 100 parliamentary constituency areas, Waller concluded that whereas in urban constituencies few differences emerged 'in rural areas there can be no doubt that the correlation between ... [the] results is much less close'.[2] Such a divergence in behaviour, according to Waller, seemed to be a function of the personal popularity of individual candidates, the existence of salient local issues, and a greater willingness to cast a vote for other than the Conservative and Labour parties in a local as opposed to a general election. A more limited study by Game of four highly politically competitive towns—Cambridge, Gillingham, Gloucester and Watford—similarly showed that thousands of electors split their parliamentary and local votes between different parties.[3] In a detailed examination of parliamentary and local elections in Liverpool, Cox and Laver show that voting for the Liberals in the city as a whole was twice as high at the local as at the general election, with two votes being taken from Labour for every one lost by the Conservatives.[4]

Since 1979 there has been growing, though necessarily indirect evidence that a significant minority of voters do not behave the same way in local and general elections. Miller has conducted two discrete pieces of survey research which help to throw light on what may be happening. In May 1986 he found that '80% of respondents had local choices for Conservative, Labour or Alliance that were exactly in accord with their party identification—and 83% in accord with their current parliamentary preference'. In other words approximately one in five voters are admitting that they make different choices for national as opposed to local elections. Moreover, whilst there was little direct exchange between Conservative and Labour preferences at the two levels, according to Miller, 'the Alliance gains more than it loses in local elections from the willingness of people to desert their national political choice'.[5] In a later study Miller compared how respondents had voted in the May local elections with their parliamentary vote five weeks later during the 1987 general election campaign. The degree of correspondence between the parties varies, but once again the analysis depicts a sizeable level of split ticket voting. Some 87% of 'local' Conservatives stayed with the party at the general election as did 80% of Labour supporters and 63% of those of the Alliance.[6] This has been confirmed by a recent analysis of British Election Study Panel data which compared the reported behaviour of voters at the 1992 general and 1994 local elections. Nearly half the sample—including a majority of Conservative and Liberal Democrat supporters—said they had voted in 1994 with local rather than national considerations uppermost in their minds. The Liberal Democrats particularly appeared to benefit from being seen as a 'localist' party and reaped an especial advantage in the few cases where they were perceived to be in control of the council.[7]

In 1997 almost half the electors in England had the opportunity to vote either for their county council or for one of the new all-purpose, unitary authorities. Following increased political competition at local level,[8] each of the major parties contested almost 90% of the county vacancies. A survey in these areas a few days before polling day, conducted by MORI jointly for the Local Government Association and Local Government Chronicle, revisited the issue of 'split-ticket' voting. MORI found that at least 10% of Conservative and Labour general election supporters intended to vote Liberal Democrat at the locals (see Table 3). This pattern accounts for the fact that according to this survey the Liberal Democrat local vote was seven per cent higher than the party's general election vote, with the Conservatives down by four per cent and Labour by five. Looked at the other way, whereas more than 90% of respondents who intended to vote either Conservative or Labour at the local elections would also support that party at the general election, fewer than three in five 'local' Liberal Democrats were likely to remain loyal—such 'deserters' favouring Labour over the Conservatives in the ratio 4:3.

3. Support for parties at local and national level

Distribution of local election 'votes' by general election 'vote'

General election vote for 1997		Con	Lab	Lib Dem	Ind	
32	Con	79	3	11	6	100%
47	Lab	2	84	10	4	100%
16	Lib Dem	2	10	77	11	100%
3	Ref	58	16	16	8	100%

Distribution of general election 'votes' by local election 'vote'

Local election vote for 1997		Con	Lab	Lib Dem	Ind	
28	Con	91	4	1	4	100%
42	Lab	2	94	3	1	100%
23	Lib Dem	17	23	57	2	100%
7	Ind	29	26	26	16	100%

Source: MORI for Local Government Association/Local Government Chronicle, April 1997.

Survey data compiled from a national sample cannot, however, accurately reflect the impact of particular electoral contexts on voters' behaviour. In order to discover how far such expressed intentions were matched in the ballot box, we have collected local election results for 30 constituencies in England where the county divisions can be aggregated into an exact match with parliamentary boundaries. We will, in time, add the results from another 35 constituencies of this type, together with about 25 cases where constituency and unitary authority ward boundaries coincide. These will prove particularly complex to analyse as multiple vacancies at the local level mean that some parties do not field a full slate of candidates and electors can split their vote not only between the parliamentary and local contests but within the local election as well. For the moment, therefore, our findings should be considered indicative rather than conclusive.

4. Aggregate general and local election voting in selected constituencies

All 30 constituencies

	Con %sh	Lab %sh	Lib Dem %sh	Ref %sh	Ind %sh	Turnout %
Local	34.1	39.4	23.4	–	3.1	73.0
General	36.0	43.1	16.2	3.3	1.3	74.0

	Con (ge) −Con (le)	Lab (ge) −Lab (le)	Lib Dem (ge) −Lib Dem (le)	Ref share	Ind (ge) −Ind (le)	Turnout ge–le
	1.9	3.7	−7.3	3.3	−1.8	1.0
With Ref candidate	1.7	4.2	−8.2	4.3	−2.0	0.6
No Ref candidate	2.7	2.0	−3.5	–	−1.1	1.2
High	11.8	13.2	9.4	8.1	1.8	4.3
Low	−4.9	−7.6	−22.3	2.3	−14.6	−2.0

20 constituencies with full local party slate and local Ind vote < 3.0%

	Con %sh	Lab %sh	Lib Dem %sh	Ref %sh	Ind %sh	Turnout %
Local	34.6	39.4	25.2	–	0.8	73.1
General	36.3	44.4	14.8	3.6	1.0	73.8

	Con (ge) −Con (le)	Lab (ge) −Lab (le)	Lib Dem (ge) −Lib Dem (le)	Ref share	Ind (ge) −Ind (le)	Turnout ge–le
	1.7	5.0	−10.4	3.6	0.2	0.7
With Ref candidate	1.1	5.3	−10.9	4.3	0.2	0.7
No Ref candidate	4.8	3.0	−7.8	–	0.0	1.0
High	9.1	13.2	−2.7	8.1	2.5	3.6
Low	−1.9	0.1	−22.3	2.3	−2.1	−2.0

The information presented in Table 4 supports a number of propositions. Both the Conservative and Labour parties attracted more support at national rather than local level whereas, and as expected from our earlier analysis, the Liberal Democrats are demonstrably more successful at garnering local votes. This is true both of our entire sample of 30 constituencies and also of the restricted analysis of 20 cases where each major party fielded a single candidate in each of the county divisions and where the intervention of Independents amounted to no more than three per cent of the total local vote in the constituency. Nor does it appear to be the case that the differences in votes are the consequence of some voters choosing to participate in one type of election but abstaining from the other. The average difference in turnout for the general and local elections is no more than one per cent and there are even instances where local turnout is higher. This amounts to clear prima facie evidence that the same voters split their ticket on 1 May.

The extent to which each party's local and general election votes diverge is, of course, the product of the aggregation of a variety of individual chopping and changing. A particular conundrum surrounds the source of the Referendum party's vote for it fielded no local candidates at all. Reading the MORI data in association with our own figures would suggest that the Liberal Democrat local vote dispersed to the almost equal overall benefit of Conservatives and Labour, and that a proportion of the Conservative local vote moved to the Referendum party. The fact that the Liberal Democrat local vote share dropped less significantly where there was no Referendum candidate, however, does indicate that some people who voted Lib Dem in the county contests switched to the Referendum party at the general election.

What happened in individual constituencies is fascinating. Although some of the more dramatic variations between local and general election votes appear to be the product of the dispersal of support for local Independent and minor party candidates (as in the 11.8% rise in the Conservative vote in Fareham and the 9.5% Labour increase in Exeter), others cannot be accounted for except by vote switching on a massive scale. In Cambridge, where the major parties were opposed by a single unsuccessful Independent, 21,000 people voted Labour and just over 18,000 Liberal Democrat at the local elections. In the parliamentary contest, which actually attracted a slightly smaller turnout, Labour polled in excess of 27,000 and the Liberal Democrats fewer than 9,000. In Pendle the Liberal Democrats slipped from a good second place locally to a poor third at the general election as their vote slumped from nearly 16,000 to just 5,460. In Canterbury, where the Liberal Democrats started the campaign as clear challengers to the Conservatives at both national and local level, not only was their local share of the vote sharply down compared with 1993 but their general election performance was even poorer leaving them third in the constituency.

Indeed, in most cases Labour appears to have been the prime beneficiary at the general election of a reduction in Liberal Democrat local support. However, where there was no Referendum candidate the issue is less clear cut. One prominent eurosceptic, Tony Marlow in Northampton North, looks to have 'shared' the Liberal Democrat windfall with Labour and another, Ann Winterton in Congleton, rarely among Conservatives at this election harvested the lion's share of local 'deserters'. In Great Yarmouth, where each party had a full local slate and where neither Independent nor Referendum candidates were present, the local and national votes were quite similar. The sole instances of the Liberal Democrat general election vote being higher were where the party had contested only a minority of county divisions. The interest in these cases centres on the turnout. In Bromsgrove where the Liberal Democrats contested two of the ten divisions only 495 more people voted nationally than locally, and in Wellingborough where none of the nine divisions featured Liberal Democrats the total local turnout was just 1,028 less than that for the general election. Even without a candidate from 'their' party to support it seems that most people are keen to use their vote once they have arrived at the polling station.

Conclusions

Even from this limited evaluation it seems clear that many more electors cast votes for different parties at the 1997 general and local elections than had done so at the comparable contests in 1979. We have long suspected, using evidence from the annual local elections, that for many voters making a choice of party at local level is something to be done independently of, and even in contradiction to, their national party preference.[9] We now know that to be true. The extent of split-ticket voting is consistent with recent evidence of a decline in party identification amongst former Conservative supporters, coupled with more effective local campaigning by both Labour and Liberal Democrat parties. From 1992–97 there has been a significant decline in the number of Conservative identifiers.[10] Some Tory voters at the general election did not support the party's candidates at the local elections. Such voters would have been the subject of targeting by the main opposition parties. Split-ticket voting now happens in both rural and urban constituencies, and it happens almost regardless of an objective interpretation of the tactical conditions prevailing in a particular constituency. What voters appear to respond to is the campaign waged by the parties, together with their own assessment of which party is best fitted to provide representation for the tier of government being elected. The combination of these two factors had hurt the Conservatives at every local election since 1993 and now they came into play at a general election too.

The appearance of such detached electors, even as a government was being chosen, must give the Conservatives, in particular, food for thought. Notwithstanding the fact that the party made gains in both seats and councils, the Conservatives suffered a worse result at the local elections than they did nationally. Even among the die-hard minority still prepared to vote Conservative at the general election, some were not sufficiently committed to support the party in local contests held at the same time. If their loyalty could not be counted on in such circumstances, what chance that they will return to the party in the 1998 or 1999 local elections?

The Conservatives may take comfort from the argument that the Labour government will enjoy an initial honeymoon with the electors, but come a period of 'mid-term blues' (discussed later by Rose) voters will return home to the Conservatives again. Here the positioning of the Liberal Democrats becomes crucial. They have established themselves as the second party of local government able to attract support at this level far in excess of their national opinion poll ratings. The party's candidates in local elections have demonstrated a strategic awareness of the prevailing electoral conditions and used that awareness to exploit, rather than be exploited by, the electoral system. At times the party has proved less popular in its overall share of the national vote than the Alliance parties during the 1980s but it has been much more successful in getting its local candidates elected. In turn, this has meant more local authorities where there is a direct Liberal Democrat input into the policy making process, either running a majority administration or involved in a power sharing arrangement on a hung council. Consequently, the Liberal Democrats have become a much more visible presence in local government and, if and when the Labour government becomes unpopular (as Rose suggests), they rather than the Conservatives may be strategically best placed to exploit any discontent on the ground. The Liberal Democrat party has already displaced the Conservatives, and become virtually the sole opposition to Labour, in urban areas such as Islington, Liverpool, Norwich and Sheffield. Current circumstances suggest that process could be extended.

Such success would further hamper the Conservatives' chances of national recovery. The general election defeat confirmed a spiral of decline that has left the party ill-suited to deal with its immediate problems. Since 1993 the party has lost thousands of council seats. The abrupt end to so many local Conservatives' political careers has also robbed the party of many of its leading activists. The stalwarts of many local Conservative constituency associations were often also the area's leading councillors. Their departure has deprived the Conservative party of a voice in local politics at precisely the wrong time. An increasingly detached electorate with weakened party ties makes it difficult for parties to communicate their message. A party without a voice in local government will be forced to make its electoral appeal principally from the national stage. When voting behaviour appears increasingly linked to electoral context that form of communication will prove a weakness since it will fail to take proper account of the prevailing local conditions. The market for votes is becoming more competitive and the Conservatives, with a depleted local power base and an ageing and declining membership, will struggle. Many have claimed the 1997 general election represents a watershed in British politics. For students of local electoral politics it merely confirmed a pattern that had long been in the making and a new order of party competition which may be hard to overturn.

---

1   D. Dorling, C. Rallings and M. Thrasher, 'The Epidemiology of the Liberal Democrat Vote', *Political Geography*, forthcoming.

2   R. Waller, 'The 1979 Local and General Elections in England and Wales: Is There a Local/National Differential?', *Political Studies*, 1980/3.
3   C. Game, 'Local Elections', *Local Government Studies*, 1981/2.
4   W.H. Cox and M. Laver, 'Local and National Voting in British Elections: Lessons From The Synchro-polls of 1979', *Parliamentary Affairs*, 1979/4.
5   W. Miller, *Irrelevant Elections?* (Oxford UP, 1988), p. 166.
6   W. Miller, H. Clarke, M. Harrop, L. LeDuc and P. Whiteley, *How Voters Change: The 1987 British Election Campaign in Perspective* (Oxford UP, 1990), p. 28.
7   I. McLean, A. Heath and B. Taylor, 'Were the 1994 Euro- and Local Elections in Britain Really Second-Order?' Paper delivered at Elections, Parties and Public Opinion Conference, London, 1995.
8   See C. Rallings and M. Thrasher, *Local Elections in Britain* (Routledge, 1997), chapter 6.
9   C. Rallings and M. Thrasher, 'Exploring Uniformity and Variability in Local Electoral Outcomes', *Electoral Studies*, 1993/4.
10 H. Clarke, M. Stewart and P. Whiteley, 'Tory Trends: Party Identification and the Dynamics of Conservative Support Since 1992', *British Journal of Political Science*, 1997/1.

Racial Politics

BY SHAMIT SAGGAR*

THE IDEA that racial politics should play a prominent part in the 1997 general election received a curious, and fairly unexpected, fillip with the launch in January 1997 by Conservative Central Office of a pre-emptive bid to woo ethnic minority voters. A high profile visit to the Indian subcontinent by John Major, a keynote address to an invited gathering of the party's ethnic minority umbrella recruitment and fund-raising outfit, the One Nation Forum, and an embarrassingly early celebration by the party of the fiftieth anniversary of Indian independence, all contributed to the freshness of the prompt. The campaign itself continued with this general theme, suggesting that racial politics—or at least a Tory instrumental spin on this front—were now back on the electoral agenda. A flurry of Labour Party rows over ethnic minority[1] candidate selections, an elusive search for true 'ethnic marginals', and periodic evidence of electoral apathy in parts of the minority electorate, all further reinforced this impression.

And yet, for a decade or more, the landscape of British electoral politics had been seemingly de-racialised. The frequent, and often ill-tempered, controversies over racial politics of the 1970s and early 1980s had been either forgotten or relegated to the margins of electoral competition. Significantly, as early as 1983 one academic commentator had remarked that the issue of immigration had fallen off the agenda of that year's general election (Crewe in the *Guardian*, 13.6.83). The issue simply failed to register in terms of its essential saliency with the electorate, in marked contrast to the picture that had prevailed in 1979. Through the campaigns of the 1980s and early 1990s, the true significance of racial politics appeared to be twofold: its constrained and often volatile impact in a small handful of constituencies, and its general failure to shape electoral politics at large. Therefore, the most immediate question in the run-up to the 1997 contest was whether, and to what degree, this election would deviate from such a pattern.

This central question can be examined by looking at a number of aspects of racial politics and electoral competition. In particular, this paper will highlight the sustained and fairly remarkable attention that was paid by the major political parties to the so-called 'ethnic vote'. This focus, together with a number of parallel developments in size, composition and political orientation of ethnic minorities, ensured the

* Senior Lecturer in Government at Queen Mary and Westfield College, University of London.

partial rediscovery of race in British electoral politics in 1997. Many commentators hoped for decisive evidence of an erosion in the Labour Party's historic command of the votes of ethnic minorities. In the event, there was little evidence to support this position. In addition, I will revisit the perennial debate over the so-called 'race card', a theme that played heavily in the long campaign run-up to May 1997. This campaign featured many descriptions of the cold logic of a deeply unpopular, incumbent Tory administration that sought a comeback by exploiting anti-immigrant and anti-minority sentiment. As I shall argue, evaluation of the actual picture is rather mixed. Finally, I shall put forward an evaluation of the scale of, and manner in which, racial politics shaped the 1997 electoral contest.

Demographic influences

Putting aside the degree of interest shown in courting ethnic minority voters, the long-term significance of this group of voters has, of course, depended on demographic characteristics. Factors relating to the size and composition of the ethnic minority population—and its chief subgroups—will shape electoral strength. Indeed, in Britain's single member constituency-based voting system, electoral power largely hangs on numbers. By the mid-1990s there appeared to be an open acknowledgement that Britain's minorities both constituted more than a demographic blip and had in places grown to become substantial local communities. The drawback with this kind of acknowledgement was that it often permitted vested interests to exaggerate the influence of minority voters. In a remarkable bid to talk up this case, an Asian-based satellite station, Zee TV, released in mid campaign a list of 36 so-called 'Asian marginals' calculated on the basis of raw numbers of Asians at constituency level without accounting for age, registration or likely turnout (*The Times*, 2.4.97). This episode was merely part of a general pattern of embellishment.

The 1991 Census showed that some three million people reported themselves as belonging to an ethnic group other than White. At 5.5% of the population, though unevenly distributed, this was up sharply from the notional figure found in the earlier 1981 Census of 2.2 million (or four per cent). A leap of around a quarter in a decade seemed more remarkable at a time when the bulk of primary, and even most secondary, immigration had tapered off. The 1991 figures showed the largest single group to be ethnic Indians, whose numbers had almost reached the psychologically important million mark (just over one in four of the minority population taken together). Table 1 below tells the wider story. Of course the size of the minority groups needs to be examined in the context of age structure. Not all of the 1.5 million Asians for instance are eligible to vote since a large slice of this population comprises those below the age of eligibility (Bangladeshis and Pakistanis in particular). Data from the Labour Force Survey has

1. Ethnic origin breakdown of UK resident population, 1991

Ethnic group	Number(000s)	% of total population	% of non-white population
All	54,889	100.0	–
White	51,874	94.5	–
All others	3,015	5.5	100.0
Black Caribbean	500	0.9	16.6
Black African	212	0.4	7.0
Black other	178	0.3	5.9
Black total	891	1.6	29.5
Indian	840	1.5	27.9
Pakistani	477	0.9	15.8
Bangladeshi	163	0.3	5.4
S. Asian total	1,480	2.7	49.1
Chinese	157	0.3	5.2
Other Asian	198	0.4	6.6
Other non-Asian	290	0.5	9.6

Source: 1991 General Census

shown that around two-thirds of the ethnic minority population are below 35 years of age (compared with around a half of their white counterparts). Over the longer run this disproportionately young population will begin to feed into a growing adult population able in principle to cast a ballot. Estimates suggest that the minority population is likely to stabilise over the next 40–50 years at around nine or ten per cent of the total population once birth and mortality rates have substantially converged.[2] In any case, allowance has to be made for the large numbers of minority children who, in proportional terms, had not by 1997 fed through into the potential minority electorate. Furthermore, the 1991 Census figures were of decreasing accuracy in estimating the minority electorate by 1997. One estimate suggested that this electorate might have grown by as much as 12% between 1991–96, to be followed by a further projected 20% expansion between 1996–2001. Meanwhile, the comparable rise across these periods in the white electorate was estimated at one and two per cent respectively.[3] A small, yet generally tightly packed, minority electorate continued to grow, even without any further fresh migration being taken into account.

Rows over ethnic minority candidates

The successive rows witnessed within the parties on the question of the selection of ethnic minority candidates were a pertinent feature of the five year electoral cycle leading up to May 1997. In 1991–92 these kind of arguments had been most closely associated with the controversial selection of John Taylor for the Conservatives in Cheltenham, with his upset defeat at the hands of an unusual Liberal Democrat swing in the election further compounding the Tories' sense of embarrassment. In 1997 it was the turn of the Labour Party to face similar—and often far worse—problems. The origins of these disputes between 1992–97 are numerous and sometimes go back many years. To begin with, the Labour Party's relationship with its minority supporters and would-be candidates has been conducted against the backdrop of exceedingly high levels of electoral backing. Table 2 shows this support in historic context. Plainly, this association has tended to stimulate expectations amongst minority activists keen to advance to candidate selection, especially in constituencies characterised by high minority settlement. A common charge of disgruntlement seen in many local disputes was that the party had been reluctant to acknowledge the vital contribution made by its minority supporters, not least in propping up morale following the electoral routs of 1983 and 1987. The relative stability of the figures shown in Table 2 reinforce this point.

2. Labour and Conservative support among ethnic minorities (%)

	1974 (Oct)	1979	1983*	1987	1992*
Lab	81	86	83	72	81
Con	9	8	7	18	10

Notes: * Recalculated average of Asian and Afro-Caribbean support levels.

Sources: Adapted from: Community Relations Commission, *Participation of Ethnic Minorities in the General Election of October 1974* (CRC, 1975); Commission for Racial Equality, *Votes and Policies* (CRE, 1980); Commission for Racial Equality, *Ethnic Minorities and the 1983 General Election* (CRE, 1984); Harris Research Centre, 'Political attitudes among ethnic minorities', unpublished dataset JN98746 (Harris, 1987); A. Ali and G. Percival, *Race and Representation: ethnic minorities and the 1992 elections* (CRE, 1993).

The 1992–97 parliament saw a significant escalation of constituency-centred arguments over the adoption of Asian candidates in particular. Especially bitter disputes occurred in seats where long-serving white MPs were due to retire and/or pressure among Asian activists had served to bring forward retirement decisions. This kind of setting had initially been witnessed in the late 1980s in Ealing Southall, where Sydney Bidwell's departure had created a valuable opportunity for Asian candidates in 1992. Now the focus was on seats such as Birmingham Sparkbrook (where Roy Hattersley was about to step down), Bradford West (where Max Madden had been successively re-elected), and Glasgow Govan[4] (where boundary changes meant that the sitting white MP had to contest the nomination). Many of these selection contests threw up allegations of dirty tricks, usually centring on claims of bogus Asian membership drives. With factionalism mounted on top of ethnic entryism, it was apparent that Labour was beginning to face a pattern of contested nominations involving racial bitterness.

Of course this pattern in itself was far from new. In the 1920s and 1930s similar battles had been waged over the motives of Irish recruits to British political parties. Further arguments ensued in the 1940s and 1950s over Jewish involvement in the Labour Party.[5] The Asian-centred rows of the 1990s seemed to perpetuate this tradition, but also differed in two vital senses. First, it was clear that the bulk of Asian would-be candidates were voluble in their claim that Labour had been historically slow to repay the Asian electorate's overwhelming support for the party.

This orientation often led to charges of exploitation, though it is striking to note that few Asian activists were prepared to flesh out threats of Asian abstention or even support for opponents. Indeed, Labour's huge membership drive between 1994–97 had included a large proportion of new Asian members, and it was possible to see an element of a repayment calculus at work in some constituencies (Pinto-Duschinsky in *The Times*, 24.3.97). Second, many Asian activists made great play of the idea that Asian votes were fundamentally cast on the basis of ethnic identity and loyalty. By stoking up the 'ethnicity-counts' argument, it was possible to convey the strong suggestion that Asian votes could be delivered—or withheld—on the say of a small handful of Asian elites. Ethnic voting, in this sense, had become something of a regular feature on the British electoral landscape.

Despite the rows, a batch of Asian candidates successfully came through selection procedures and stood in promising seats for Labour. Table 5 later in this chapter shows their progress. Meanwhile rather fewer new black candidates were adopted by any of the main parties, and indeed only one managed to capture a fresh winnable seat. The black parliamentary presence had therefore progressed minimally since its 1987 level when three black Labour politicians had been selected in safe seats.

Targeting minority voters

Perhaps the most predictable feature of the 1997 campaign was that, once again, attention veered to so-called ethnic marginals. This perspective was rooted in the claim that, despite their modest overall numbers, ethnic minorities wielded greater potential electoral influence as a result of their concentration in marginal seats. This claim was applied to both Conservative and Labour held seats, and even a single Liberal Democrat seat. In 1997 the chief proponent of the ethnic marginals thesis was 'Operation Black Vote' (OBV), a pressure group established a year earlier by Charter 88 and others to press the case for greater minority democratic participation. OBV released figures suggesting that up to 49 seats depended on the voting power of minorities. Interestingly, OBV's estimate in fact only related to black voters. A parallel argument was advanced by an Asian satellite television station, Zee TV, who claimed that the fate of 45 seats hung on the Asian vote. There were, perhaps inevitably, problems with both estimates. First, they failed to adjust for the differential age profile of minorities in comparison with whites; second, no allowance was made for differential registration rates, a surprising oversight given OBV's interest in trying to boost registration levels; and third, despite great improvements over the years, there remain doubts about the turnout levels of minority voters. A well-publicised MORI poll of black people in summer 1996 seemed to portray a black electorate noticeably detached from the democratic process; for instance just 40% reported that they were certain to vote

(*Guardian*, 8.7.96). Ironically, if true, these figures had the effect of undermining claims about potential black electoral clout.

Such miscalculations and exaggerations aside, what, then, was the ethnic marginals potential in 1997? A rather different perspective was put forward by the Confederation of Indian Organisations which identified just eight seats in which Asian voters were likely to have a crucial influence. It is possible to identify the seats where minority concentrations were well placed to shape results, adjusting downwards for their considerably younger age profile. These seats are calculated in which the majority of the sitting MP is equalled or exceeded by the size of the local ethnic minority electorate. Accordingly, in 1997, there were 17 Conservative-held, 36 Labour-held, and one Lib Dem-held ethnic marginals. The key message from this list is that, with 54 seats, it is somewhat shorter than the combined estimates publicised during the campaign by OBV and Zee TV respectively. Indeed, once age is taken into account, the potential number of ethnic marginals shrinks by almost a half. Many putatively convincing ethnic marginals do not turn out to be good cases at all. To take just one example, Eltham in South East London, was often thought of a classic ethnic marginal held on a notional majority of 3.8% of the vote; however, the probable minority electorate was around 3.6%, making it difficult to sustain the ethnic marginals claim. Furthermore, it is striking that the Labour list (36) is double that of the Conservatives (17), reflecting the continuing reality of minority geographical concentrations in urban areas more likely to return Labour representatives. Those Tory ethnic marginals that did exist were strongly bunched amongst the party's 30 most marginal seats; with Labour, ethnic marginals were spread across a much larger range of its defending seats, with a fair number among constituencies with double digit Labour majorities.

The significance of these figures should not be confined to the length of this list. Indeed, they merely illustrated a potential, itself crucially dependent on evidence of differential swing across ethnic groups. Whilst broadly different inter-ethnic voting patterns can be shown through survey evidence, there is little to show that such differential swing existed in 1997. To be sure, the secret ballot system makes it exceedingly hard to further such a line of enquiry, and it is entirely reasonable to conclude that ethnic marginals behaved precisely in line with other comparable marginal seats. The implication must be that, in the absence of compelling local evidence, minority voters, although often poised disproportionately to influence local results, in fact had a negligible impact. The 1997 campaign again included polling evidence of strong Labour support among minority voters,[6] but little, if anything, to show that local swings were substantially larger—or smaller—as a result of an appeal to minority voters. The exceptions were few and stand out, such as the contests in Bethnal Green and Bow, and in Bradford West.

Claims about, and evidence for, ethnic floaters?

Underlying the ethnic marginals controversy there remained the age-old question of the electoral loyalties of minority voters. As Table 2 above made clear, studies over a twenty year period had pointed to more-or-less steady and unwavering support for the Labour Party. Conservative organised attempts to attract minority supporters may have first begun as long ago as 1976, but these efforts had shown few dividends despite the Tory landslides of the 1980s. The question underscoring the 1997 campaign therefore was as before: how promising were the prospects for a Tory breakthrough, especially amongst targeted middle class Asian voters?

Only two significant polls—both by MORI—were carried out prior to polling day. The first related to black voting intentions and was commissioned the best part of a year ahead of the election itself. The second surveyed Asians and appeared in February 1997. Table 3 summarises their findings. As these figures reveal, the prospects appeared pretty weak. Conservative support among minorities has, historically, been fairly low—usually around 10–20%. The 1997 contest was unlikely to be an exception, chiefly because all the indicators leading up to the election suggested it was going to be a poor year for the Tories. In the event, it was rather perverse to pursue the claim that minorities generally, and Asian specifically, were somehow exempt from such a well established national trend.

3. Voting intentions, Asians and blacks, 1996–97 (%)

	Asian*	black**
Conservative	25	8
Labour	70	86
Lib Dem	4	4
Other	1	1
Undecided/refused/not voting	22	21

Notes: * Of those naming a party (689); ** All except those certain not to vote (703).

Sources: MORI, 'Asian Voting: preliminary results', February 1997; MORI, 'Black Britain', *British Public Opinion*, July 1996.

With such a bleak picture, what, then, inspired the Tory bold onslaught to woo minority voters? Three rationales carry weight in the context of 1997. First, the 'ethnic campaign', if it can be dubbed as such, signalled the extent to which party strategists appeared to believe that the 1997 election could have been won and that Asian voters might play a crucial role in snatching a surprise victory. As the long campaign progressed through 1996–97, commentators—and even some Tory loyalists—remained bemused by the party leadership's insistence that a fifth consecutive victory was assured. One strategy that appeared to make this possibility seem tangible was the idea that the Conservatives ought not to concede any group of voters as unwinnable. Targeting ethnic minorities, traditionally heavily Labour-leaning, signalled (mainly for party morale) that the incumbent party was prepared to come out and campaign for victory, however unlikely.

Second, in terms of putting together a winning coalition of voters, Tory strategists recognised they were operating within tough constraints. For one, many among the skilled, affluent working class appeared reluctant to back the Conservatives, despite a track record of having supported the party over several elections since 1979. In their absence, any convincing electoral strategy required a substitution effect, whereby new sympathisers to the Tory cause would be the raw material of first-time Conservative voters. This amounted to an effort to poach Labour supporters, notably among the growing Asian middle class. Significantly, however, very little of the content of the 1997 Tory 'ethnic campaign' in fact involved class-based appeals. Party strategists chose yet again to emphasise a distinctive cultural-based message to Asian voters in particular. By concentrating on a set of abstract bourgeois values, the message pushed out by a succession of One Nation Tory politicians revolved around the slogan that 'Your values are our values, and our values are your values'.

Third, it is quite reasonable to think that the Tory onslaught was prompted by a longer term agenda. Somewhat inverting the logic of the previous arguments, Tory strategists in 1997 accepted neither the likelihood of a surprise victory nor the chances of a breakthrough among middle class Asian voters. Instead, the 1997 blitz represented an early move to increase the chances of such a breakthrough in 2002 or even 2007. The notion of 'pipeline politics' perhaps best explains the 1997 imperative to create a favourable electoral legacy: the targeting of younger, educated and aspiring Asians who might reasonably be expected to come on stream in the next, or next but one, general election.[7]

The Labour Party meanwhile chose to pursue a very low key campaign towards ethnic minorities. Revealingly, just one sentence on race found its way into the party manifesto declaring an intention to be tough on immigration! Plainly the party viewed the need to court minorities with relatively low priority, arguably reinforcing the impression of paternalism, approaching exploitation, among some of its critics.

The 'race card' revisited

Arguably, given the largely predictable failure to establish a genuine Conservative voting breakthrough among minority voters, the real significance of the 1997 election for racial politics lay in the silence of the so-called 'race card'. The long run-up to the election itself had been characterised by a series of predictions that the electorally unpopular Tories would inevitably exploit anti-minority and anti-immigrant popular sentiment in an ill-principled bid to secure re-election. These arguments, broadly, were not borne out by events. The 1992–97 period had, indeed, seen a steady escalation in the saliency of, and controversy over, the treatment of refugees and asylum seekers. Most notably, some of the spin off from the Conservative administration's 1993 Asylum and Immigration Appeals Act undoubtedly reinforced the impression of an uncompromising government stance to bear down on immigration and also to respond to populist pressure. This populist trend in the Home Secretary's steer was typified by the political editor of the *Daily Telegraph* in spring 1995: 'Proposals for immigration curbs in the next Queen's Speech are an attempt to woo back Tory supporters attracted by the more moderate policies espoused by Tony Blair'. Such a suspicion received fresh credibility in autumn 1995 when the Labour Opposition made an (unsuccessful) bid to try to bury the immigration issue—and presumably its own sense of vulnerability on it—by seeking to have the new Asylum Bill debated by a special, ad hoc committee of the House of Commons (*The Times*, 16.11.95). Against this backdrop, momentum had built up which suggested that the 1997 contest was more likely than not to rekindle the kind of 'race card' electoral politics seen in earlier elections such as 1970 and 1979.

Yet, the momentum had moved attention in a spurious direction, and the 1997 contest turned out to have little in common with these previous episodes. Three central factors best account for this dog which did not bark in the night. First, and most pivotal, the leadership factor within Tory ranks served to blunt the cutting edge of any potential 'race card' campaign that may have been planned or hoped for. Mr Major's special association with the British Asian and Afro-Caribbean communities had been a discernible feature of his term as party leader. Indeed, the idea that he was the first Prime Minister who, for purely generational reasons, was comparatively at ease with the emergence of a multiracial society, had been the subject of informed comment during the early part of his tenure (*Independent*, 1.11.91). Previously, his known reputation as gut fighter against his party's anti-immigrant wing had stayed with him since his Lambeth council days. A few weeks before the campaign start, Mr Major sought, with some effectiveness, to re-establish in a Commons speech his earlier liberal credentials, 'In the past 18 years we have seen the most extraordinary changes and improvements in race relations in this country. I think that it is immensely important and I am certainly not going to lend my voice or my policy to anything that would damage that improvement.' (*Hansard*, 4.3.97). Also, few insiders had forgotten the fact that in 1992 Major, in alliance with his then party chairman, Chris Patten, had moved quickly to quash any serious attempts to play an overt anti-immigrant card. Then, the Tories' efforts had extended only to a familiar move to tarnish their Labour opponents with the label of weakness and indecision. The Conservatives' former Director of Research, Andrew Lansley, went on the record in the mid-term of the 1992–97 parliament to boast that negative campaigning on a set of issues including immigration had been profitable for the Tories in 1992 (*Observer*, 3.9.95). The claim was repeated when he suggested in late 1995 that the weak Major administration might try a pincer movement around the popular Opposition leader in order to try to inflict damage on the latter's image as being tough on questions of crime, immigration and individual responsibility. In any case, the Lansley intervention can be accounted for in terms of batting at a familiar crease for Tory leaders: Labour's old 'soft' reputation on immigration had managed to endure into the 1990s and few could deny the basic logic of sticking to reliable defensive strokes. The question of how far Tory strategy took on a fresh impetus to attack new Labour on race in 1997, as a *core* battleground issue, is therefore doubtful.

Second, if the political logic to exploit race in 1992 had, as claimed, been strong, it remains a puzzle to account for the even greater missed opportunity of 1997. The 'race card' thesis rests heavily on the notion that right of centre parties have an in-built advantage over their leftist rivals, and that a core test for this in Britain ought to be election and re-election bids by the Conservatives in unfavourable electoral climates. The 1997 election, with a Tory poll deficit in double figures for over two years up to polling day, appeared therefore to be a prime 'race card' scenario. The reason why the scenario was not played out as smoothly as the thesis suggests, perhaps has to do with the reasons why other related negative attacks failed to hit target in 1997. That is to say, the basic purpose of Tory attacks on Labour's reputation on crime and immigration, to take two prime examples, would have been to under-mine the latter's credibility and essential competence. However, the task in 1997 must be set against the context of the Conservatives having to fight to re-establish their basic competence on an even wider range of issues such as allegations of corruption, economic mismanagement, and internal indiscipline (see Gavin and Sanders in this volume). Such a context meant that any Tory attempt to exploit race would have been seen as a primary technique for re-election, rather than a secondary instrument to drive home any competence advantage that the party might have enjoyed (as in 1992).

Third, the reservoir of potential votes that might conceivably be gained from exploiting anti-immigrant sentiment has tended to become shallower during the 1980s and 1990s. Issue voting around the immi-gration question arguably reached its high water mark in the 1960s, and was most notably linked with an unexpected, and arguably critical, surge in Tory fortunes in the 1970 election. Issue voting on immigration could be cited in the 1970, 1974 and 1979 contests, in a way that has not been the case in more recent elections. More importantly, the immigration issue commanded considerable saliency in this earlier era. Butler and Stokes classically (and the BES thereafter) measured the electorate's strong passions on the question in the 1960s and 1970s: 45, 46, 46, 43 and 40% reported that they felt very strongly that 'too many immigrants had been let into the country' in 1964, 1966, 1970, 1974 and 1979 respectively.[8] As late as 1979, 51% of all voters felt that the best way to improve race relations was by stopping further immigration, whilst 63% recognised this policy position to be also that of the Conservative Party (against only 10% crediting it to Labour).[9] In sharp contrast, by 1997 it was virtually impossible to cite even a single poll that showed any meaningful interest in the issue by the electorate. Furthermore, tests of issue voting usually require clear evidence of inter-party divergence on policy and that this distinction be understood by the electorate. In the case of immigration policy, a Labour Opposition's reluctance to make overt policy concessions coupled with a campaign strategy to be seen to be minimising policy distance from the Conservatives, meant that little, if any, sense of Labour-Tory policy contrast was widely observed by the electorate. A pre-emptive move was launched to neutralise the issue in 1995 by then Shadow Home Secretary, Jack Straw: 'We should not allow so much as a cigarette card to come between the Labour Party and the Tory Government over immigration.'[10]

Immigration in this traditional form may not have counted for a lot on the electoral landscape, but behind it there remained considerable disquiet about multiculturalism in modern Britain. The sole intervention on the immigration issue during the national campaign—by Nicholas Budgen in the Tory marginal of Wolverhampton South West—should perhaps be viewed in this broader context. In making a direct appeal to curb further immigration, the Budgen campaign plainly missed the point that comparatively little fresh immigration was contemplated by the major parties.[11] However, in citing the 'substantial social problems ... immigration had brought' that had caused 'many West Midlanders [to] feel themselves to be strangers in their own pubs, schools and streets', Budgen was undoubtedly aiming at a rich seam of unmarshalled support. That said, the real difficulty with this local version of the 'race card' thesis, as epitomised by Budgen, is that it signally failed. For one thing, Budgen went down to defeat with no tangible evidence to suggest that voters locally rewarded—or indeed unduly punished—him on the race question. Additionally, the local swing against him (−9.94%) was entirely in line with the fate of Conservative candidates in neighbouring contests.[12] Against this evidence, it would be hard to argue that race even served to limit the damage endured locally by the Tories.

Meanwhile, the electoral resurrection of anti-immigrant sentiment was to be found in a few pockets in 1997. The persistence of the BNP in several London constituencies showed beyond doubt that such sentiment could be channelled into electoral strength. However, these cases were fairly small in number and restricted to local circumstances. A prime example was in Bethnal Green and Bow, where the adoption of minority candidates by all three major parties was widely greeted by BNP officials as 'music to their ears'. Some 3,350 local voters agreed.

Polling evidence and trends

At the time of writing no reliable indicators can be cited on voting patterns of minorities in the 1997 election. Firm evidence on this front will be forthcoming from the British Election Study.[13] Thus, any discussion must rely on the two MORI polls during 1996–97 cited previously, both confirming strong Labour advantages over other parties among Asian and black voters. So much is not disputed and fairly unremarkable given the strong performance of the Opposition in the lead up to the election itself. However, the pre-election polling evidence contains some incisive pieces of data on Asian and black electoral outlooks which are worthy of brief comment. Looking at Table 4, it is apparent that there were very strong similarities between Asian and general public voting turnout intentions. The position among black respondents was rather different, with a long tail of those seemingly disinclined to vote. This contrast is worth noting, perhaps because it tells us that, while this measure of black political integration lagged behind that of other minorities and the general public, it by no means describes a politically alienated ethnic group.

4. Voting turnout, black, Asian and general public, 1996/97 (%)

	black	Asian	general public
Certain not to vote	13	10	8
Not very likely to vote	11	7	7
Quite likely to vote	14	11	11
Very likely to vote	17	13	15
Certain to vote	40	58	57
Don't know	5	1	2

Sources: MORI, 'Asian Voting: preliminary results', unpublished briefing notes, February 1997; MORI, 'Black Britain', *British Public Opinion*, July 1996; data on general public from nationwide survey by MORI on behalf of *The Times*, January 1997.

The MORI poll of Asians also highlights two conundrums for the Conservatives, significant for future efforts to court this group. The first of these was that total Tory support stood at a fairly impressive 25% of Asian respondents. This figure implies something of a modest growth in Tory support among Asians, even though recent support in the 1980s and early 1990s never broke through the psychologically important 20% mark. Asian voters, in other words, although heavily skewed to Labour, had not abandoned the Conservatives in the large numbers seen amongst the electorate as a whole. MORI's own newspaper-commissioned polls in early 1997 described quite considerable haemor-rhaging in Tory support among the electorate as a whole. Asians, to that extent, were bucking the national trend. Secondly, just 15% of Asians declared that the Conservatives were the party they most trusted to look after the interests of Asian people, or rather fewer than the proportion who said they were intending to vote for the Conservatives. This difference suggests that, whilst the Tories lag far behind the Labour

Party (51% most trusted Labour), the influences behind party choice are unlikely to be shaped by Asians' views of Asian interests alone. Indeed, the broader issue agenda, overwhelmingly made up of mainstream policy questions, seemed to drive the 25/70 Tory/Labour split. The message for future strategy presumably must be that the Conservatives must regain general public confidence as *the* route to improving the party's rating among Asians.

Performance of minority candidates

The 1997 election witnessed a significant expansion in the numbers of black and Asian parliamentary candidates (a record 44 were selected among the three major parties, up from 24 in 1992). The real focus, however, was on those in promising seats, with a likely scenario of three, perhaps four, additional minority members joining the ranks of those elected in 1992 and 1987. The downside appeared to the fragile position of Nirj Deva in west London whose grip on his seat was likely to blown away on just a tiny swing to Labour. Table 5 describes the fortunes of all forty-four. These results largely confirmed most informed projections that were made before polling day. As expected, minority Labour Party candidates taking over safe seats (three in total) were elected to the Commons, and the only Tory defending a notional majority (Deva) went down to a heavy defeat. Additionally, Kumar was returned in a north east Tory marginal with no difficulty whatsoever, taking the overall new minority intake to four. The 1997 total thus rose to a new record of nine MPs from the ethnic minorities (all Labour).

5. Performance of ethnic minority candidates (major parties), 1997

	1992	1997	Average change in share of vote	N
Labour candidates	5	9	+5.1	14
Conservative candidates	1	0	−8.9	11
Lib Dem candidates	0	0	−2.8	19

Notes: includes ethnic Chinese candidates.
Sources: Author's calculations based on: 'Election Results 1997', *The Times*, 3 May 1997; British Parliamentary Constituencies 1992–97 database; and P. Norris, *UK Election Results* (Harvard University, 1996).

The real twist in the candidacies of most of the new intake appeared to be their general failure to enjoy — or contribute to — Labour's quite decisive swing, most notably from the Tories. Most starkly of all, Oona King's triumph in London's East End was somewhat deflated by the almost unique case of a local pro-Tory swing away from Labour. Plainly, whatever was said by Labour officials and activists in the constituency before polling day, her prospects were very definitely squeezed by the other major parties' decisions to select ethnic Bengali candidates to tempt a largely Bengali electorate. An ethnic penalty appears to have been paid by Labour in this seat, even though survey data indicates that Asians are often reluctant to back same-ethnicity candidates on grounds of ethnic origin alone. Elsewhere, Sarwar experienced a considerably smaller pro-Labour swing than comparable, neighbouring Labour candidates. His poor showing might be explained in terms of a strong SNP push throughout Glasgow. Singh in Bradford appears simply to have done an ineffective job of delivering the Labour vote. The former's honeymoon was particularly short-lived when, a fortnight after victory, he found himself embroiled in fresh and serious allegations of electoral malpractice. His case had two immediate effects: first, Sarwar's fate became an early, and perhaps unwelcome, test of the new Labour administration's approach to 'sleaze' controversies, and second, the collective reputation of minority parliamentarians received an equally unwelcome setback.

Meanwhile, it is striking to note that several incumbent Labour minority MPs matched or even exceeded Labour's generally strong performance. In London, Khabra, Boateng and Grant (though not Abbott), managed to match or exceed Labour's already-impressive swing in Greater London (13.3%), whilst also adding substantial growth to Labour's already-large vote. The significance of their performance is that it contrasts sharply with the shaky performances of many of the new minority MPs, and it is worth recalling that several of today's incumbents underwent similar baptisms of fire when first returned in 1987 and 1992. Small, yet discernible, racial penalties were inflicted on most of them when first returned, and the 1997 figures suggest a continuing pattern at work. However, in all cases, the incumbents have successfully built up something of a small personal vote in their constituencies, which one might speculate could prove to be vital in the event of a future reversal in new Labour's fortunes.

Implications for British politics

The 1997 general election was remarkable in the development of racial politics in a very limited number of ways. At the same time, the election signalled several points of continuity, extending and reinforcing earlier trends. Where the election broke new ground was the degree to which party competition for minority votes became a well-established, if exotic, feature of the intensive campaign period. In 1997 it would have been hard to fail to note the overt Tory effort in this direction. Whereas previous elections (notably 1987) represented rather better prospects for the black and Asian Conservative cause, in 1997 key markers were laid by a party, though set for defeat, that remained conscious of the need to nurture a new winning coalition for the future. The attention heaped on Asian voters, for instance, tended to exaggerate the actual electoral leverage of this group.

All this, of course, took place against the backdrop of little or no explicit interest shown by the major parties in race relations or indeed immigration. What few policy positions the parties did hold singularly failed to be articulated in a curiously non-racial election. There are two views of this kind of backdrop. One view, continuously heard among minority politicians and in the minority press, argued that electoral silence signified disinterest and disregard. The politics of racial equality had been frozen out of the election because too few votes could be swayed and too many lost, according to this view. A counter viewpoint, however, claimed that the low exposure given to racial affairs was to be welcomed as there was little evidence to show that the issue agenda of minority voters were significantly different from their white counterparts. Political parties, by neglecting any race agenda, were doing the job of broad interest articulation and aggregation, as rational party competition theory might suggest. If racial politics and concerns fell between the cracks, so much was to be expected, if not universally welcomed. In that respect, the 1997 contest signalled a pattern that is more likely than not to be followed in future elections.

1   The term 'ethnic minority' is used interchangeably with 'minority' throughout the paper, and is a direct reference to those resident in Britain whose recent ethnic origins lie in South Asia, the Caribbean and Africa. No particular political or sociological inference should be read into the use of these largely descriptive terms though the author accepts that these terms have been the subject of a protracted debate in recent years. Demographic accounts of these groups, except where indicated, are taken from the ethnic origin question in the 1991 General Census.

2   R. Ballard and V.S. Khabra, *The Ethnic Dimensions of the 1991 Census* (University of Manchester, 1994), p. 15.

3   Estimates provided by the Centre for Research in Ethnic Relations, Warwick, as quoted in *The Runnymede Bulletin* (March 1997), p. 5.

4   At the time of writing, the newly-elected Labour MP for Glasgow Govan, Mohammed Sarwar, was facing both a police and internal party inquiry into allegations of corruption during the election campaign.

5   See A. Geddes, 'Labour and 'ethnic entryism': participation, integration and the party context', *New Community*, forthcoming.

6   'Black Britain', *British Public Opinion* (MORI, July 1996); 'Asian Poll', (MORI, March 1997).

7   S. Saggar, 'Pipeline Politics', *India Today*, March 1997, p. 52.

8   D. Butler and D. Stokes, *Political Change in Britain* (Macmillan, 1974), p. 461.

9   BES, May 1979, Election Survey.

10 A. Lansley, 'Race Issue Leaves Straw Blowing in the Wind' (*Observer*, 10.12.95).

11 The sole exception was Labour's promise to scrap the 1983 'primary purpose' immigration rule, a change it quickly confirmed once in office after the election.

12 Wolverhampton NE and Wolverhampton SE recorded Conservative to Labour swings of 11.9 and 9.3% respectively.

13 An ethnic minority booster sample of the BES cross-section (designed by Shamit Saggar (QMW) and Anthony Heath (Nuffield), in conjunction with CREST and Social Community Planning Research) will provide data on this and other related points.

Gender Politics: A Breakthrough for Women?

BY JONI LOVENDUSKI*

THE 1997 general election will be remembered as the long awaited breakthrough for women's representation in the House of Commons. The 120 women who won now constitute about one fifth of all MPs, up from 60 in 1992. Labour women are not just backbenchers: there are five women in the Cabinet, eighteen women ministers, two women whips in the House of Commons, one in the House of Lords and Betty Boothroyd continues as Speaker of the House of Commons. Much of this achievement is due to Labour policies to increase their proportion of women candidates. The extraordinary sight of 120 women taking their seats in the Commons on 6 May 1997 will provide a lasting and powerful image of the new parliament. Even as Westminster reconvened, however, there were complaints from women's rights advocates that the new feminine image belied a persisting masculine reality. The virtual absence of women from the national election campaigns was widely noted. Tony Blair's failure to deliver on the promise of a separate, cabinet level minister for women was criticised by feminists who also expressed anxiety that efforts to promote women would falter well before equality with men was achieved.

Whether such efforts will fail depends upon whether the new women MPs will pull the ladder up after them. That is unlikely. Feminists have contended for some time that only when a critical mass of women is present will long standing masculine biases in politics be altered. This assertion has some intuitive appeal but, in the absence of a significant presence of women in British politics there has been no opportunity to test it. The new intake of women will probably generate a spate of studies all investigating what difference having more women makes to British parliamentary politics. Answering such a question is a complicated matter. The new women MPs did not simply arrive there, like all MPs they came through complex processes of qualification and selection, suggesting that a series of related changes led to their success.

It is useful here to make a distinction between women's issues and women's perspectives. Women's issues mainly affect women, either for biological reasons, (for example, breast cancer screening, reproductive rights), or for social reasons, (for example, sex equality or childcare policy). Women's perspectives are women's views on all political concerns. Many analysts argue that, although women and men agree

* Professor of Politics at Southampton University.

that broadly the same issues are significant, women perceive those issues in a different way to men. For example, in 1996 the Fawcett Society found in a survey of women's and men's concerns that both sexes prioritised economic issues.[1] But women were more concerned about part-time work, low pay and pension rights, while men were more concerned about unemployment.

Arguments for women's representation hold that only women can be relied upon to bring women's issues to the political agenda, and that it is necessary to have full representation of women in parliament to ensure that women's perspectives are as extensively represented as men's. In using this distinction it is important to keep in mind that women, like men, are a diverse group rather than a unitary political category. Only by acknowledging both the diversity of women and their differences from men is it possible to consider the ways in which politics are gendered and to assess whether the substantial increase of women in British politics will have an impact.

This article considers the implications of bringing a large group of women into the House of Commons. The discussion follows the logic of the electoral process, looking first at the selection of women candidates, then at the campaign in terms of media coverage, women voters and policy issues, and concludes by considering whether more women MPs will make a difference to British parliamentary politics. The discussion concentrates on Labour Party politics which, between 1992 and 1997, was the main site of activity to increase women's representation in British politics.

The selection of women candidates

Mainland parties nominated 371 women candidates, representing a slight increase on 1992. Success rates differed dramatically by party (see Table 1). As in the past, what was important was where the candidates were standing as British political parties have tended to place their women candidates in unfavourable seats. In 1997 many of Labour's 159 women candidates were well placed to win since women fought fourteen seats where Labour MPs were retiring and half of Labour's 86 target marginals. The swing brought in a record-breaking 102 Labour women, or one quarter of the new parliamentary party. In contrast, following their devastating defeat, in total only thirteen women Conservative MPs were returned, representing eight per cent of Tory Members in the new parliament. It would have been even worse, since

1. Women Candidates and MPs, 1987–1997

| | Conservative | | Labour | | Liberal Democrat | | PC/SNP | |
	Cand	MP	Cand	MP	Cand	MP	Cand	MP
1987	46	17	92	21	105	2	15	1
1992	63	20	138	37	143	2	22	1
1997	67	13	159	102	142	3	23	2
(1997 %)	(10.3)	(7.9)	(24.8)	(24.2)	(22.0)	(7.2)	(21.2)	(33.3)

five of these women could have lost with another 2.5 per cent swing to Labour, including Teresa Gorman for Billericay, Virginia Bottomley for Surrey South West and Gillian Shephard for Norfolk South West. Only three Liberal Democrat women candidates were returned, Ray Michie for Argyll and Bute, Jenny Tonge for Richmond Park, and Jackie Ballard for Taunton (representing in total seven per cent of their party's MPs). The SNP returned their two sitting women MPs, Margaret Ewing for Moray and Roseanna Cunningham for Perth, while Plaid Cymru's women candidates all fought seats which would have required a swing of more than 25% to win, and none was returned.

The reason for the breakthrough of Labour women can be found in the selection process. The party composition of the House of Commons is determined by the electorate, but party members select individual candidates. In each party, in each constituency, a protracted and complex selection process takes place in the year or two prior to a general election. Over the last few electoral cycles all three major parties have promised to increase their proportions of women MPs, but only Labour has been successful. This reform is best understood as part of women's long march through the Labour party, a part of the organisational politics that have characterised Labour's modernisation. In this politics the left, centre and right of the party formed alliances and coalitions that mobilised different regions, trade unions, and party sections. Only one new set of actors was evident, organised feminist party women. In the years after 1979 feminism slowly gained footholds in the Labour party, in many of the affiliated unions and in party branches, regions and sections. Changes in the party offered the opportunity for women to make effective demands for representation and by 1992 they had secured quotas for women on all party decision making committees. Entry to the Parliamentary Labour party, however, proved slow and elusive. Despite a steady increase, only 37 Labour women MPs were returned in 1992, or 14% of the parliamentary party.

Frustration with slow progress led to growing demands for compulsory quotas of women candidates. In 1993 the annual conference agreed that there should be women candidates in half of all Labour seats where MPs were retiring and half of all their most winnable (target) seats. The mechanism to implement the quotas was 'all women shortlists', a device which meant simply that certain constituency parties would be allowed to select from only women applicants. The 'all women shortlists' decision went almost unnoticed at the time, given other heated debates on the conference floor about union-party relations, but objections were soon raised, and the procedure was confirmed after an extensive debate at the 1994 party conference. The party held regional 'consensus' meetings to determine which seats in each region should have all women shortlists and its National Executive Committee (NEC) intervened where regional targets were not achieved. The NEC had the power to impose all women shortlists where a constituency proved recalcitrant.

This decision came as part of a range of measures designed to improve women's representation in the party. New rules about the representation of women in internal party positions were important in the implementation of the candidate quotas. Under the regulations at least three of the seven constituency party officers had to be women. All seven officers were invited to consensus meetings so it became a simple matter to check that the composition of officers met the requirements. In addition new women constituency officers were often (but not inevitably) sympathetic to the idea of promoting women candidates.

Efforts to improve women's prospects had the full support of John Smith and were backed by the Labour Coordinating Committee, various trade unions responding to claims by women members, and by a number of internal feminist women's advocacy groups including Labour Women's Network, EMILY, and Labour Women's Action Committee. Implementation of the quotas met with mixed responses and early in 1996, with 35 women selected on all women shortlists, two disgruntled male aspirants won their case against the policy at an Industrial Tribunal held in Leeds on 8 January 1996 (*Jepson and Dyas-Elliott v The Labour Party and Others*). The Industrial Tribunal accepted the argument that the selection procedure by a political party facilitates access to employment and is therefore subject to the Sex Discrimination Act. Anxious to complete its selections in good time for the general election, and concerned not to jeopardise the positions of women already selected under the policy, the NEC decided not to appeal the decision. Instead they established a working party to identify effective and legal ways to maximise the number of women candidates nominated and selected in the remaining vacant Labour seats. This decision disappointed feminist advocates in the party who believed that the Blair leadership was lukewarm toward issues of women's representation and too unwilling to take controversial decisions to improve it. In fact, very few women were selected for target or inheritor seats after the Tribunal decision. According to party officials the tendency was for selections to go to the candidate who fought the seat in 1992 and these were normally favoured sons rather than daughters. At the end of the selection period the NEC women for Bethnal Green and Bow, Don Valley, Warrington South and Pontefract and Castleford. The latter two were selected from all-women shortlists drawn up by the NEC by-election panel. In three last minute selections the panel imposed candidates (all men) in three constituencies—Dudley North, Kingston upon Hull West and Hessle, Kilmarnock and Loudoun.

Although the policy had to be abandoned, the all-women shortlists were very successful in achieving their objectives. All women candidates chosen by this process were elected. The timing of the quotas was especially important. If the 1997 general election had been missed, later opportunities would not be as good. As Peter Coleman, the party official in charge of candidates remarked in late 1996 'If we didn't do it for

1996/7, all the opportunities that arise because we're going to have, hopefully, a swing that will take a lot of new members in. If we didn't achieve it that time, we lost it for another decade because the people that get elected this time, in the main I would have thought, would have been reselected to fight the next election. So its not just one parliament, we're actually closing the door for two parliaments. And then the only way to get through is to get selected in Labour held seats where Members of Parliament are retiring. And they will be in traditional seats, and that is going to be even more difficult . . .'.[2]

Selection continues to be an issue for Labour. A working party on Parliamentary Representation has been meeting since the autumn of 1996 to draw up policies for the selection of candidates for the European Parliament, the proposed Welsh and Scottish Assemblies, and to revise mechanisms for choosing candidates for the House of Commons. The working party has explicit instructions to devise ways of selecting adequate numbers of women. It has heard that most experienced party officials think there is little way of guaranteeing further selections of women without legal compulsion.

Neither the Conservatives nor the Liberal Democrats altered their candidate selection procedures to increase the nomination of women. The return of only thirteen Conservative women was a consequence, not only of their overwhelming defeat, but also of the rather limited efforts they made to promote women candidates. The party's strategies included periodic exhortations that more women should come forward, and training for women candidates was offered by the party women's section, often with disapproval from other leading officials. Officially the Conservatives claim to be opposed to positive action and they were very critical of Labour's policy. But former Conservative Vice President in charge of women, Emma Nicholson, suggests that in fact the Conservative women's organisation parallels the whole party structure—which itself reserves places for women at each level. She regards the 'approved list', of acceptable candidates as anomalous in not having a quota of women. The reason is timing, she believes, and had the approved list first been set up in the 1930s or 1940s, rather than later, it would have had a quota.

Conservative women complain privately but the ethos of unity means little gets stated publicly. Typical is the comment by Theresa May, candidate for Maidenhead 'I became a candidate on my merits . . . I have no burning desire to promote women's parliamentary rights.' (*The Times*, 22.4.97). The low key strategy most affects the supply of candidates as relatively few women are willing to stand for office. Only five women were selected to fight vacant Conservative seats, a further four were selected for new seats which would have been Conservative in 1992 , and five were selected for the thirty seats that needed a swing of less than two per cent for a Conservative win. Yet the official note for the future is relentlessly optimistic. Dame Angela Rumbold, the Vice

Chairman in charge of candidates, noted a qualitative change in those coming forward. '. . . women are beginning to understand the rules of the game. And this is the first time . . . and whereas before, you would have a number of women who were fighting the seat for the first time, and were bitterly upset in their forties that they didn't get anywhere, now I'm getting twenty-five year olds and thirty year olds fighting seats, and that is very much healthier.'[3]

The Liberal Democrats fielded 142 women candidates but almost all were in hopeless seats. No women were selected to replace the six MPs who stood down, although Jenny Tonge (Richmond Park) and Jackie Ballard (Taunton) were well placed in classic Liberal Democrat margin-als. Liberal Democrats oppose positive discrimination measures such as compulsory quotas but they do insist that women are placed on shortlists where these contain at least two aspirant candidates. A significant number of their shortlists, however, contain only one name and there are no special rules to help to place women in winnable seats.

Coverage of women in the election campaign

Turning to the election campaign, all parties ran leadership-focused campaigns and the predominance of men in these top slots, therefore, meant few appearances by women. A similar pattern had been evident in 1992. One significant difference in 1997 was the active intervention of feminist advocacy organisations determined to raise the profile of women in the election. These included the Fawcett Society, the new Women's Communication Centre, as well as organisations inside the parties and think tanks, especially DEMOS and Barbara Follett's 'British Women' project at the IPPR. These organisations produced reports, commissioned polls, issued press releases and kept up a steady stream of information about women voters and candidates. Their work, in a long election campaign with journalists hungry for any new informa-tion, was regularly reported. In addition the Equal Opportunities Commission and the Women's National Commission intervened, launching a National Agenda for Action on women's representation and women's issues. The EOC/WNC initiative included press confer-ences, a statement of key issues and, in February 1997, a specially commissioned NOP poll on women's preferences and attitudes.

The Fawcett Society, an organisation that dates from the campaigns for women's suffrage at the turn of the century, was especially active. As well as commissioning polls and conducting focus groups, Fawcett monitored television news for one week between 4 and 10 April.[4] During that week male politicians appeared 169 times including 26 appearances by government spokespeople, while women politicians made eight separate appearances (including Margaret Beckett, Diane Maddock, Mo Mowlam, Clare Short, Edwina Currie, Theresa Gorman and Margaret Ewing). On women's issues the study found two television news stories about childcare and one on parental leave. Similarly, the

Loughborough University study of election broadcasts found that Margaret Thatcher was the only women to rank among the ten most seen politicians in all the media. Women made seven per cent of all appearances: three per cent were front bench politicians, four per cent other politicians and one per cent leaders wives. The three party leaders accounted for 43% of all appearances in all media of any candidate (*Guardian*, 5.5.97). Even the *Daily Express* felt moved to write about the absence of women from Labour's campaign.

Although its tone varied from the supportive to the patronising or hostile, some of the press coverage seemed like something from a previous era — for example an emphasis on arguments between women. Rumbold's feuds with other women are 'legendary'. She once accused Emma Nicholson, the Conservative defector of being 'a bit menopausal'. Miss Nicholson called her 'a very heavy cannon, a loose cannon on a sinking ship', which all seems very mild by comparison to what the Tory men were reportedly saying about each other. In the same article Rumbold, who is an experienced and tough politician was described as 'with her flame coloured hair and high cheekbones she has been compared to a retired French dancer.' (*Daily Telegraph*, 16.4.97). Normally the right wing press reserved venom of this kind for Labour women. For example, the *Daily Mail* reported a debate in the five way women contest at Hampstead and Highgate where Glenda Jackson was defending her seat under the headline of 'Not such a gentle reminder as the claws come out'; the article read 'Last night relations between the sisters grew even less fraternal when they exchanged vicious insults at an old style public meeting.' (*Daily Mail*, 18.4.97). But the 'insults' detailed in the report were indistinguishable from the normal run of party political argument. There was no real story that women were especially vicious to each other on that occasion. Norma Major featured in the *Sunday Mail* (20.4.97) under the heading of 'Why are these people trying to destroy my husband', while Major's daughter got more coverage than most Tory women candidates. It seems that little has changed since the 1992 campaign when leaders wives made more appearances and attracted more attention than all women politicians put together. As usual, some of the coverage was self referential — one amusing example was the running story in both the *Daily Mail* and the *Daily Express* on Barbara Follett's refusal to give them interviews, and some emanated directly from party press offices, the coverage of Mo Mowlam's treatment for a brain tumour was an example of a managed news story. The tabloid press adapted their normal offerings to their electoral coverage. For example, the *Mirror* treated its readership to 'Blair's Babes', a series of pin up photos in which the caption offered Labour motifs, while the newly 'new Labour' *Sun* began its coverage by placing Tony Blair's letter to its readers next to its page three pin up, a juxtaposition that provoked protest from Clare Short and other feminists in the early days of the campaign. The reference to 'Blair's Babes' passed from the left to the right of the tabloid spectrum when the *Daily Mail* used it as the caption for its group photograph of the new Labour women MPs on 6 May.

Parties could and did have a role in the kind of images the media received, hence even within the context of a leader centred campaign they had the capacity to present senior women politicians. But little effort was made to do this. For example, Margaret Beckett found herself sidelined, left 'shuffling papers at one daily conference, given no chance to speak by Gordon Brown (*Guardian*, 1.5.97). As Michael Billig noted Labour 'has not woken up to something commercial advertisers take for granted: lectures by men are not the best way to impress female consumers. The more Blair publicly does his leadership bit, the more he excludes women in his team in front of an electorate which comprises more women than men. Men in suits are still setting the gender of political debate.' (*Guardian*, 5.5.97) This observation applies to all the major parties.

Voting and the gender gap

The gender gap in voting had been a feature of electoral behaviour for almost all post war elections. Comparing women and men in surveys from 1945 to 1992, Pippa Norris confirmed a long standing gender gap in Britain whereby women were more likely than men to vote for the Conservative party. The Conservative advantage peaked in the 1950s, fluctuated in the 1960s and 1970s and closed to insignificance in 1987, only to reopen in 1992 when the gap was greatest among older women, while younger women actually preferred Labour.[5] The overall pattern hid the most interesting phenomenon: among younger voters more women than men were sympathetic to Labour, while the pattern reversed among older voters, with women pensioners giving the winning edge to the Conservatives. Evidence of the gender generation gap appeared in the opinion polling and focus groups up to the day of the general election.

In this election Labour made a sustained effort to convince women voters. Attention was paid to differences in women's and men's media consumption, interviews were given to women's magazines, efforts were made to modify political language and style, and a substantial set of policies designed to appeal to women was devised. Feminists inside the Labour party used the gender generation gap to argue that more should be done to target women voters. Reckoning that their lead would decrease in the course of the election campaign, Labour had reason to be worried about the gender gap in voting intentions. In the event, Labour appeared to have solved its problem as women swung more heavily toward them than did men. The NOP BBC exit poll shows that Labour increased its lead by 11% among women but by only eight per cent among men reversing a long standing gender differences (see Kellner this volume Table 1).

Recent studies have attempted to identify the political agendas of British women. Wilkinson and Diplock suggest that men and women care about the same issues but think about them in different ways.[6] They found that older women were particularly concerned about pension provision and the availability of public transportation. Working women were most interested in the minimum wage and provision for part time workers, reflecting the concentration of women in part time, low paid jobs. Mothers were most interested in levels of child benefit, and which is more important than tax cuts for their incomes. Younger women wanted reassurances that they would be enabled to balance work and family life and childcare. These priorities do not mean that women are not concerned about the economy, health, and law and order. What they demonstrate is that there is a set of issues which is especially important to specific groups of women voters.

A similar study by Adcock aimed to identify women's political concerns and to relate those to party policies.[7] Because it was based on 10,000 self-selecting responses the survey lacks scientific validity, but its findings are interesting and give some indication of what the perspectives of British women might be. Adcock found that women's issues (defined as policies on childcare, domestic violence, part time workers rights, low pay and equal pay, support for carers) did not feature strongly in the mainstream policy agenda although such measures are discussed in special policy documents aimed at women. Moreover women expressed different priorities about mainstream policy concerns. For example, for women the key employment issue was not unemployment, the issue highlighted by the three main parties, but equal pay, equal access to pensions, access to childcare, and part time workers rights. On Europe, women mentioned not the single currency or national sovereignty but social rights. Such differences were apparent on all economic issues. Finally women expressed great concern about personal security and protection from violence.

Policies for women were developed by all three main parties but did not play a prominent role in manifestos. Prior to the campaign a set of policies were developed by the parties and publicised among women's advocacy organisations. In government the Conservatives established a substantial government machinery on women's issues including the sex equality branch of the Department for Education and Employment and the Ministerial Group on Women's Issues. Labour promised a Cabinet level Minister for Women and offered a series of documents setting out its thinking on women's issues. All three parties addressed women's issues in their campaign guides with proposed strategies, and pledges to enhance women's public representation. Considerable efforts were made to publicise strategies to the organised women's movement. For example, the Liberal Democrats launched their 'Fair Deal for Women' at their 1995 annual conference when Paddy Ashdown declared it to be the most important event at the conference. The Conservative Government held a series of 'feedback meetings' following the 4th UN World Conference on Women at Beijing in 1994 to report its policies to invited representatives of major women's advocacy organisations. Labour appointed a series of Shadow Ministers for Women who cultivated close contacts with women's organisations and other women's advocates. During 1996, Tessa Jowell conducted a widely publicised 'women's tour' meeting with women's groups and organisations throughout the country. The aim was to listen to women's concerns targeting groups such as the Townswomen's Guilds and Women's Institutes. These meetings aimed to attract women who had not previously been Labour supporters. During her tenure as Shadow Minister for Women, Clare Short ran a series of seminars at Millbank Tower that brought together experts on women's issues. These activities led to the production of a series of policy documents including 'Listening to Women' (1997), 'Strategy for Women' (1996) and 'Peace at Home' (1995).

Yet the women's agendas were not highlighted in party manifestos. The Liberal Democrats manifesto offered a separate chapter on 'opportunities' with a section on women that pledged greater opportunities at work, pension equality and the improved representation of women in public life. The document led on education and offered strong images of women throughout. Labour took mainstreaming a step further and did not include a separate section on women, although it did refer to its progress in 'making major strides to rectify the underrepresentation of women in public life'. Its five 'deliverable' election pledges made no direct promises to women. The Conservatives continued their traditional appeal to 'families' offering no special appeal to women in their 25 campaign pledges. A special section on women promised affordable high quality childcare. Not only were the policies on women's issues absent from the manifestos, they played little part in the national campaigns. The Liberal Democrats' day on women's issues led by Shirley Williams was an exception.

Making a difference

In the aftermath of the women's victories many claims were made that Parliament and politics will change. These claims varied from general remarks that women, who are used to organising their lives efficiently, will not tolerate the time-wasting conventions of the Commons, to specific claims such as Shirley Williams' comment that 'No woman would set up a system of pensions based on a lifetime's ability to work when it is obvious that it will not provide for many women.' (*Independent*, 17.4.97) Certainly many women MPs think it will make a difference. Clare Short contends that it will bring a change in the 'ya-boo' culture of the House of Commons. Feminist advocates argue that having more women makes the Commons better able to reflect a range of social concerns and to ensure that issues of special concern to women—health education, part time work, transportation, equality and social care will be better placed on the political agenda. They might also point to the new role models offered by Mo Mowlam (Secretary of State for Northern Ireland) and Margaret Beckett (President of the Board of Trade) who have taken on portfolios not typically associated with women.

The press is ambivalent. On the one hand it has welcomed the new intake of women but at the same time it has trivialised the implications of their presence. Stories range from items about the absence of women's lavatories at Westminster and the replacement of the 'gentleman's' barber with a unisex salon, through features on the house husbands who will support the women MPs, to reasoned critiques and assessments of the interests and qualities of the new women. Other coverage has been more critical. Both the *Guardian* and *Independent* reported concerns that Labour did not establish its promised separate Minister for Women at Cabinet level, but instead, belatedly, added it to Harriet Harman's Social Security portfolio.

How should such contentions be assessed? It is important not to make too much of the women's breakthrough. With a women's presence of 18.2%, Britain now ranks about twentieth in the world in its proportion of women in the national legislature.[8] Whilst much has been accomplished, it is not even clear that the critical mass, the movement from a small to a large minority that made a difference in other countries, has been achieved. All but a few of the new women MPs are part of a massive Labour majority. Their room for manoeuvre is limited and their position is insecure. Many are in marginal seats. As one Labour official remarked 'If we had a disastrous Labour government for five years and we lost all the seats we won . . . women would be the first to go.' Party loyalty will determine much of what they will do.

For women to make a difference to parliament it is necessary for women MPs to have distinct views on women's issues, to bring a 'women's perspective' into political decision making, or to bring a different style and set of role expectations to politics. It will be a matter for research to explore whether (1) there are distinctive women's perspectives and issues (2) whether women representatives share these perspectives and issue positions and (3)whether women representatives act decisively on the basis of such differences.

Some evidence is available to support the view that women MPs do bring a distinct set of perspectives to parliament. The *1997 British*

2. Approval of measures to promote women's representation

% Approve or approve strongly	Men	Women
All women short lists	16.4	29.2
Quotas/affirmative action	40.0	61.2
Better childcare in Parliament	87.8	93.4
Financial support for women candidates	26.0	65.7
Reserved seats for women	6.2	23.7
N	743.	178.

Source: The British Representation Study 1997 (N.999) of candidates and MPs.

Representation Study of 1,000 politicians (candidates and MPs from all parties) asked if respondents approved of a series of measures designed to increase the proportion of women in parliament, including all women shortlists, positive quotas and other affirmative action measures, better childcare facilities in parliament, financial support for women candidates, and reserved seats for women. The results suggest that women politicians are consistently more likely to take a pro-woman line than men. BRS data also indicate that women representatives are more likely than men to support a pro-choice line on abortion, to favour equal opportunities policies, and to agree that women should have access to a variety of social roles.[9]

The final question is whether women MPs will act on the basis of these preferences. Here there is little evidence yet on which to draw. Within a few weeks of taking their seats, however, it became clear that the Labour women MPs had already formed a network and would work together on suitable issues. Whether more women in parliament will make a difference, only time will tell.

1   Fawcett Society 'Winning Women's Votes: The Gender Gap in Voting Patterns and Priorities', 1996.
2   Interview with Peter Coleman, 14 June 1996.
3   Interview with Dame Angela Rumbold, 12 June 1996.
4   Karen Ross, 'Watching Women', Fawcett Society, 1997.
5   P. Norris, 'Mobilising the Women's Vote: The Gender-Generation Gap in Voting Behaviour', *Parliamentary Affairs*, 1996/1.
6   H. Wilkinson and S. Diplock, 'Soft Sell or Hard Policies: How Can the Parties Best Appeal to Women?', *Demos Commentary*, London 1996.
7   Charlotte Adcock What Women Want on Politics' Women's Communication Center, March 1997.
8   Interparliamentary Union 'Men and Women in Politics: Democracy Still in the Making', 1997.
9   The British Representation Study of candidates in the 1997 general election was directed by Pippa Norris in collaboration with Joni Lovenduski, John Curtice, Anthony Heath and Roger Jowell.

Turnout

BY DAVID DENVER* AND GORDON HANDS†

MOST COMMENT on the results of the 1997 general election has focused—not surprisingly—on the scale of the Conservative defeat, the huge swing to Labour as compared with 1992 and the success of the Liberal Democrats in winning 46 seats. Less attention has been paid to turnout in the election, despite the fact that the sharp decline from 1992 was a very significant aspect of the results and may, indeed, have contributed to Conservative losses. Like party support, turnout in elections varies in three main ways—from election to election, from place to place and from elector to elector—and previous analyses of turnout in Britain have utilised both survey and aggregate data to investigate the causes and effects of variations in participation by the electorate. Analysis of who votes and who does not, and why, requires survey data, however, and must await the availability of the 1997 BES surveys of the electorate. In this paper we use aggregate data to explore changes in turnout over time—both nationally and at constituency level—and spatial variation across regions and constituencies in the 1997 election.

National turnout 1950–97

During the 1997 campaign fears were expressed that the electorate might be 'turned off' by the length of the campaign and by the saturation media coverage. Such fears seem to have proved well founded, for the election saw the lowest turnout in any general election during the postwar period (71.6%). Table 1 shows the overall turnout in Great Britain in general elections since 1950. The two elections of 1950 and 1951 had quite exceptionally high turnouts—higher than in any election between the wars and never bettered since. The lowest turnout, until 1997, was in 1970 (72%) which was the first election after the voting age had been lowered from 21 to 18, resulting in an increase of more than three million in the size of the electorate as compared with 1966. No such structural factors can account for the very low turnout in 1997.

Comparing turnout across general elections is not quite as straightforward as this, however. Turnout as officially reported is defined as the number of people who voted as a percentage of the number on the

---

* Reader in Politics at Lancaster University.
† Senior Lecturer in Politics at Lancaster University.

1. Overall turnout in general elections, 1950–1997

	Reported	Adjusted
1950	84.1	86.9
1951	82.6	91.7
1955	76.9	81.5
1959	79.0	87.6
1964	77.2	85.7
1966	76.1	79.3
1970	72.0	77.0
1974 (Feb)	79.1	81.7
1974 (Oct)	73.0	81.0
1979	76.2	80.8
1983	72.7	77.8
1987	75.6	80.9
1992	77.9	82.0
1997	71.6	75.4

Notes: These figures exclude Northern Ireland. The adjusted figure is reported turnout as a percentage of (100 minus 0.82, times the number of months between the compilation of the register and the date of the election).

electoral register. The register is drawn up annually in October but does not come into force until the following February. In the interim, of course, some people will have died and others will have moved from their place of registration, and with every month that passes the register becomes increasingly inaccurate. Since dead people cannot vote and those who have moved have to make special arrangements to vote, a more accurate comparison of turnout at different elections can be made if an adjustment is made for the age of the register at the time of the election. This is done in the second column of Table 1 on the basis of a formula devised some time ago by Richard Rose.[1] In these terms the 1951 election was clearly still exceptional but, as before, turnout in the 1997 election was the lowest of the series.

Turnout and change in turnout in the standard British regions since 1992 are shown in Table 2. The South West had the highest turnout in 1997 (75.1%) as it had in 1992 (81.1%), but three regions (North, Yorkshire & Humberside and Greater London) fell below 70%. In terms of change, Scotland had much the smallest decline (– 4.0%) while the North West and East and West Midlands had the largest (– 7.3%).

2. Regional turnout, 1992–1997

	1992	1997	Change
Scotland	75.4	71.4	−4.0
Wales	79.7	73.5	−6.2
North	76.5	69.5	−7.0
Yorks & Humberside	75.4	68.4	−7.0
North West	77.3	70.0	−7.3
West Midlands	78.2	70.9	−7.3
East Midlands	80.6	73.3	−7.3
East Anglia	80.0	74.6	−5.4
South East	80.2	73.8	−6.4
Greater London	73.8	67.8	−6.0
South West	81.1	75.1	−6.0
Great Britain	77.9	71.6	−6.3

The overall decline in Great Britain (– 6.3%) was the largest recorded between any pair of elections in the postwar period. Analysis of changes in turnout at constituency level is severely restricted by the extensive boundary changes which took place between 1992 and 1997, since there is no way of reliably estimating what the 1992 turnout might have been in many of the new constituencies. We shall return to the question of change in turnout below, however. First we deal with variations in turnout across constituencies in the 1997 election itself.

Variations in constituency turnout

As in previous general elections, turnout in 1997 varied markedly across constituencies. The lowest turnout was in Liverpool Riverside (51.9%) and the highest in Brecon and Radnor (82.2%). Only nine constituencies had a turnout of over 80%, while in 33 it was below 60%. Almost all of the latter are inner city constituencies, including 10 in inner London, four in Glasgow and four in Greater Manchester. Overall, the standard deviation of constituency turnout in 1997 was 5.6—an increase in the amount of variation as compared with 1987 (mean 75.4%, s.d. 4.5) and 1992 (mean 77.5%, s.d. 5.5).

Clearly variations of this kind demand investigation and previous research has suggested a number of relevant explanatory factors. One source of variation between constituencies relates simply to the practicalities of voting and the measurement of turnout. An example of a practical matter affecting constituency turnouts occurred at the 1992 election. The election took place during a university vacation and, since most students had returned home, constituencies with large resident student populations recorded turnouts which were much lower than usual.[2] In 1997 the election was held in university term-time and, as a consequence, turnout was closer to its normal level in the constituencies concerned. The decline in turnout in Cambridge (– 1.6%) and City of Durham (– 3.7%), for example, was much smaller than the overall decline in their respective regions (– 5.4% and—7.0%). In general, however, practical considerations relate to the accuracy of the electoral registers upon which turnout calculations are based. If some constituencies have registers which are more inaccurate than those in others— because they include more people who have moved away from the area or have died—then they will appear to have lower turnouts. Very low turnouts tend to be found in inner-city constituencies, for example, but these also tend to be areas in which there are large floating populations, and it seems likely that the low turnout figures are in part a consequence of electoral register inaccuracy. Denver and Halfacree tackled this problem more generally. They argued that in areas of high out-migration electoral registers will become more inaccurate more quickly than in areas of more stable population, and they demonstrated that the level of out-migration from a constituency has a significant negative effect on recorded turnout levels.[3] People who move residence can, of course, apply to vote by post, but many do not apply since this involves a significant extra 'cost' in terms of time and effort.

Apart from these practical issues, investigations of turnout variation have drawn attention to two main sorts of explanatory factor—the social composition of constituencies and variations in the electoral context across constituencies. The method of analysis normally used is to try to account for variations in the dependent variable—constituency turnout—by reference to a series of independent variables, employing correlation and regression techniques, and we also use this method in what follows.

Social structure and turnout

Investigations of social influences upon constituency turnout levels are hampered by the fact that the censuses, from which details of the social composition of constituencies are derived, are held only once in every ten years. As a result, the data on social composition will be out-of-date when applied to an election which is some distance in time from the census date. Thus, analysis of the 1997 election has to be based on census data that are already six years out of date. Nonetheless, there is little dispute over the nature and extent of the relationships between turnout and the social composition of constituencies. In broad terms, turnout tends to be lower in poorer areas and in those in which a large proportion of the electorate live in privately rented accommodation, and tend therefore to be relatively transient, and higher in more affluent areas and those which have a relatively stable population. Table 3 shows simple correlation coefficients measuring the strength of the relationship between eleven indicators of the social composition of constituencies and turnout at the 1997 election.

The figures show, firstly, that there was a clear relationship between the occupational structure of constituencies and turnout. More middle-class constituencies tended to have higher turnouts and more working-class constituencies lower turnouts. Variations in patterns of housing tenure were even more strongly associated with variations in turnout. The coefficient for percentage owner occupiers is strongly positive, while other housing categories produce negative coefficients. This is generally interpreted as reflecting the fact that areas with high levels of

3. Correlations between social composition and constituency turnout, 1997

% Professional and Managerial	0.502	% in agriculture	0.378
% Manual workers	−0.332	Persons per hectare	−0.649
% Owner occupiers	0.690	% Aged 18–29	−0.595
% Private tenants	−0.298	% Aged 75+	0.152
% Local authority tenants	−0.554		
		% Households no car	−0.809
		% Ethnic minority	−0.488

Notes: All coefficients are significant, p <.001, N = 639. West Bromwich West (where the Speaker was not opposed by the Conservatives or Liberal Democrats) and Tatton (where there were no Labour or Liberal Democrat candidates) are excluded from this and all subsequent constituency analyses.

owner occupation tend also to be areas that are relatively affluent and relatively stable in terms of population movement. In contrast, where there are high proportions of people who privately rent their housing there is also typically a large transient population. Up to the 1980s there was no significant correlation between turnout and the percentage of households which rented their accommodation from the local authority. As owner occupation has expanded, however, it is increasingly the case that those living in council accommodation are among the poorest and most deprived sections of the community and turnout has fallen in these areas, in relative terms. As can be seen, in 1997 the more council tenants there were in a constituency, the lower was the turnout.

Survey studies find that younger voters are significantly less likely to vote than other groups and this is reflected in the strong negative correlation found using the constituency data, although it is also the case that more urban areas tend to have larger proportions of young people in their population. One might expect that areas which have large proportions of older folk would also have lower turnouts, since such voters might have difficulty in getting to the polls, but in fact the relationship with turnout is positive and significant, although not substantial. This might be explained by the fact that retired people may have more time to go to the polls or may regard voting as an opportunity to get out and meet people. It is also possible, however, that the positive correlation reflects more accurate electoral registers in areas with larger proportions of older people since the old are more settled and less likely to move around than the young. Finally, the proportion of workers in agriculture and the number of persons per hectare in a constituency are indicators of the extent to which it is an urban or rural area. The figures show that turnout in 1997, as before, was lower in more urban areas—and especially in those with a very high population density—than it was in more rural areas. The proportion of households with no car can be taken as an indicator of the general level of poverty or affluence constituency and was strongly negatively related to turnout—indeed, among the variables examined this was the single best predictor of turnout levels. Finally, the larger the proportion of ethnic minority residents in a constituency the lower was the turnout in 1997.

Three cautionary points need to be made about the interpretation of these correlation coefficients. Firstly, as noted above, the social composition variables are derived from the 1991 census so that, although the data would have given an accurate picture of the social make-up of constituencies at the time of the 1992 election, they were six years out of date by the 1997 election. Secondly, the coefficients are derived from aggregate data and refer to the characteristics of constituencies, not individuals. We cannot infer from these data that owner occupiers turn out in greater numbers than other people or that ethnic minority electors tend not to vote. Rather, the figures tell us that the greater the proportion of owner occupiers in a constituency the higher, usually, is the overall turnout in the constituency, and the more ethnic minority voters there are the lower is the turnout. Thirdly, the various measures of social composition are themselves highly inter-correlated. Thus constituencies in which a large proportion of households have no car tend also to have large proportions of ethnic minority voters, council tenants, manual workers and young people, as well as high population density. Sorting out which variables are the most important influences on turnout requires multivariate analysis, which allows us to say whether a particular variable still exerts a significant influence when all others are held constant, and we return to this below.

Electoral context

There are a number of aspects of the structure of the electoral contest facing electors which might influence the decision of electors to vote or not. Firstly, there is the number of candidates available to vote for. It may be that a larger number of candidates makes for a more vigorous local campaign, but it might also be the case that if a contest offers a wider than normal range of choice then this might encourage some people to vote who would not otherwise do so. On the other hand, in some constituencies large numbers of 'other' candidates stand, but each gets only a few hundred votes. A more reliable measure than the number of candidates standing may therefore be the percentage of the vote gained by all candidates not representing the major parties.

A second element of the electoral context which varies from constituency to constituency is the tactical situation facing voters and it may be that this too will affect turnout levels. Awareness of the potential impact of tactical voting has greatly increased in recent years as the two major parties have been more vigorously challenged by the Liberal Democrats (and their predecessors) and by the nationalists in Scotland and Wales. Since electors who might previously have considered their votes 'wasted' may now recognise that they can be used more effectively in certain situations, we might hypothesise that electoral contests in which tactical voting appeared to be a realistic option would have higher turnouts than those where it did not. In order to test this, we devised a simple scale designed to give a rough indication of the scope that existed for tactical voting in each constituency. It is generally agreed that the likelihood of tactical voting is influenced by two considerations—the size of the combined vote of the second and third placed parties compared to that of the winner, and the distance between the second and third parties. On our scale a constituency scores zero if, in the previous election, the winner was more than 10 per cent ahead of the next two parties combined. The remaining constituencies are scored from 1 to 4. This score was created by adding together a score based on the lead of the winning party over the other two parties combined (1 if it was up to 10% ahead; 2 if it was up to 10 per cent behind; 3 if it was more than 10% behind) to one based on the difference between the second and third parties (0 if it was up to 10% and 1 if it was more than 10%). Thus, a score of 4 would indicate that the winning party was more than 10% behind the combined shares of the other two parties in the previous election with a gap of more than 10% between the second and third parties.

Previous experience suggests, however, that by far the most important aspect of the electoral context so far as turnout is concerned is the marginality (or, to put it the other way round, the degree of safeness) of the constituency in the previous election. Unsurprisingly, it is usually the case that the more marginal a seat is perceived to be, the higher is the turnout. In our previous work on turnout in British general elections from 1959 to 1979, we found that there were strong associations between the marginality of constituencies and their turnout even after taking account of a variety of other social and political factors.[4] It is not difficult to explain the importance of marginality. In the first place, the parties usually put a much greater campaign effort into more marginal seats and their efforts at voter mobilisation result in higher turnouts. Secondly, many electors will get to know whether their constituency is safe for one of the parties or whether it may change hands, and reason that it is more important to vote in more marginal seats.

In our earlier publications we found that the relationship between marginality and turnout steadily strengthened between the 1964 and 1979 elections. We confidently expected this trend to continue in future elections since voters were becoming more sophisticated and parties were targeting their campaign efforts more systematically into marginal seats. In fact, contrary to our expectations, the simple correlation between the two variables actually became markedly weaker in 1983 (0.27), fell further in 1987 (0.16) and remained at a low level in 1992 (0.17). No convincing explanation for this apparent weakening of the impact of marginality has been offered, and all analyses of turnout in recent elections find that it remains, nonetheless, a significant variable in multiple regression equations. In other words, once a variety of social composition and other variables are taken into account the marginality or safeness of constituencies is clearly associated with turnout levels.

Applying our measures of marginality and of the scope for tactical voting to the 1997 election is, of course, made problematical by the constituency boundary revisions which we referred to above. However the parties made their own calculations about the situation in the new constituencies and also made extensive use of a specially calculated set of 'notional' 1992 results which estimated the distribution of 1992 votes for the parties in the new constituencies.[5] These were also widely used, at least in the quality press, to give voters information about the status of the new seats. We too have used these notional results in what follows where the distribution of votes in 1992 is relevant to our analysis.

4. Correlations between electoral context variables and turnout, 1997

Constituency marginality	0.258
Scope for tactical voting	0.181
% vote for Referendum party	0.111
% vote for 'others'	−0.260

Note: N = 639. All coefficients are statistically significant at p <.001 except for Referendum party vote share which is significant at p <.05.

Table 4 shows the relationships between the aspects of the electoral context that we have discussed and 1997 turnout. We have separated support for the Referendum party from support from 'other' parties and individuals since it was a fairly significant new player in the electoral game. As can be seen, support for 'other' parties is significantly associated with turnout, but in the 'wrong' direction—the greater this support, the lower the turnout. Simple inspection of the election results suggests that this is because large numbers of 'other' candidates tend to be found in inner city constituencies, which as we have seen tend to have low turnouts for other reasons. On the other hand, the presence of Referendum party candidates appears to have encouraged some people to vote who would not otherwise have done so—the correlation is significant and positive, although not very strong.

'Scope available for tactical voting' is also associated with higher turnout, but (apart from the clearly aberrant figure for 'other' share of the vote) the strongest relationship among these variables is with previous marginality. Despite the uncertainties caused by the boundary revisions, the more marginal a seat was in 1992 (or was deemed to be by the notional results), the higher was the turnout. Indeed, the size of the coefficient suggests that marginality was a greater influence on turnout than it had been in the previous two general elections. If we consider only the 238 seats which had no boundary changes or only minor ones (involving 5% or less of the electorate)—in which, it might be surmised, the marginality of the seat and the tactical situation would have been more widely understood—we find that the marginality coefficient rises to 0.287 and that for scope for tactical voting to 0.243.

Multivariate analysis

We noted above that many of the social composition variables which correlate strongly with turnout are themselves interrelated and the same is true of marginality and 'scope for tactical voting'. Multiple regression analysis enables us to examine the effect of one variable while holding all others constant and also to assess the extent to which combinations of factors can explain variations in turnout. Table 5 reports the results of two such analyses, based on a stepwise regression procedure.

The first column shows the standardised coefficients (which indicate the relative importance of each of the variables) in a multiple regression equation predicting constituency turnouts on the basis of the *social composition* variables described above. When all other variables are

5. Predicting constituency turnout on basis of social composition and electoral context, 1997

	I	II
% Households no car	−0.479	−0.451
% Owner occupiers	0.465	*
% Local authority tenants	0.392	*
% Manual workers	−0.217	−0.256
Persons per hectare	−0.167	−0.192
% Private tenants	0.099	−0.108
% Aged 18–29	−0.098	−0.147
% Ethnic minority	−0.068	−0.105
Marginality	–	0.255
% Referendum party	–	−0.104
Scope for tactical voting	–	*
% others	–	*
Constant	70.82	85.55
R²	0.730	0.797

Note: the figures reported are standardised regression coefficients. Only statistically significant coefficients are reported (* = not significant).

controlled for simultaneously, eight remain significant. Six have an impact in the expected direction, but % of council tenants is now associated with higher turnouts, as is % of private tenants. Taken together, these eight variables account for 73% of the variation in turnout, with % households with no car, % owner occupiers, % local authority tenants and % manual workers being the most important influences. The second column shows what happens when the four electoral context variables are added to this basic equation. Two are significant—previous marginality and % vote for the Referendum party—but the latter, contrary to the impression given by the simple correlation in Table 4, is now seen to be associated with lower turnout. Two of the housing variables drop out of the equation, and % private tenants now shows the expected relationship with turnout. The addition of the electoral context variables sharply increases the variation explained to 79.7%, which reaffirms the argument that an explanation of turnout variation must take account of political as well as social factors.

These multivariate analyses confirm that variations in constituency turnout in 1997 can be predicted with a good deal of accuracy on the basis of variations in their social composition. As in previous elections, poorer, urban, working-class seats with larger than average numbers of ethnic minority and young voters had much lower turnouts than more affluent suburban, small town and rural seats. In addition, however, the marginality of constituencies was important—enhancing the predictive power of our basic equation substantially. Indeed, just three variables— % households with no car, % manual workers and previous marginality—together account for 69.6% of the variation in turnout. Marginality appears, then to have assumed more importance in the 1997 election than it did in 1992.[6] This suggests that there may have been an above average decline in turnout in safer seats, which takes us back to the question of turnout change.

Change in turnout 1992–97

Explaining variations in change in turnout is always more difficult than explaining variations in turnout itself. To start with, change in turnout is of course much smaller than turnout—the average change in turnout in pairs of elections between 1950 and 1997 was only 3.7%, whereas the average turnout in these elections was 76.7%. This means that random or 'accidental' factors—such as the local weather, a recent by-election, the timing of elections in relation to local holiday periods—will have a much greater impact on change in turnout than on the absolute level of turnout, and may 'swamp' the effects of social or political factors. For this reason, standard regression analyses of change in turnout consistently produce smaller r^2 figures than similar analyses of absolute turnout. Secondly, whereas there is a considerable body of evidence about the relationship between social factors and constituency turnout, there are no very obvious general hypotheses about the relationship between social factors and change in turnout. In addition, the changes in constituency boundaries to which we have already referred mean that a full analysis of change in turnout in 1997 is not possible.[7] We can, however, explore the topic to some extent by focusing on the 238 constituencies in which there were no boundary changes or in which the changes involved 5% or less of the electorate. In these constituencies the mean 1997 turnout was 71.4%, with a standard deviation of 5.31—very close to the figures for the constituencies in which boundary changes were more extensive (mean 71.5%, s.d. 5.65).

We described above the decline in turnout between the elections of 1992 and 1997 in Britain as a whole and in the standard regions. As we saw, there was a sharp drop in overall turnout (6.3%) and this calls for explanation, especially since it has been argued that it was a significant factor in the Conservative rout. In fact two main explanations for the fall in turnout have been put forward. The first suggests that voters were simply bored by the length and lack of excitement of the campaign, and by the perceived absence of significant policy differences between the major parties. The fact that the decline in turnout was well-nigh universal suggests that there was indeed a 'boredom factor' which affected the whole country, and the dramatic decline in audiences for television news programmes during the campaign is persuasive circumstantial evidence in support of this view. In none of the constituencies where direct comparison was possible did turnout increase, and in only one (the most marginal seat of all, Vale of Glamorgan) was turnout unchanged. There were only small declines in the idiosyncratic Western Isles (− 0.3%), and in Edinburgh South (− 0.6%) and Dumfries (− 1.0%), but in the remainder the fall ranged from − 1.3% to − 12.2% (Thurrock).

But the very fact that there were significant variations in the size of the fall in turnout implies that some considerations other than general boredom affected the electorate. The second explanation that has been put forward for the fall in turnout is that many former Conservatives decided not to vote.[8] This is certainly a plausible hypothesis, given the sharp drop in the Conservative share of the vote. If it were true, however, we would expect the decline in turnout to be greatest in constituencies in which the Conservative vote was highest in 1992. Thus if, across the board, 10% of previous Conservatives did not vote in 1997, and nothing else changed, then this would produce a sharper drop in turnout in Conservative-held seats (and especially in safe seats) than in Labour seats, and very little change where there were few Conservative votes to start with.

But examination of the constituency data provides little evidence to support this view. To start with, Table 6 shows the mean changes in different groups of seats in England and Wales where comparison between 1992 and 1997 can be made.[9] If we focus on seats held (notionally, at least) by the Conservatives in 1992, the fall in turnout was indeed very slightly smaller in marginal than in safe seats. And similarly in the seats held by Labour in 1992, the fall in turnout was slightly smaller in safe Labour seats, where the Conservative vote would have been lowest.[10] But overall the drop in turnout was clearly smaller in seats that were held by the Conservatives in 1992 (−5.8%) than in those that were Labour held (−7.9%) or held by the Liberal Democrats (−7.2%). Moreover, the drop in turnout in Conservative-held seats was very similar in those that they retained in 1997, those that they lost to Labour and those lost to the Liberal Democrats.

6. Mean changes in turnout in comparable constituencies, 1992–97

Con held 1992	−5.8	(107)	Lab held 1992	−7.9	(103)
majority >20%	−5.9	(41)	majority >20%	−7.6	(55)
majority 10–20%	−5.9	(27)	majority 10–20%	−8.1	(22)
majority <10%	−5.6	(39)	majority <10%	−8.3	(26)
Con held 92 and 97	−5.8	(35)	Lib Dem held 92 and 97	−7.2	(6)
Con lost to Lab	−5.8	(58)			
Con lost to Lib Dem	−5.9	(14)			

Note: the figures refer only to constituencies in England and Wales, N = 219.

This analysis is confirmed by Table 7, which shows correlation coefficients measuring the association between the change in turnout in English and Welsh constituencies and a variety of other factors. The figures tell a clear story. If we look first at correlations with the major parties' vote shares in 1992, we see that the larger the Conservative (and Liberal Democrat) share of the vote in a constituency the *smaller* (i.e. less negative) was the fall in turnout; by contrast, the larger the Labour vote in 1992 the steeper was the decline. If the drop in turnout was mainly due to 'stay-at-home' Conservatives we should expect the opposite. It may be, of course, that the turnout of anti-Conservatives varied dramatically, increasing in Conservative areas and decreasing

7. Correlations with changes in turnout, 1992–97

% Con 1992	0.258*	% Professional and managerial	0.536*
% Lab 1992	−0.356*	% Manual workers	−0.515*
% Lib Dem 1992	0.253*	% Owner occupiers	0.177#
		% Private tenants	0.364*
		% Local authority tenants	−0.379*
Change in % Con 1992–97	0.032	% in agriculture	0.269*
Change in % Lab 1992–97	−0.023	Persons per hectare	−0.126
Change in % Lib Dem 1992–97	0.053	% Aged 18–29	−0.133#
% Referendum party 1997	−0.051	% Aged 75 +	0.351*
		% Households no car	−0.306*
		% Ethnic minority	−0.070

Note: the figures refer only to constituencies in England and Wales, N = 219; * = statistically significant, p <.001; # = statistically significant, p <05.

substantially in their own areas, but it is difficult to think of any hypothesis which would explain such differential behaviour and it remains inherently implausible. The second part of the table, which gives correlations with changes in the parties' vote shares between 1992 and 1997, shows that changes in turnout were in fact unrelated to the election outcome in any systematic way. It is worth noting that this applies also to the Referendum party—the proportion of the vote it won was not associated with the pattern of turnout change. It would appear, then, that even though the fall in turnout that occurred in 1997 was very sharp, it actually had little systematic impact on the election result.

But we are left, then, with something of a paradox. Both the Conservative vote and turnout fell sharply, yet the two are unrelated. By contrast, Labour won the election with a substantial increase in its vote share, yet the turnout was lowest, and fell most sharply, in Labour areas. Though we cannot here explore matters in detail, it seems likely that three factors account for the peculiar pattern of events. First, although the Conservative vote fell, many of those who voted Conservative in 1992 switched their vote to one of the other parties in 1997, rather than abstaining. Figures from the BBC exit poll referred to in Pippa Norris's introduction to this volume provide some striking evidence on this point. Although by definition it can tell us nothing about those who did not vote in the election, it shows that as many as 28.5% (or 4 million) of 1992 Conservative voters switched to another party. Second, there does seem to have been a substantial across the board decline in turnout. Whether this was due to the long campaign, or because voters thought the result was a forgone conclusion will have to wait for more detailed analysis on the basis of survey evidence, but it seems that this was a general trend across the whole country. Third, superimposed on this general trend there was a tendency for turnout to fall most among groups which traditionally have lower turnout and are more likely to support Labour. Further evidence for this is provided by the right-hand column of Table 7, which shows that fall in turnout was highest in constituencies with high proportions of manual workers, those owning no car, local authority tenants, and high population density, and lowest in those with high proportions of professional and managerial workers, agricultural workers and old people.

Thus, although we cannot properly infer it from the constituency data, the evidence does suggest that there was a tendency for past and potential Labour supporters to stay away from the polls in larger numbers. This may have been due to a belief that the election was 'in the bag' or to disillusion as a consequence of Labour's abandoning traditional policy stances and ideology. Whatever the reason, it can be concluded that, although the election results were a damning indictment of the Conservative government, they hardly constituted a ringing endorsement of the new Labour party. More generally, the turnout figures for 1997 show that there is a substantial section of the electorate concentrated in poor, inner city areas, but not confined there—where the electorate's engagement with democratic politics is slight. Whether this indicates disaffection, lack of interest or a pragmatic response to the alternatives offered is not clear, but this is certainly an issue to which all the parties ought to give some attention.

1   See R. Rose, *Electoral Behaviour* (Free Press, 1974), p. 494.

2   J. Curtice and M. Steed, 'The Results Analysed' in D. Butler and D. Kavanagh, *The British General Election of 1992* (Macmillan, 1992) p. 347.

3   D. Denver and K. Halfacree, 'Inter-Constituency Migration and Turnout at the British General Election of 1983', *British Journal of Political Science* 22, 1992.

4   D. Denver and G. Hands, 'Marginality and Turnout in British General Elections', *British Journal of Political Science* 4, 1974; D. Denver and G. Hands, 'Marginality and Turnout in British General Elections in the 1970s', *British Journal of Political Science* 15, 1985.

5   The 'notional' 1992 results are to be found in C. Rallings and M. Thrasher, *Media Guide to the New Constituencies* (Local Government Chronicle Election Centre, University of Plymouth, 1995).

6   For a recent assessment of the impact of previous marginality in 1992 see C. Pattie and R.J. Johnston 'Voter Turnout at the British General Election of 1992: Rational Choice, Social Standing or Political Efficacy?', *European Journal of Political Research*, forthcoming.

7   The Boundary Commission for England did not use 1992 electorates to define the new constituencies. The 'notional' 1992 results found in Rallings and Thrasher's *Media Guide to the New Constituencies* are intended only as estimates of the distribution of votes in the new constituencies and should not be used to estimate 1992 constituency turnouts.

8   Garret Fitzgerald argues (*The Times*, 12.5.97) that 'the whole of the two million fall in the total poll was accounted for simply by Tories staying at home'.

9   The 19 comparable Scottish seats are excluded since the fall in turnout was much lower in Scotland and there is a heavy preponderance of Labour held seats.

10   There were, of course, many more Conservative-held than Labour-held seats in 1992 so that, as we have suggested, the smaller decline in turnout in Conservative marginals will have contributed to the increased importance of marginality in predicting turnout overall.

The Electoral System

BY PATRICK DUNLEAVY* AND HELEN MARGETTS†

ALTHOUGH the UK's electoral system is widely seen as the simplest possible method of voting it still has a capacity to surprise us. In recent years political scientists have recognised that we still do not fully understand how complex plurality rule elections are, and how many component effects need to be measured to gain an accurate picture. The impacts of an electoral systems on the political process can be measured in two rather different ways. The conventional approach is an *institutional* one, concerned chiefly with how the system alters or distorts the competition between parties and leaders for political power.[1] Here the focus is exclusively on winners and losers, majorities and advantages for one party over another, and how the distribution of seats might have turned out differently. These issues are important ones. But they do not tell the whole story. A second *experiential* approach focuses instead on how the system of voting affects citizens themselves, by recognizing and making effective some of their choices and filtering out others. Here the focus is on how the electoral system provides feedback to citizens which tends to reward and confirm some kinds of behaviour, but to ignore or discard the remainder.

One immediate application of this approach is to explain why large numbers of people (by no means all Labour supporters) saw the result of the 1997 election as a positive experience, a breath of fresh air and a reaffirmation of democratic control. This widespread reaction, remarked on by numerous commentators, occurred immediately after the results, despite the low turnout at the polls themselves and the poor level of public interest in the election campaign. Was this feeling just 'time for a change' in a new guise, or relief that after eighteen years leadership succession was still feasible in Britain? Or did it have some objective basis in people's own experiences of how their votes were processed to produce a result? We explore briefly how the main institutional indicators moved in 1997, and in the second section turn to the experiential measures. The conclusions explore some of the implications of the 1997 outcome for the debate about electoral reform which will probably occur during the coming Parliament, with a referendum on changing the voting system for the House of Commons before 2002 promised in the Labour and Liberal Democrat manifestos.

* Professor of Government at the London School of Economics and Political Science.
† Lecturer in Politics at Birkbeck College.

Institutional indicators

There are many different possible indicators of electoral system performance, but serious comparative work on electoral systems has tended to focus on a number of important and intuitively understandable measures, especially the concepts of 'deviation from proportionality' and the 'effective number of parties' in a political system (which is measured at two levels in terms of votes and in terms of seats inside the legislature).[2] *Deviation from proportionality* is accepted universally as one of the key dimensions of an electoral system, showing how in a given election the allocation of seats across parties in a political system deviates from the allocation of votes. Table 1 shows how to calculate simple deviation from proportionality[3] (hereafter termed the DV score) for the 1997 result in Great Britain.[4] We simply subtract the percentage of votes a party received from its share of seats gained in the Commons to give a deviation for each party. The largest deviation is often a good indicator of how distorting an electoral system is, and in 1997 this measure was 21% (the exaggeration in Labour's seats share). But to check more carefully we simply add up the deviations for all parties (discarding their plus or minus signs, which would otherwise mean that they cancel out) and then divide by two,[5] giving again a DV score of 21% for the 1997 general election.

1. Deviation from proportionality, 1997

Party	% votes (1)	% seats (2)	(2)–(1) deviations
Conservative	31.4	25.7	−5.7
Labour	44.4	65.4	+21.0
Liberal Democrats	17.2	7.2	−10.0
Scottish National Party	2.0	0.9	−1.1
Plaid Cymru	0.5	0.6	+0.1
Referendum Party	2.7	0	−2.7
Others	1.7	0.2	−1.5
Total	100	100	

Total deviations (ignoring + or −signs)	42.1
DV score = total deviations/2	21%
Largest deviation (for Labour)	21%

Deviation from proportionality can be simply understood as the fraction of MPs who are not entitled to their seats in the legislature in terms of their party's national share of the vote. Under a pure proportional representation system over one fifth of 1997 seats would switch to a different party. This figure is much the same as the DV scores in most elections since the mid-1970s, when substantial third party voting became an established feature of British politics. The 1997 landslide is slightly below the 1983 DV score of 23%, when Margaret Thatcher won a large majority over Michael Foot's divided Labour party. The almost unique feature in Table 1, however, is that Labour's gains (its huge 'winner's bias') did not come solely from third parties, but in large part also from the under-representation of the main party in opposition.

This election was only the third time since 1918 that the Conservative seats/votes ratio has slipped below one, the other occasions being in 1945 and (marginally) in 1966. Liberal Democrat under-representation is their lowest since 1970 in terms of percentage deviations, and their seats/votes ratio at 0.4 is their highest postwar score. The connected patterning of Liberal Democrat seat gains, solidly established in south-west England with 'critical mass' and stretching eastwards to reach some urban centres in the south-east and the south-west London suburbs, greatly enhances their possible threat to Tory hegemony in these areas.

The main reason for the Conservative under-representation was their precipitate decline in votes since 1992, with a quarter of their total vote share vanishing over five years. Britain's plurality rule electoral system heavily discriminates against political parties which fall below a threshold of around 33%. By dropping to just 31% of the poll, five points below their previous worst score this century (in October 1974 under Ted Heath), the Conservatives have created a mountain for themselves to climb at the next election (see Norris this volume). But they have also opened up a real (if still outside) possibility that the Liberal Democrats could try to displace them as the main non-Labour party, a feat which they have achieved in most major cities at the local government level.

One consequence of immense significance is that the Tories have also ceased to be a national party (see McAllister, this volume). Table 2 shows that they achieved seats/votes ratios close to one in only six out of 18 regions of the country, while getting scores of below 0.3 in eight regions.[6] Even in the London suburbs, the Conservatives were under-represented by one third in 1997. The Tories' heartland areas (those with significant over-representation) were reduced dramatically to East Anglia and the south-east outside London, with the party faring

2. Seats/votes ratios for political parties in 18 regions of Britain, 1997

Region	Cons	Lab	Lib Dem	4th party	4th party is:
Central Scotland	0.0	1.8	0.3	0.0	SNP
Yorkshire: conurbation	0.0	1.7	0.2	0.0	Others
Scotland: Highlands	0.0	1.6	1.5	0.7	SNP
South Wales	0.0	1.6	0.0	0.0	Plaid Cymru
Scotland: South	0.0	1.5	1.7	0.6	SNP
Mid and North Wales	0.0	1.5	0.8	1.4	Plaid Cymru
North West: conurbation	0.2	1.5	0.3	0.0	Others
London: middle	0.2	1.6	0.2	0.0	Others
West Midlands: conurbation	0.4	1.6	0.0	0.0	Others
North East	0.4	1.4	0.2	0.0	Others
North West: rest	0.5	1.6	0.0	0.6	Others
London: suburbs	0.6	1.5	0.8	0.0	Others
East Midlands	0.9	1.4	0.0	0.0	Others
West Midlands: rest	0.9	1.5	0.2	0.0	Others
Yorkshire: rest	1.1	1.3	0.3	0.0	Others
South West	1.2	1.1	0.9	0.0	Others
South East	1.5	1.0	0.3	0.0	Others
East Anglia	1.6	0.9	0.0	0.0	Others

proportionally also in the south-west and in Yorkshire outside the conurbation areas. The Liberal Democrats achieved higher seats/votes ratios than the Tories in seven regions out of the 18, and were almost treated proportionately in the south-west. But the third party also had seats/votes scores of zero in five regions. Labour fought its election on a one-nation campaign, and secured uniform seats/votes ratios around 1.5 in all but three regions—the south west, south east and East Anglia—although even here the party fared proportionately. There were no clear relationships between party fortunes and regional variations in turnout, with all but one region showing turnout rates between 68 and 76%; the exception was the middle of London, where turnout fell to a depressing 64% (see Denver and Hands, and McAllister in this volume).

We next turn to a second key measure of how the electoral system behaved, the effective number of parties (ENP), measured in terms of vote shares and seat shares. Political scientists have always confronted some problems in deciding how many parties are in competition with each other. Many commentators still speak of the UK as a 'two party system', because of the Conservative and Labour joint monopoly of government, describing them as 'major parties'. The Liberal Democrats are relegated to the status of a 'minor party', although in any other liberal democracy in Europe their vote share since 1974 (ranging between 15 and 26%), and their central position on the left-right spectrum, would make them a very important coalitional actor. Half-hearted attempts to accommodate them using the concept of a 'two and a half party' system clearly broke down in 1997, when the Referendum Party brought strong elements of four party competition into the English election, while four or more party struggles have long been the norm in Scottish and Welsh constituencies.

There are problems in 'counting' parties, as Lijphart has noted: 'The practical problem in measuring the number of parties is how to count parties of unequal size, and in particular how to count very small parties. The assumption in the comparative politics literature has long been that some kind of weighting is necessary'.[7] Weighting is much better than simply discounting the smaller parties by fiat, as the 'two party system' idea does. By incorporating a weighting mechanism, ENP has become a central measure for the analysis of electoral systems. The ENP measure is simple to operate, as Table 3 shows. We express the vote shares of all parties in decimal fraction form—so that Labour's share is 0.444, for instance, instead of 44.4%. Then we square each party's vote share, which always converts them into even smaller fractions. Squaring makes very small parties' fractions almost zero, but leaves larger parties with still substantial fractions—for instance the figure for Labour is now 0.197. Finally we add up these squared vote shares, and then divide one by this total to get the ENP score. The calculation for ENP shown in Table 3 results in a figure of 3.06 which

3. Calculating the effective numbers of parties for votes

Party	Decimal vote share	Squared decimal vote share
Labour	0.444	0.197
Conservative	0.314	0.099
Liberal Democrats	0.172	0.030
SNP	0.02	0.0004
Plaid Cymru	0.005	0.000025
Referendum Party	0.027	0.0007
Others	0.017	0.0003
	Sum of squared vote shares	0.327
	1/sum of squared vote shares	3.06

suggests that there were effectively three parties in competition at the 1997 election in Britain. Of course, there are limits to such indices, like all measures which involve squaring numbers, but it provides a useful basis for comparing Britain with other countries such as with the US with its uniquely perfect ENP score for votes of 2.0, or other west European liberal democracies where ENP scores are usually above 3.[8]

Once we have calculated the ENP score for vote shares, we can do the same thing for shares of seats in the House of Common—and doing so discover that the effective number of parties securing representation in the legislature is much less—in fact the score is 2.0 exactly. Labour's large share of seats and the under-representation of the Tories and Liberal Democrats largely explain this difference from ENP for votes. We can give a precise measure of the difference using the 'relative reduction in parties' (RRP) index. We express the reduction in parties (which is 1.06, obtained by subtracting the number of parties in the legislature from the number of parties in the electorate) as a percentage share of the number of parties in the electorate (which is 3.06). This gives an RRP score of 34%. This result can be interpreted as the extent to which the electoral system fails to represent people's vote choices in the Commons. Again an RRP score of this level is very high by comparison with other liberal democracies, and by British historical standards. With Thatcher's victory in 1983 the RRP score touched 31%, its then highest level in the postwar period, but then in 1987 it dropped down to 28 and in 1992 to 24%. The 1997 score is a new record in the postwar period.

Finally, it makes sense to look briefly at a traditional but now rather discredited concept which perfectly expresses the institutional concern with the power implications of the electoral system—the concept of the 'wasted vote'. The idea here is to distinguish those voters who were efficacious in the highly restrictive sense that their support was absolutely essential to return the MP elected in their local constituency. By definition voters who are efficacious cannot have supported defeated candidates. But people who supported locally winning candidates, but whose support merely went into enhancing those candidates' winning margin, also were not efficacious on this view. Thus total 'wasted votes' includes all losing votes in a constituency, plus any surplus majority votes (that is, votes more than N_2+1, where N_2 was the votes total of the runner up). Traditionally critics of Britain's plurality rule elections have argued that the House of Commons reflects the views of only a minority of efficacious voters, and that the system condemns most voters to cast 'wasted' votes. There are considerable difficulties with this line of argument, however. For instance, no voter who makes up part of a winning majority can possibly know if their individual vote will form part of the surplus majority or the 'efficacious' vote (although they may well know in advance the approximate probabilities of a surplus majority). Defenders of the status quo have been most hostile to the concept, arguing that it is a wholly artificial construct, relies on an absurdly narrow criterion of efficaciousness, and ignores many of the complex reasons why voters support political parties.

Nonetheless, if we bear in mind the need to maintain 'score' quotes around 'wasted', this criterion is an interesting one, which captures one part of the many facets of electoral system performance, especially when we look at variations in the index across regions. Table 4 shows that the proportion of surplus majority votes was highest in safe Labour areas, touching nearly half of all votes in the south Wales region, for example. And it was over a third of voters in four other regions (the north, the north-west conurbation area, middle London, and the Yorkshire conurbations). The narrowest surplus majorities came in the south-west, East Anglia and the south-east because the Conservative vote came under pressure there, and other parties won seats there by narrow margins. Losing votes showed much less variation across regions, amounting to 37% as a minimum and 55% as a maximum. Putting the two elements together to make the 'wasted' vote total shows a fairly sharp variation. 'Wasted' votes are at a maximum in south Wales where they account for around four out of five ballots, dropping to two thirds of the total in seven out of the eighteen regions.

4. 'Wasted' votes by region, 1997

Region	Surplus majority votes (%)	Losing votes (%)	'Wasted' votes (%)
South Wales	45	37	81
North East	41	37	78
North West: conurbation	38	39	76
Scotland: South	25	50	75
London: middle	35	41	75
Scotland Highlands	21	52	74
Mid and North Wales	21	52	73
Central Scotland	32	45	77
Yorkshire: conurbation	33	41	71
West Midlands: conurbation	27	44	71
Yorkshire: rest	22	49	70
North West: rest	22	46	69
East Midlands	19	49	68
East Anglia	13	55	68
South East	14	54	68
West Midlands: rest	17	50	67
South West	12	55	67
London: suburbs	15	51	66

Whether or not we accept the normative implications of the 'wasted' votes label, the data in Table 4 emphasize the narrow basis on which electoral success can strictly be founded under plurality rule. For instance, if all the currently losing voters in south Wales kept voting on their current pattern (without becoming more cohesive or reducing the fragmentation of their votes between parties) then in principle a mere 19% of the current electorate could keep the region safe for the winning incumbents in 1997 (almost all of whom are Labour). This kind of statistic has some important links to political practice, notably in the complaints voiced during the election campaign that the three main parties' activities were exclusively directed to 200,000 or so 'swing' voters in marginal seats.

Experiential indicators

Shifting focus, we ask now how voters experienced the voting system in 1997 in different regions of Britain—as an accurate set of devices for measuring their preferences, or as a distorting mirror with no apparent logic of equal treatment? The institutional approach to the analysis of electoral systems focuses on phenomena according to the extent that they shape or influence control of political power and the state apparatus at national level. In contrast, the hallmark of the experiential approach is to compile measures and indices which capture how people are affected (consciously or unconsciously) by political events, regardless of their salience for political outcomes. The essential step to getting closer to voters' experiences is to disaggregate, going below the national picture on disproportionality to detect underlying patterns, in this case at regional level.[9]

The difference in approach may be illustrated by applying experiential criteria based on the standard Census regions to the indicators described earlier. The British score for deviation from proportionality, for instance, is normally misleadingly low if compared with other countries because areas of pro-Conservative deviation in the south-east are partly offset by areas of pro-Labour deviations in Scotland and the north. In 1992 the national DV score was just 18%, but looking closer at regional patterns of DV demonstrated that much higher scores than this were common in most regions.[10] Across south-east England where the Conservatives won 97% of seats on the basis of 55% of the votes (leaving all other parties virtually unrepresented), the 1992 regional DV score was 43%—just about as high as it is possible to get and still regard the political system as a liberal democracy. In central Scotland there was an equivalently unfair system, although with fewer seats at stake.

Figure 1 shows that in 1997 differences between the national DV score and regional DV patterns were just as sharp, although the pattern of electoral unfairness across regions shifted dramatically. Twelve of the eighteen regions had DV scores above the 21% national level, and in

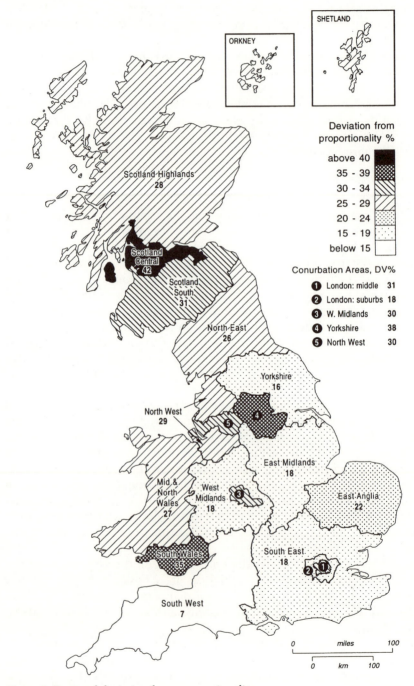

SHETLAND

ORKNEY

Deviation from
proportionality %

above 40	■
35 - 39	
30 - 34	
25 - 29	
20 - 24	
15 - 19	
below 15	

Conurbation Areas, DV%

① London: middle 31
② London: suburbs 18
③ W. Midlands 30
④ Yorkshire 38
⑤ North West 30

Scotland Highlands
28

Scotland
Central
42

Scotland
South
31

North East
26

Yorkshire
16

North West
29

East Midlands
18

Mid &
North
Wales
27

West
Midlands
18

East Anglia
22

South Wales
35

South East
18

South West
7

0   miles   100

0   km   100

Figure 1. Regional deviation from proportionality

ten regions the DV scores either rose or stayed constant compared with 1992: all the areas involved lay in northern or conurbation England, plus Scotland and Wales. But in three critical areas, the south east, south west and the London suburbs, deviation from proportionality was cut substantially. Conservative hegemony in these areas was challenged and Labour or the Liberal Democrats or both broke through the barriers imposed by plurality rule elections to win substantial numbers of seats. We can use the data given in Figure 1 to try and assess how these conflicting trends affected voters at large, by computing an average 'experiential' DV score across the regions, but one which is weighted by the population size of the regions so as to represent the amount of electoral system disproportionality experienced by the average voter in Britain. The results show interesting contrasts with the normal (institutional) DV scores across the last two general elections:

Great Britain DV scores on:	Institutional Basis	Experiential Basis
1992	17.4	29.2
1997	21.1	23.8

According to the conventional way of measuring national DV (in terms of the under-representation of the different political parties at *national* level), in 1997 the electoral system became more unfair and disproportional than before. Yet according to the experiential DV score (measuring how likely it was that an average voter's choice would be discarded or ignored in the allocation of seats at a *regional* level) the system became appreciably fairer.

The origins of these divergent indications lie in the trends in two groups of regions in the period since the 1980s. Figure 2 shows that in the Tory 'heartland' regions the 1997 result produced sharp declines in

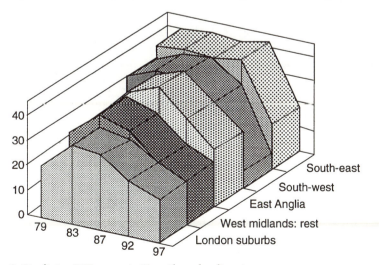

Figure 2. Declining DV scores in Tory 'heartland' regions

DV scores in the south-east and south-west. In other regions where DV scores increased considerably in the 1980s under Thatcher, the 1997 result only confirmed an already established trend across several elections for disproportionality to lessen, notably in the London suburbs and the west midlands outside the conurbation areas. Thus the electoral system has become fairer in Tory areas of strength, but at the same time in Labour heartland regions the DV scores have been increasing from their low points in the mid 1980s, as Figure 3 demonstrates. Here the change is much more sharply and uniformly confined to 1997 alone, reflecting both Labour's substantially increased vote share and the Conservatives' lurch into unpopularity. But because the Conservatives' heartland regions were larger their trend (towards greater proportionality) shapes the overall downward movement of the experiential DV score.

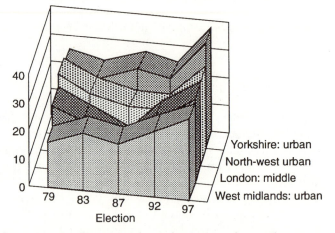

Figure 3. Disproportionality restored in Labour areas of strength

Turning to the other key aspect of the electoral system's operations, looking at the spread of relative reduction in parties scores across regions again reveals that the voting system operates in an extreme way not captured by the institutional or national RRP score considered earlier. Figure 4 shows that while the Great Britain data show the system discarding over a third of the parties voted for by the electorate, at a regional level the RRP score can go as high as 62% in central Scotland, 57% in the Yorkshire conurbation area, and above or very close to 50% in four other regions. Eleven out of eighteen regions had RRP scores above the institutional score. Only one region had an RRP score of the level (close to 10%) which would be expected in the US or any west European proportional representation system. This exceptional area was south west England, where Conservatives, Liberal Democrats and Labour each won seats in rough proportion to their vote shares, despite the potential for erratic outcomes with a fairly even multi-party split under plurality rule elections. Again, computing the

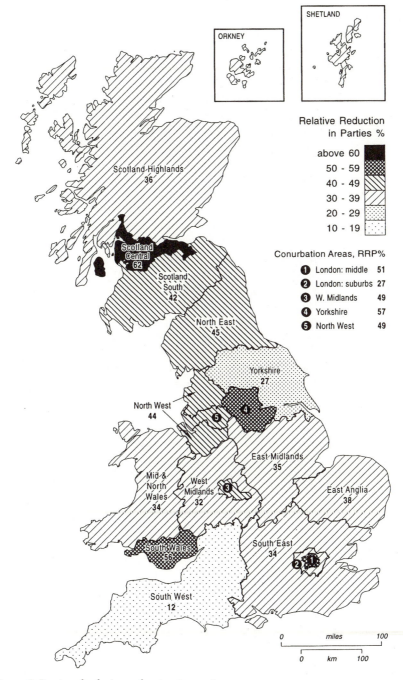

Figure 4. Regional relative reduction in parties

average of the regional RRP scores (while weighting the regions for their different population sizes) allows us to calculate the reduction of choice experienced by British voters as a whole. In 1997 this experiential RRP score was 39%, a remarkably high score for any liberal democracy, even amongst plurality rule countries. However, the experiential score shows a slight fall from 41% in 1992, whereas we noted earlier that institutional RRP went up.

A final dimension of the experience of voting harks back to the 'wasted' vote calculations we considered earlier, which focus on how many voters were essential to determine results, and how many were apparently supernumerary, able to be screened out of influencing the eventual party balance of the House of Commons. The experiential approach has no place for a concept like 'wasted vote', however. There is no reason to believe that voters who supported a decisively winning candidate thereby felt that their vote was devalued in any way—rather the contrary. Just as the *Sun* in 1992 proudly proclaimed itself 'the paper with the big majority', most people seem to like backing 'big winners', regarding their behaviour as successful, and increasing the likelihood that they will repeat it in future (other things being equal). And when we examine the concept of losing we need to be just as careful to specify what is entailed. Most people (except rational choice theorists!) can appreciate that a general election is a large-scale social process, which in the UK involves the collective choice of tens of millions of people, and this process operates at several levels. At the constituency level the election determines the choice of an MP. Nationally people's choices (as mediated by the constituency contests) determine the choice of Prime Minister and government. Someone can be successful in getting the local MP they wanted, but not get the government they wanted, and vice versa. In addition, many voters will look outside their immediate local constituency in assessing how the election result affected them: indeed in many cases people may not accurately know which constituency they are voting in, especially in 1997 when the boundaries in three quarters of British seats changed in some degree. People may pay attention to how parties fared generally in their region, noticing especially when they support a dominant party regionally—in which case they will tend to feel supported or reinforced in their alignment. Hence voters may experience the general election as successful from their point of view in three ways—by electing the MP they want, obtaining the government which they want, or finding that they support a dominant party in their region. We implement this last criterion restrictively, setting a 'dominant party' to mean one which wins at least 70% of seats in that region.

Table 5 shows the results of applying these criteria of success to the 1997 election result. Obviously all Labour voters were winners in one sense, that the party they supported nationally became the government. Nearly one in six voters not only secured the government they wanted,

5. Winners as a percentages of all Great Britain voters, 1997

	Lab	Cons	Lib Dem	Other	Total
Triple winner	16.3	0.0	0.0	0.0	16.3
Double winner:					
National/local	18.9	0.0	0.0	0.0	18.9
National/regional	0.8	0.0	0.0	0.0	0.7
Regional/local	0.0	0.0	0.0	0.0	0.0
Single winner:					
National	8.4	0.0	0.0	0.0	8.4
Regional	0.0	0.0	0.0	0.0	0.0
Local	0.0	12.6	3.3	0.7	16.6
Triple loser	0.0	18.8	13.9	6.2	39.0
All voters	44.4	31.4	17.2	6.9	100.0

however, but were also triple winners, with Labour MPs winning locally and their constituencies being located in Labour-dominated regions (there were no Conservative-dominated regions by our criterion). An additional fifth of all voters (all of them Labour) were double winners, at both national and constituency levels. Two groups were single winners only. One in eight voters, all Labour, secured the government they wanted, but saw their votes lose locally and did not live in safe Labour regions. One in six voters were single winners only in their local constituency, supporting non-Labour parties—the biggest group of them being Conservatives. Finally, nearly two in five voters failed to see their choices reflected by the election outcome at any level, locally, nationally or in a pattern of regional party dominance.

Table 6 looks at what proportions of voters *for each party* came away from the election with some degree of success, and compares that picture with the 1992 general election. In 1992 nearly half of all Conservative voters were triple winners, but in 1997 the same was true of only 37% of Labour voters. In 1992 one in six Tory voters saw their party win nationally without being successful at either regional or local level, while the figure was slightly higher for Labour in 1997. While one in fourteen Liberal Democrats were winners in 1992, this proportion rose above one in six by 1997. For the Conservative voters, of course, the change from 1992 to 1997 was a considerable one, with the proportion registering any form of success for their vote dropping to

6. Winners as proportions of each party's supporters, 1997 and 1992

1997 election	Lab	Cons	Lib Dem	Other	All voters
Triple winner	37	0	0	0	16
Double winner	44	0	0	0	20
Single winner	19	40	19	10	25
Triple loser	0	60	81	90	39
Total	100	100	100	100	100
1992 election	Lab	Cons	Lib Dem	Other	All voters
Triple winner	0	48	0	0	21
Double winner	32	36	0	0	27
Single winner	50	16	7	10	25
Triple loser	18	0	93	90	27
Total	100	100	100	100	100

two fifths. Across both elections the proportion of people who were some kind of winner declined appreciably, from nearly three quarters in 1992 to just three in five in 1997. In 1992, although Labour was in opposition, their supporters had a much more secure base of local constituencies and regional dominance to fall back on than Conservative voters in 1997.

Conclusions: The electoral system and electoral reform

The electoral system normally runs in the background of British politics. Its operations attract little attention except for what they might mean for the fortunes of political parties. In addition critics and reformers of the electoral system often deplore its unfairness but see little hope of change in the near future. The aftermath of the 1997 general election is qualitatively different for a number of reasons. Before the election, at the end of March 1997, Labour and the Liberal Democrats issued the report of a joint commission between the two parties on constitutional reform which seemed to foreshadow a period of unprecedented cooperation on devolution, House of Lords reform, other constitutional measures, and even electoral system change. After Labour's landslide victory cynics were quick to conclude that this prospect of joint action would be speedily jettisoned, especially once a new generation of ministers and Labour MPs began to appreciate the seductive attractions of government power. Nonetheless the joint agreement still stands, and most of it was reflected in fairly explicit promises in the Labour manifesto. These pledges were admittedly vague on timings and details, but they may not now be easily evadable by a Labour leadership which assured the British people that it would keep all its promises.

Electoral reform will very probably happen in Scotland and Wales, where two slightly differing forms of the 'additional member system' (AMS) are likely to be adopted for electing the Scottish Parliament and the Welsh Senned. Both involve a large majority of locally elected constituency MPs, plus a sizeable minority of 'top-up' MPs elected in larger subregions, a provision which is likely to be the saving of the Conservative party in both nations. The joint commission document also looked forward to the appointment of a government committee or commission to draw up a question for a referendum on the House of Commons' voting system. The two parties pledged to offer voters a choice between the status quo and a single 'proportional' alternative — almost certainly a version of AMS, probably with around 75% of the seats in local constituencies and minimal 'top-up' seats. Some Labour voices proclaim that the alternative vote and other non-proportional systems are still in play, but most accept that these alternatives have been side-lined. Many Liberal Democrats retain a strong affection for the single transferrable vote (STV), but recognize that they have little chance of overcoming Labour's resolute opposition to any form of multi-member constituencies. Finally it was announced that some form of regional list PR system will be adopted in time for the 1999 European elections. And in the even more remote future there is a dim prospect of elections to a reconstituted House of Lords, if Labour confronts this issue during a second term in government.

How does the evidence about the electoral system's performance relate to this sudden incursion of electoral reform issues into practical politics? We have seen that gauging how parties and voters were treated is not a simple task, but requires consideration of a number of different aspects. In many ways the 1997 result continued the history of plurality rule much as it had gone before. Deviation from proportionality measured in conventional terms rose; the relative reduction in parties increased in many regions of the country; safe Labour regions and seats multiplied, even while Conservative heartland areas began to show more pluralism in their politics. 'Plus ca change, plus c'est la meme chose', one might well conclude. The political pendulum swung, the previous plurality became a minority, the previous leading minority became the plurality, and that was all.

On the other hand we noted the zeitgeist of satisfaction with the election result which followed Labour's landslide, the Liberal Democrats' partial breakthrough to greater efficacy as a party, and the Conservatives' large-scale loss of votes and seats. The experiential DV and RRP figures considered above shed some interesting light upon this reaction — for they suggest that in objective terms the extent to which the electoral system ignored or discarded voters' preferences actually fell somewhat in 1997, despite Labour's seats landslide and the Conservatives' under-representation in the Commons. We might naturally expect that some Labour voters (and perhaps even some Liberal Democrats) will react to their party's newfound success by assigning increased legitimacy to a voting system which they have previously criticized. And to some degree the experiential measure of DV lends some support to this change. Yet not all experiential measures moved in the same way. The system constraints and limits have not changed in any across the board way. We showed, for example, that in fact far more voters (73%) derived some kind of winning benefit from the election result in 1992 than in 1997 (when this figure fell to 61%).

A full interpretation of the 1997 results must await a detailed consideration of how the election not just mapped out under plurality rule, but also how it would have turned out under alternative voting systems.[11] This information is not yet available, but there are some preliminary results of a major survey (conducted by ICM for the authors) which shed a little light on how British voters felt about proportional representation reform proposals immediately after the election. We asked voters to agree or disagree with two statements, and their responses showed significantly different patterns, depending on the slant of the question towards or against electoral reform.

Responses to the first question do not suggest that public opinion on

7. Attitudes towards electoral reform, 1997

	Agree	Disagree	Neither or DK	Majority for PR
This country should adopt a new, voting system that would give parties seats in Parliament in proportion to their votes	55%	27%	19%	+28
	Agree	Disagree		
We should retain the current voting system as it is more likely to produce a single party government	35%	43%	22%	−8

Source: Survey conducted by ICM, May 1997: Sample size 1901.

electoral reform has changed all that much in the immediate aftermath of the general election from the configuration broadly supportive of voting system change which had emerged by the early 1990s; in 1992, 57% of a sample of 10,000 agreed with the same question.[12] Responses to the second question were 43% in favour of the status quo in both 1992 and 1997. In 1992, 39% of respondents were in favour of changing the system; the four per cent decrease in 1997 might be accounted for by the first flush of enthusiasm for the election. The differences in response across the two questions and the continuity over time at the least suggest that there is still all to play for in the outcome of a eventual referendum on changing the Commons voting procedures. If Conservative and Labour elites can continue to agree on the advantages of the status quo, and communicate that message successfully to citizens within a re-legitimized system of government, then a voting systems referendum may yet 'entrench' plurality rule rather than reform it. If reformers can successfully highlight the high levels of disproportionality under plurality rule, which were undoubtedly evident in the 1997 outcome, then the prospects of winning a referendum majority still look bright.

We would like to thank Jane Pugh of the LSE Geography Department for creating the maps and Brendan O'Duffy of Queen Mary and Westfield College for help on data assembly.

1   See J. Curtice and M. Steed, 'Appendix 2: The Results Analysed' in D. Butler and D. Kavanagh (eds), *The British General Election of 1992* (Macmillan, 1993) , p. 323.

2   A. Lijphart, *Electoral Systems and Party Systems* (Oxford University Press, 1993), Chapter 3 provides a clear explanation. Lijphart in fact recommends a more complex version of the DV score known as the 'least squares' measure. Since this index is harder to explain, and in our view has some peculiar and undesirable mathematical properties of which Lijphart seems unaware, we concentrate on the simpler DV measure here. The conclusions of our analysis are not affected by the choice of measure.

3   R. Taagepera and M. Shugart, *Seats and Votes* (Yale University Press, 1989), Chapter 10.

4   We exclude Northern Ireland, because it is essentially a quite separate party system.

5   It is necessary to divide by two because in the process of adding the absolute values, the numbers have in effect been doubled. This formula gives a range of values for DV that can range between 0 and 100% (although in practice it rarely exceeds 50 and it is theoretically possible for it to rise above 100), a desirable property for such an indicator. Omitting the division by two would mean that DV ranged between 0 and 200%. See Taagepera and Shugart, 'Appendix C', p. 260 for a full discussion.

6   Our regions are based on the government 'standard regions', but we separate out major conurbation areas from the rest of the regions. Thus in the north west the conurbation area includes Liverpool, Merseyside and Greater Manchester; in Yorkshire both former metro-counties in south and west Yorkshire; and in the west Midlands the former metro-county area. We also distinguish between the middle of London (a somewhat broader area than the historic 'Inner London') and the outer suburbs.

Scotland is split into three regions—the Highlands, the central lowland area and the southern uplands. Wales is divided between south Wales and the mid and north area.

7 Lijphart, *Electoral Systems and Party Systems*, p. 67.

8 For a full discussion and cross-country comparisons see P. Dunleavy and H. Margetts, 'The Experiential Approach to Auditing Democracy' in D. Beetham (ed.), *Defining and Measuring Democracy* (Sage, 1994), p. 155.

9 It should be noted that citizens' experiences of political processes are not necessarily the same as their subjective perceptions of such processes. 'Experience' is defined by the *Concise Oxford Dictionary* as 'actual observation of or practical acquaintance with facts or events; knowledge or skill resulting from this; an event regarded as affecting one ([as in] 'an unpleasant experience'); the fact or process of being so affected ([as in] 'learning by experience')'. For example, political experiences may build up bit by bit over long time periods all the while generating adaptive responses, without citizens being aware of their own responses.

10 See D. Beetham, *Defining and Measuring Democracy*, pp. 155–81.

11 See P. Dunleavy, H. Margetts and S. Weir, *Replaying the General Election of 1992: How Britain Would Have Voted Under Alternative Electoral Systems* (LSE Public Policy Group, 1992).

12 For details of the 1992 survey, see P. Dunleavy, H. Margetts and S. Weir 'Replaying the Election', *Parliamentary Affairs*, 1992/4.

The New Labour Government:
On the Crest of a Wave

BY RICHARD ROSE*

VICTORY is sweet, but the aftertaste becomes bitter as election-night euphoria is followed by the 'no win' problems that sooner or later confront every government. Opinion polls and by-election results act as memento mori—reminders of the mortality of politicians and parties. After the 1966 election, Harold Wilson proclaimed that Labour was the natural party of government, and John Major's 1992 election victory was similarly hailed as demonstrating that the Conservatives could rule into the next millennium. Such pride soon went before a fall. Politicians riding the crest of a wave face a one-way option: down. The scale of Labour's landslide victory means that it can lose lots of seats and still hold office after the next general election, and the vagaries of the first-past-the-post electoral system gives Labour more seats than the Conservatives for a given number of votes. But before new Labour can win a second term of office, it must get through four or five years as the government of the day. As such, it is a hostage to every misfortune that hits the country, including many beyond its power to control. It is also a hostage to 'own goals' scored by ministers deficient in political skills. The Prime Minister and his apparatus will find that the skills they used to great effect in transforming the Labour Party and campaigning against a Conservative government differ from those required in government. This is especially so when government is on the defensive, due to actions outside its control or to problems of its own creation.

Winning with a surge in short-term support

The Labour Party, of which Tony Blair became leader in 1994, was down but not out. Long-term changes in British society had reduced the normal Labour vote to about a third of the electorate, while leaving the Conservatives' share at just under two-fifths of the vote. In an election in which short-term influences on the vote were equal, the Conservatives would expect to win by a margin of about six per cent. But short-term forces are rarely if ever equal, resulting in each election showing a deviation from the notional normal vote. In 1974 the Conservatives did worse than their normal vote, and in 1983 this was true of Labour. In the 1992 election Labour polled its long-term normal support, and this spelled its defeat. Yet the same model showed that if Labour were

* Director of the Centre for the Study of Public Policy, University of Strathclyde.

favoured by short-term factors and the Conservatives handicapped, then Labour would win 39% of the vote and enjoy a small working majority in the House of Commons.[1]

Short-term factors worked against the Conservatives. The disastrous collapse of the pound in September 1992, dropped support for the government to 30% in the Gallup poll by November 1992. Concurrently, support for Labour, under its new leader, John Smith, rose to 51%. But Labour politicians could not regard this as a forecast of victory, for the party had been even further ahead in April 1990. Labour's subsequent defeat indicated that for it to win office it needed 'the biggest shake up in the British party system in generations'.[2] Tony Blair delivered just this. The Blair campaign rejected political Micawberism, the belief that sooner or later victory would turn up for the Labour Party. It accepted that in a changing society the old Labour appeal based on class, the poor and state responsibility for welfare was a big electoral handicap. Unlike predecessors, Blair had no inhibitions about dropping shibboleths and commitments to which classic Labour supporters were attached. By 1997 it had fewer similarities with the party of Harold Wilson or Hugh Gaitskell than it did with the new Democrats of President Clinton, not a party in the textbook sense but a campaign apparatus with a single clear goal, electoral victory.

By definition, a new party must attract new voters if it is to have a chance of winning. The strategic art of the new Labour initiative is that, while it offered a new face to the electorate, it carried with it almost all the normal vote of old Labour, an asset that the breakaway Social Democratic Party lacked. To emphasize newness, Blair openly broke with old Labour's commitment to social democratic as well as Clause IV socialism. Instead of fighting Thatcherism, the Blair team sought to co-opt the popular parts of the Conservative government's record, including the promotion of opportunity and opposition to increases in income tax. In place of left/right differences accepted by Margaret Thatcher as well as old Labour politicians, Tony Blair campaigned on 'style' or 'valence' issues,[3] linking his appeal with consensual goals positively valued by the electorate, such as competence, honesty, unity, community, and freshness. To win votes, such an appeal must distinguish one party from another. The Major government played into Blair's hands, as disunity erupted over Europe and hardening of the political arteries led to incompetence and sleaze. When Cabinet ministers were not shooting themselves in the foot, they were shooting at colleagues more than in any postwar British government. The result was that the 1997 Conservative vote was down 11.2%, an even bigger drop than that suffered by Labour when Michael Foot led old Labour's suicidal 1983 campaign.

The combination of the structural change from old to new Labour, and from an effective campaign machine to Conservative disunity, delivered a landslide parliamentary majority to Tony Blair. But even with many short-term factors helping, new Labour failed to win as large a share of the popular vote as old Labour did in losing the 1959 general election. New Labour's vote was up 9.9% from its normal vote for the period 1974–92, but up only 4.1% from the peak of the electoral cycle for old Labour. Blair's winning coalition of voters had a very broad base (see Table 1). A fifth were converts from the Conservative, Liberal Democrat or Nationalist parties, more than double the proportion of conversions secured by Harold Wilson in Labour's 1964 Labour victory. Reciprocally, the share of old Labour vote was less than Wilson had secured, and the accession of young voters and abstainers was barely more than half that on which Labour's 1964 victory was based.[4] In short, new Labour primarily owed its victory to gains from people who had rejected old Labour. Blair recognized this, telling with pride about an old Labour supporter who voiced his suspicions of the party's revolution by saying that he even knew Tories who were voting New Labour. Blair replied, 'Long may it continue'.[5] Yet, short-term support is most subject to loss in the face of short-term setbacks.

1. Sources of Labour's 1997 vote

Old Labour voters	65
Ex-Conservatives	12
Too young, abstained	15
Ex-Liberal Democrat	6
Other, Don't know	2

Source: NOP/BBC Exit Poll, 1.5.97.

How long and how deep are mid-term slumps?

If a week is a long time in politics, then the life of a Parliament can seem like eternity, with the only uncertainty whether one goes from purgatory to heaven or hell. After a post-election honeymoon, comes the mid-term slump. Some governments recover sufficiently to win the next general election, but others do not. The mid-term is always a severe test for a prime minister, for the politics of losing ground are different from the politics of winning ground. Analytically, the two questions about a mid-term slump are: How far does it go? How fast does it happen? The answers can be found in the monthly Gallup poll questions about how people would vote if an election were held tomorrow. In the first decade after World War II, the mid-term slump was hardly in evidence. Intermittent Gallup polls showed support for the governing party almost always in the range of 40 to 49%, and no government lost a by-election. The slump became evident in the prime ministership of Harold Macmillan. In September 1957, Conservative popularity fell to 33% in the Gallup poll. Following recovery and victory in the 1959 general election, the Macmillan government's support slumped again to 31%. The norm for mid-term slumps remained the same under Harold Wilson's first government, and under Ted Heath.

Three-party competition since 1974 has reduced the support of the election winner. Whereas previously 44 to 49% of the vote was needed

2. The scale of the mid-term slump

		Won with (% share of voters)	Low in Gallup poll	Month when lowest poll recorded
1955–59	Con	50	33	29 th
1959–64	Con	49	31	32 th
1966–70	Lab	48	28	26 th
1970–74	Con	46	31	38 th
1974–79	Lab	39	30	25 th
1979–83	Con	44	26	30 th
1983–87	Con	42	24	28 th
1987–92	Con	42	28	33 th
1992–97	Con	42	20	30 th

Note: Governments with a duration of less than two years are excluded from the above calculations.

Source: Gallup poll data from D. Butler and G. Butler, *British Political Facts, 1900–1994* (Macmillan, 1994).

to win, since 1974 the winning share has ranged between 37 and 44%. The government's vote has also been less committed and made large-scale by-election losses routine. The Thatcher government saw its support drop as low as 24 per cent within 28 months of its landslide 1983 victory. John Major's government holds the record for the depth of the mid-term slump, falling as low as 20% by December 1994. Between 1955 and 1997, the governing party has seen its popular support average a fall of 17 percentage points when at its nadir. Usually this point is reached in its third year of office, when defeat at the next general election looms increasingly large, and a prime minister's past victories become less significant. The popularity of party leaders shows higher peaks, for the prime minister's popularity normally runs well above that of his or her party, but for that reason the troughs reflect a big drop in personal popularity. Harold Macmillan was approved by 79% of the electorate at his peak, and by only 30% at his nadir; Harold Wilson's rating fluctuated between 69 and 27% between 1964–70, and John Major varied between 59 and 18%.[6]

The implications for Tony Blair are clear: even while in office you won't always be on top, insofar as this is measured by the latest opinion poll. A fall in support for the Blair government to 27% could be described as better than average, but it would be sufficient to send shock waves through the New Labour government. Similarly, if Blair's personal popularity rating falls to 29%, this would be better than the average fall since Jim Callaghan entered Downing Street—but still a bruising ride down. Thus, the question is not whether the New Labour government will have a mid-term slump, but how soon it will come, and how far down it will go.

Facing up to the mid-term slump

Since a government can only lose office if the opposition wins, the state of the Conservative Party offers some reassurance to New Labour. The readiness of Tony Blair to steal the most popular parts of the Thatcher programme, has led many Conservatives to move toward the further shores of the right in order to remain distinctive. The Conservatives will find it harder to demonstrate 'competence' from the opposition benches than from the government benches. Moreover, the election of a new leader in summer 1996 will not be the party's last fight during this Parliament, given that divisive European issues will continue to appear on the political agenda. However, in a multi-party system New Labour is also vulnerable to attack from 'third' parties. The Liberal Democrats, an acceptable alternative for Conservative moderates, have enjoyed their best general election success since 1929, and the large number of Labour seats in Scotland makes the party vulnerable to attack from Nationalists too.

Given the scale of its parliamentary majority, a mid-term slump does not threaten the New Labour government with a loss of office. But a party leader who shows signs of becoming an electoral liability finds it much harder to assert his or her authority on Cabinet colleagues and on Parliament. In the worst case, a leader can be challenged or even unseated by a revolt of the disaffected. But Blair has interpreted New Labour's election victory as giving him a mandate to maintain iron discipline over the parliamentary party (measures in the first session of Parliament have been crafted to have broad appeal, and the Liberal Democrat contingent in the House provides Blair with additional sources of support). Blair's centralization of power in the leader's office in opposition has been carried over into Downing Street in a way unprecedented in modern British history. But this means that if any mistakes are made by the New Labour government, Blair will get the blame. He has left few buffers between himself and blame for anything and everything that might go wrong. And inevitably, some things will.

Amateurishness and inexperience, rather than hardening of the political arteries, is the most obvious hazard of a new government. A prime minister in Blair's position need not hesitate to dismiss Cabinet colleagues for specific errors or generalized incompetence. But a dismissed minister who pursues a grudge cleverly and consistently can make trouble for the government. The government's large majority means that during the Parliament more than a hundred MPs will realize that they have no chance of getting office, and they will be ready to voice dissatisfactions and disenchantment. If the prime minister no longer appears an election asset, the threat of discipline diminishes. As the number of the unruly increases, the capacity to intimidate falls, for a party that deselects dozens of its sitting MPs invites the formation of a breakaway party, and the embryo of such a party already exists, in the form of Old Labour.

In government, the prime minister will find that the methods used to dominate an opposition party will be insufficient to deal with many substantive problems in the environment of which British government is but one part. The government can anticipate, influence or respond to economic difficulties or developments in the European Union, but in an interdependent world it cannot order businessmen or foreign governments to do what it wants. In this sort of context the economy is the most predictable source of trouble, since there is a reversal in the economic cycle every two years or so. Conservative government efforts to create a pre-election 'feel good' factor are likely to intensify the post-election 'feel bad' factor. The standard political response is to accept a recession in the middle of a Parliament in order to have the economy booming again in the run up to the next general election. In other words, it is in the interest of a government to engineer a mid-term slump. This strategy does not guarantee a subsequent election victory, as John Major and Ken Clarke found out this spring. But a Blair administration can try to ride out economic difficulties by blaming problems on their predecessor, and claiming that tomorrow will be better than the present.

From time to time, the prime minister is going to be put on the spot by problems currently unforeseeable. How many Cabinet ministers knew about BSE before the British beef crisis broke over their heads? How many Cabinet ministers besides Michael Heseltine ever thought that their behaviour in the arms-for-Iraq case would ever be publicly scrutinized by a Scott report? And how many backbenchers or ex-backbenchers expected arrangements entered into for private profit or pleasure would be splashed in the Sunday papers?

Tony Blair is establishing a SW1 regime that makes him first without equal rather than just first among equals. But in the European Union a British prime minister is only one among fifteen. The Prime Minister has promised that while he 'would not be dogmatic', New Labour's policy will be to put British interests 'first, second and last'.[7] To underscore the point, he met, and let it be known that he met, Baroness Thatcher prior to a major meeting of the Council of Ministers in the Netherlands in late May 1997. Blair's goal is easy to state: EU policies that are acceptable to the British House of Commons, and to the British electorate at a general election or referendum. But the German and French governments have the same goal, but different interests, different governing coalitions and different electorates. Chairing meetings of the EU Council of Ministers in the first six months of 1998 will give Blair great prominence. But it will also expose him to great pressures from other countries to give a clear-cut declaration whether Britain really wants to be part of Europe or not. Except for Ted Heath, no British prime minister has given a straight answer to that question. Europe is an issue that divides Labour as well as the Conservative Party, and it divides British voters too. At some point in the next five years negotiations within the EU may offer the Prime Minister the Hobson's choice of being accused of sacrificing the 'sovereignty' of Parliament or opting out of major EU developments while the other 14 members move ahead and leave Britain behind.

Within Britain, a Scottish Parliament will raise novel challenges. The risk for Labour is not that its plans on devolution will fail, but they are in place, leading to the election of a Scottish Parliament in autumn,

1999. Labour expects to dominate the new Edinburgh Parliament, though it has never won as much as half the vote in Scotland, and in 1997 it won 78% of Scottish seats at Westminster with less than 46% of the Scottish vote. The Scottish National Party came second in the share of votes (with 22%), but trailed behind the Liberal Democrats in seats. The introduction of proportional representation for the four-party system of Scotland creates opportunities for new coalitions and new party splits.

The election of a Scottish Parliament could well be a 'second order' election, in which voting reflects attitudes toward the current performance of British government rather than purely Scottish issues. This phenomenon is familiar in voting for the European Parliament, and in local elections too.[8] When the Scottish election is held, the New Labour government is more likely to be near its low point rather than on the crest of a wave—and its declining popularity is likely to rub off on Labour's candidates in Scotland. Moreover, the Scottish Nationalists are sure to make an issue of Blair's 1997 campaign statement to Scottish journalists that, notwithstanding devolution, 'Sovereignty rests with me as an English MP, and that is the way it will stay'.[9]

While the mid-term slump is a certainty, how New Labour responds remains to be revealed, and the same is true of the electorate. Precedent, as symbolized by the swing of a pendulum between two, and only two, political parties, is an increasingly unreliable guide since 1974. In this Parliament, referendums, devolution and a debate about proportional representation threaten the centralization of power represented by the Crown in Parliament, the device Blair has seized on to impose his will on new Labour. By definition, unprecedented challenges cannot be predicted, but they happen nonetheless. The events that produce the mid-slump will provide a severe test to the commitment of supporters won over in 1997, and to the apparatus that Tony Blair built up to win Downing Street.

1   For the theory and calculations of the normal vote, see Richard Rose, 'Long-Term Structural Change or Cyclical Fluctuations? The 1992 Election in Dynamic Perspective', *Parliamentary Affairs* 1992/4 at 452ff.

2   Richard Rose, 'Long-Term Structural Change or Cyclical Fluctuations?' at 452.

3   The distinction between valence and position issues comes from Donald E. Stokes, 'Spatial Models of Party Competition', *American Political Science Review* 57/2, 1963.

4   Compare Table 1 and David Butler and Donald Stokes, *Political Change in Britain* (London: Macmillan, 1974) 2nd edn, Table 12.4.

5   Tony Blair, *New Britain* (London: Harper Collins, 1996) at 54.

6   See Richard Rose, 'A Crisis of Confidence in British Party Leaders?', *Contemporary Record* 9/2, 1995 at 278.

7   Quoted in Robert Peston, 'Blair ledges fresh start in Europe', *Financial Times* 10.5.97.

8   See Karlheinz Reif and H. Schmitt, 'Nine Second-order National Elections: A Conceptual Framework for the Analysis of European Election Results', *European Journal of Political Research* 1980/1 at 3–44; William L. Miller, *Irrelevant Elections? The Quality of Local Democracy in Britain* (Oxford: Clarendon Press, 1988).

9   Quoted in James Blitz, 'PM attacks Blair over Scotland', *Financial Times* 5.4.97.

AUTHOR INDEX

SUBJECT INDEX

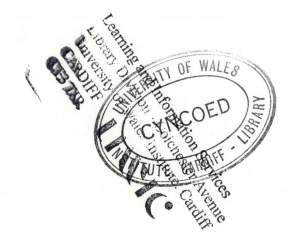